BORDER MATTERS

REMAPPING AMERICAN CULTURAL STUDIES

José David Saldívar

University of California Press
Berkeley   Los Angeles   London

University of California Press
Berkeley and Los Angeles, California

University of California Press, Ltd.
London, England

Parts of the introduction appeared, in different form, in *The American Literary History Reader,* edited by Gordon Hutner (New York: Oxford University Press, 1995); parts of chapter 1 in *The Columbia History of the American Novel: New Views,* edited by Emory Elliott (New York: Columbia University Press, 1993); most of chapter 2 in *Cultures of U.S. Imperialism,* edited by Amy Kaplan and Donald Pease (Durham, N.C.: Duke University Press, 1993), and in *Blackwell's Companion to American Thought* (Oxford: Blackwell, 1995); portions of chapter 3 in *Confluencia* 1 (Spring 1986); portions of chapter 4 in *Stanford Magazine* (September 1993); portions of chapter 5 in *Mester* 12/13 (Fall 1993/ Spring 1994); and an early version of chapter 7 appeared in *Revista Casa de las Américas* (July–September 1996). Grateful acknowledgment is made for permission to reprint this material.

Library of Congress Cataloging-in-Publication Data
Saldívar, José David.
    Border matters : remapping American cultural
studies / José David Saldívar.
        p.   cm. — (American crossroads ; 1)
    Includes bibliographical references and index.
    ISBN 0-520-20681-9 (cloth : alk. paper). — ISBN 0-520-20682-7 (pbk. : alk. paper)
        1. Mexican-American Border Region—Civilization.
    2. Popular culture—Mexican-American Border Region.
    3. Mexican American arts—Mexican-American Border
    Region. 4. American literature—Mexican American
    authors—History and criticism. 5. Mexican-American
    Border Region—Intellectual life. 6. Biculturalism—
    Mexican-American Border Region. I. Title. II. Series.
    F787.S19   1997
    306'.0972'1—dc21   96-49209
                                                                    CIP

Printed in the United States of America
9 8 7 6 5 4 3 2

Contents

Illustrations

Preface

This book locates the study of Chicano/a literature in a broad cultural framework, going beyond literature to examine issues of expression and representation in folklore, music, and video performance art. Additionally, it looks at the recent theorizing about the U.S.-Mexico border zone as a paradigm of crossings, intercultural exchanges, circulations, resistances, and negotiations as well as of militarized "low-intensity" conflict.[1] How do the discursive spaces and the physical places of the U.S.-Mexico border inflect the material reality of cultural production? By analyzing a broad range of cultural texts and practices (*corridos*, novels, poems, paintings, *conjunto*, punk and hip-hop songs, travel writing, and ethnography) and foregrounding the situated historical experiences facing Chicanos/as, *Border Matters* puts forth a model for a new kind of U.S. cultural studies, one that challenges the homogeneity of U.S. nationalism and popular culture. The seven chapters argue for inclusion of the U.S.-Mexico border experience within cultural studies and strive to show how to treat culture as a social force, how to read the presence of social contexts within cultural texts, and how to re-imagine the nation as a site within many "cognitive maps" in which the nation-state is not congruent with cultural identity. Although what follows is not a definitive statement about border discourses on a global scale, it is an attempt to place the histories and myths of the American West and Southwest in a new perspective—what Gayatri Chakravorty Spivak calls "the emerging dominant" in American studies (1995, 179).

As I was bringing this project to a close, I found myself riveted by a Public Broadcasting System *Firing Line* debate in which William Buckley and Ariana Huffington faced Ed Koch and Ira Glazer on the topic of immigration, both legal and illegal. Buckley and Huffington called for new enforcement measures against the "hordes" of illegal immigrants flooding across our nation's borders. Huffington, a recent immigrant herself (from Greece), called, without irony, for more guards, more border fences, and the use of sophisticated military vehicles and technologies left over from Desert Storm to patrol the U.S.-Mexico border. Koch rebutted Huffington's position by reminding her that had the national borders been closed and more draconian restrictions placed on immigrants by the U.S. government in the 1960s, she would never have had the chance to become a hyphenated ethnic-American herself. This debate about immigration laws and border crossings highlights, I think, how the mass media are constructing a popular narrative of national crisis.

As I reflect on the hegemonic Proposition 187 passed by voters in California in 1994, a measure denying undocumented immigrants public education, health services, and other benefits, I cannot help but see such unconstitutional measures as fundamentally colonialist discourses whereby U.S. Latinos, Chicanos, Mexicanos, Central Americans, and Asian Americans are cast as an illegal outside force, an alien nation "polluting" U.S. culture. I wholeheartedly agree with the Panamanian activist-intellectual and *salsero* Rubén Blades, who contends in his border song "Desahucio" (Evicted) that "la ley aplicada mal deja de ser ley" (the law applied badly ceases to be law) (1995). How can we begin making connections between moral panic about border-crossing migrations and the drift into a militarized law-and-order society? Can these events be linked and articulated together in the construction of a narrative of reality in which "illegal aliens" become the signifiers of the present crisis in U.S. society? If this crisis is not a crisis of "ethno-race,"[2] is ethnorace the lens through which this crisis is seen in the American West?

Almost all of the artists and writers explored in *Border Matters* answer that we are here to stay and we are not going away (*aquí estamos y no nos vamos*).

In this time of anti-immigrant hysteria, when, as the border ethnographer Ruth Behar puts it, "stories of homelessness, violence, and suffering are falling on ears that no longer bear to listen" (1993, xii), border discourses about the United States and Mexico are destined to become more central in remapping American studies. I have written this book about the U.S.-Mexico border precisely because the government is gearing up to implement a new "battle plan" against border-crossers from the South into the North, a plan involving a complex network of support from the military, the National Guard, and local police departments. The border-control program, at a cost to the Immigration and Naturalization Service (INS) of $2.6 million a month, will militarize areas along the border in California and Arizona.[3] This militarization of the U.S.-Mexico border, as the historian Timothy Dunn has documented in detail, has a broader historical and political context, for "three different U.S. presidential administrations from the two major U.S. political parties" have implemented a doctrine of "low-intensity conflict" to enforce immigration and drug laws. According to Dunn, this doctrine, especially under the Reagan and Bush administrations, included the deployment of "military surveillance equipment by police agencies" —AH1S-Cobra helicopter gunships, OC-58Cs reconnaissance helicopters, small airplanes with TV cameras and forward-looking infrared night-vision sensors, and a variety of seismic, magnetic, and acoustic sensors to detect movement, heat, and sound as well as "low-tech" construction of chain-link fences. Even more, it involved the "large-scale" use of "military forces to maintain security and stability," that is, joint state and federal law enforcement agencies with military support (1996, 148).

What is significant about this intensive militarization of the U.S.-Mexico border is the extent to which it led not only to a "loosening" of the Posse Comitatus Statute (which outlawed the use of the military in the domestic sphere) but also to new alliances between the civilian police and the military to enforce drug and immigration policies. Briefly, for Dunn, the militarization of the U.S.-Mexico border disciplined and punished "undocumented workers coming into the United States, and hence [led to] their economic subordination." Further, it extended Reagan's and Bush's undeclared wars in Central America, "signal[ing] and subject[ing] to especially punitive immigration enforcement measurements" refugees and immigrants from El Salvador and Guatemala (163).

If Reagan's and Bush's low-intensity conflict doctrine in the 1980s largely targeted racialized border-crossers from the South, it also led to the creation of what the Native American novelist Leslie Marmon Silko calls "the Border Patrol State."[4] "Since the 1980s," Silko writes, "on top of greatly expanding border checkpoints" in the Southwest, "the Immigration and Naturalization Service and Border Patrol . . . implemented policies that interfer[ed] with the rights of U.S. citizens to travel freely within the U.S." (1996, 118). To support her claims, Silko turns to the powerful evidentiary form personal testimony, describing how in December 1991, when traveling by car from Tucson to Albuquerque for a book signing of her border-crossing novel *Almanac of the Dead*, she was detained at a border checkpoint near Truth or Consequences, New Mexico, despite presenting a valid Arizona driver's license and conversing with the government agents in English. Meanwhile, other travelers who were "white," she recalls, "were waved through the checkpoint" (121). For Dunn and Silko, immigration and drug enforcement laws single out for punishment racialized border-crossers from the South while they simultaneously target "people of color" from the North by restricting their free movement within the nation's borders.

I hope that the writers, activists, musicians, and artists I have brought together in *Border Matters* can help begin to undo the militarized frontier "field-Imaginary"[5] in American culture by reconfiguring it within an emerging U.S.-Mexico *frontera* imaginary, where migration and immigration do not mean what Silko calls locking the nation's door.

In the past ten years the terms *border* and *borderlands* in Chicano/a studies have come to name a new dynamic in American studies—a synthesis of articulated development from dissident folklore and ethnography; feminism; literary, critical-legal, and cultural studies; and more recently gender and sexuality studies.[6] The impact of all this on American studies has been broad and deep. As Carl Gutiérrez-Jones argues in "Desiring (B)orders," "throughout Chicano/a Studies as a field, the figures of the border and the borderlands have acted as central components in a revisionary project that has been largely motivated by historiographic designs" (1995a, 99). While Gutiérrez-Jones is absolutely right about Chicano/a studies' revisionist historiographic project, I also believe that the paradigm of the border involves us in an ontological question: What kinds of world or worlds are we in? As we will see in the chapters that follow, U.S.-Mexico border writers and artists such as Los Tigres del Norte, Américo Paredes, Carmen Lomas Garza, and John Rechy work through the issue of what happens when different social worlds confront one another, or when boundaries between worlds are crossed.

If (since Frederick Jackson Turner's 1893 address, "The Significance of the American Frontier in American History") the frontier field-Imaginary in mainline American culture has become, in the historian David Wrobel's words, "a metaphor for promise, progress, and ingenuity" (1993, 145), the Chicana/o studies invocation of *la frontera* has a "more realistic" potential for understanding what the historian Patricia Nelson Limerick calls "the legacy of conquest" in the American borderlands, where "trade, violence, . . . and cultural exchange" shaped nineteenth-century America and where "conflicts over the restrictions of immigration, disputes over water flows, and . . . a surge of industrial developments [such as *maquiladoras,* or assembly factories] punctuated late twentieth-century America" (in Grossman 1994, 90).

For many new Americanists, the field-Imaginary of Chicano/a studies has begun to redress what the literary historian Amy Kaplan sees as "the conceptual limits of the frontier, by displacing it with the site of the borderlands" (1993, 16). For Kaplan, Chicano/a studies links "the study of ethnicity and immigration inextricably to the study of international relations and empire" (16). In other words, the invocation of the U.S.-Mexico border as a paradigm of crossing, resistance, and circulation in Chicano/a studies has contributed to the "worlding" of American studies and further helped to instill a new transnational literacy in the U.S. academy.

If the Chicano cultural critic Rafael Pérez-Torres is correct that "the borderlands make history present . . . the tensions, contradictions, hatred, and violence as well as resistance and affirmation of self in the face of that violence" (1995, 12), a quick look at the way in which the paradigm of the borderlands has traveled, shifted, and been appropriated by official U.S. culture indicates how enmeshed the American frontier field-Imaginary continues to be in our culture. It seems that everyone, from traveling performance artists to writers of television commercials, has started "running for the border," often with their "blue suede huaraches," as the Chicano singer El Vez puts it (1994). Only by "contextualizing" the borderlands paradigm within a Chicana studies subaltern tradition—as Yvonne Yarbro-Bejarano suggests—can we begin to "avoid the temptation to pedestalize or fetishize" it (1994, 9).

With these criticisms and lessons in mind, *Border Matters* begins by mapping a discourse about the U.S.-Mexico borderlands that has emerged from the historical experience of the American West, to provide a broad genealogy in which a range of border writings operate across both nineteenth-century and late twentieth-century contexts. Indeed, this book is fundamentally shaped by Michel Foucault's famous statement that "it is in discourse that power and knowledge are joined together. And for this very reason, we must conceive discourse as a series of discontinuous segments whose tactical function is neither uniform nor stable. To be more precise, we must not imagine a world of discourse divided between accepted discourse and excluded discourse, or between the dominant discourse and the dominated discourse; but as a multiplicity of discursive elements that can come into play in various strategies" (1980, 100).

It is precisely this uneven discursive terrain of the border in the American western field-Imaginary of the American West that *Border Matters* reconstructs: the things said and concealed about migration and immigration; the enunciations required and those forbidden about the legacy of conquest in the Americas. In my view, border discourse not only produces power and reinforces it but also undermines it, makes it fragile, and allows one to map and perhaps thwart the cultures of U.S. empire. Because this message about the legacy of conquest has not gotten through to official American culture, *Border Matters* joins the dynamic work of new western American historians, new Americanists, and cultural studies workers in critiquing how the American imaginary continues to hold to the great discontinuity between the American frontier and *la frontera.*

I am grateful for fellowship support during the past five years from the American Council of Learned Societies and the University of California's President's Fellowship in the Humanities.

Sections of this book were presented at the American Studies Association; Dartmouth College; the Huntington Library; the Smithsonian Institution; Stanford University; the University of California at Berkeley, Irvine, Los Angeles, San Diego, and Santa Cruz; the University of Washington; and the Universidad Nacional Autónoma de México in Mexico City. I would like to thank the people who arranged these visits. Special thanks are due Houston Baker, Jr., for his invitation to participate in the Presidential Forum at the meetings of the Modern Language Association in 1992. I am also grateful to the editors of the following books and journals, where portions of this book appeared earlier, in different form: *The American Literary History Reader,* edited by Gordon Hutner (Oxford University Press, 1995); *The Columbia History of the American Novel: New Views,* edited by Emory Elliott (Columbia University Press, 1993); *Cultures of U.S. Imperialism,* edited by Amy Kaplan and Donald Pease (Duke University Press, 1993); *Blackwell's Companion to American Thought* (Blackwell, 1995); *Confluencia* 1 (Spring 1986); *Stanford Magazine* (September 1993); *Mester* 12/13 (Fall 1993/Spring 1994); and *Revista Casa de las Américas* (July–September 1996).

Grateful acknowledgment is also made to the artists and publishers for permission to reprint excerpts from *Between Two Worlds* by Américo Paredes (Houston: Arte Público Press / University of Houston, 1991); "Border Brujo," copyright 1993 by Guillermo Gómez-Peña, reprinted from *Warrior for Gringostroika* with permission of Gray-wolf Press, Saint Paul, Minnesota; *East Side Story* by (Kid) Frost (Arturo Molina), produced by Virgin Records, 1992; *Graciasland* by El Vez (Robert Lopez), produced by Sympathy for the Record Industry, 1994; "Jaula de Oro" by Los Tigres del Norte, produced by Profono Internacional, 1985; *Restless Serpents* by Berenice Zamora (Menlo Park, Calif.: Diseño Literarios, 1976); "Los Vatos" by José Montoya, in *El Espejo / The Mirror,* edited by Octavio I. Romano (Berkeley, Calif.: Quinto Sol Publications); *Whispering to Fool the Wind* by Alberto Ríos (New York: Sheep Meadow Press, 1982); and *Five Indiscretions* by Alberto Ríos (New York: Sheep Meadow Press, 1985).

I owe enormous debts to the following colleagues and friends, who in a variety of ways left their mark on this book: Juana Alicia, Tomás Almaguer, Margarita Barceló, Mary Patricia Brady, Héctor Calderón, Angie Chabram, Gaston A. Donato, Catherine Gallagher, Mario García, Carmen Lomas Garza, Susan Gillman, Gordon Hutner, Amy Kaplan, José E. Limón, Gerald López, Lisa Lowe, Jesús Martínez, José Montoya, Donald Pease, Carolyn Porter, Mary Louise Pratt, Vicente Rafael, John Rechy, Roberto Fernández Retamar, Alberto Ríos, Renato Rosaldo, Ramón Saldívar, Sonia Saldívar-Hull, Rosaura Sánchez, Helena Viramontes, and the anonymous reviewers for the University of California Press. Monica McCormick of the University of California Press and Eileen McWilliam of Wesleyan University Press have supported the book with great rigor and generosity, and Sheila Berg edited the book with attentive care.

Border Matters was written during my affiliations with the Center for Cultural Studies at the University of California at Santa Cruz, the Center for Chicano Research at Stanford University, and the Department of Ethnic Studies at the University of California at Berkeley. It reflects, moreover, the brilliant guidance of my colleague James Clifford, who was more than willing to share with me the fruits of his own research and writing on diaspora's borders. I would also like to thank Norma Alarcón, Mitchell Breitweiser, Judith Butler, Patricia Penn Hilden, Elaine Kim, David Lloyd, Michael Omi, Genaro Padilla, and Julio Ramos, my new colleagues at the University of California at Berkeley who have offered their extraordinary support and insights. Bonnie Hardwick, director of the manuscript division of the Bancroft Library, helped me to begin answering questions about María Amparo Ruiz de Burton and the nineteenth-century Californio's *testimonios.* Additionally, I would like to thank my students and colleagues Arturo Aldama, Chris Breu, Scott Davis, Michelle Habell-Pallan, Sergio de la Mora, and Raúl Villa for their sustained encouragement. Skilled research assistance was supplied by Berkeley graduate student Josh Kun, who helped me track all the border soundings and more. As always, I am privileged to be able to acknowledge Laura Escoto Saldívar and David Xavier Saldívar, my best and sternest critics, who daily remind me—as the *salsa* song says—*que nunca olvides cuanto te quiero, porque un amor de verdad vence a los dolores.*

Berkeley, California
1997

INTRODUCTION

Tracking Borders

> For many musicians around the world, "the popular" has become a dangerous crossroads, an intersection between the undeniable saturation of commercial culture in every area of human endeavor and the emergence of a new public sphere that uses the circuits of commodity production and circulation to envision and activate new social relations.
>
> George Lipsitz, *Dangerous Crossroads* (1994)

Let us begin by considering the effects of shifting critical paradigms in American studies away from linear narratives of immigration, assimilation, and nationhood. Is it possible today to imagine new cultural affiliations and negotiations in American studies more dialogically, in terms of multifaceted migrations across borders? How do musicians, writers, and painters communicate their "dangerous crossroads" to us? How do undocumented and documented migrants in the U.S.-Mexico borderlands secure spaces of survival and self-respect in light of the government's doctrine of low-intensity conflict and in regions undergoing what social theorists call "deindustrialization"—the decline of traditional manufacturing? What kinds of cultural formations are thematized by artists who sing about regions such as El Valle de Silicon in northern California, where workers now produce computer chips instead of fruits and vegetables?

In the early 1970s Los Tigres del Norte, together with their musical director, Enrique Franco (fig. 1), migrated from northern Mexico to San Jose, California. Los Tigres del Norte have had a significant historical importance for *norteño* music in California (both Alta and Baja), for in 1988 they became one of the first undocumented bands to receive a Grammy Award for best regional Mexican-American recording, for their album *Gracias—América sin fronteras* (Thanks—America without Borders). Los Tigres del Norte's use of "the circuits of commodity production and circulation," as the cultural critic George Lipsitz suggests (1995,

Figure 1. Enrique Franco, leader of Los Tigres del Norte. Photo by Craig Lee. Courtesy of *San Francisco Examiner*.

12), allows us to examine one recent historical instance in which the musical traditions of the U.S.-Mexico border acquired what Pierre Bourdieu calls "symbolic capital" (1977, 171). Los Tigres del Norte's border music is simultaneously national and transnational in that it affects everyday life in the local (Silicon Valley) region and thematizes the limits of the national perspective in American studies.

In the story of Los Tigres del Norte's discrepant crossings, we can discover the shifting pattern of un/documented circulations, resistances, and negotiations. More important, the border migrations of Los Tigres del Norte provide us with a fascinating example of the problems that attended the passage of rural *norteño* musical forms to the mass-mediated culture industries of the overdeveloped Silicon Valley region. Originally from Mocorito, in the northern state of Sinaloa, Los Tigres del Norte migrated first to the border city of Mexicali, before they were hired by a local musical promoter in San Jose. Since the early 1970s they have lived and recorded their *conjunto* music in this capital of Silicon Valley. It was not until 1975, however, that their commercially successful "crossover" came, when they recorded the *corrido* (border ballad) "Contrabando y Traición" (Contraband and Betrayal). Los Tigres del Norte have recorded more than twenty-four records and scores of musical anthologies and have even starred in and produced border movies and music videos based on *corridos* such as their international hit "Jaula de Oro" (The Gilded Cage).

I emphasize the band's undocumented migration north from Mexico because, although Los Tigres are well known in Mexico, Cuba, Latin America, and what Chicanos/as call *el otro México* (the other Mexico)— areas of the American West, Southwest, and Midwest—they are virtually unknown to cultural studies workers in our own backyard, Silicon Valley. As the political scientist Jesús Martínez writes, "The musical style and subject matters of the songs recorded by the group are alien to the values and lifestyles of the rest of the population," reflecting the "sharply segregated society" (1993a, 9).

It goes without saying, Martínez continues, that the real stars of Silicon Valley are the high-tech scientists, engineers, late capital managers, and multinational entrepreneurs such as David Packard, William Hewlett, Steve Jobs, and Stephen Wozniak. Their fandoms are celebrated by the two hundred thousand Silicon Valley professionals who work at Apple, Hewlett-Packard, and IBM, among other companies (9). At the low-tech end of the occupational spectrum are the scores of documented and undocumented workers who listen to, dance to, and eagerly consume the music of Los Tigres del Norte. For the same circuits of late capitalism that brought low-wage jobs to California also carried the band's *conjunto* sound to Silicon Valley and beyond. "By posing the world as it is against the world as the socially subordinated would like it to be," the border music of Los Tigres del Norte supplies what the postcolonial cultural critic Paul Gilroy says ethno-racial music in general provides—"a great deal of courage to go on living in the present" (1993, 36).

In 1985 Los Tigres del Norte recorded the best-selling *corrido* "Jaula de Oro," a shattering portrait of an undocumented Mexican father and his family. The interlingual, accordion-driven ballad surges with lived feelings.

> Aquí estoy establecido en los Estados
> Unidos. Diez años pasaron ya en que
> cruzé de mojado. Papeles no me he
> arreglado. Sigo siendo ilegal.

> Here I am established in the United States.
> It's been ten years since
> I crossed as a wetback. I never
> applied for papers. I'm still illegal.

And it focuses, like most *corridos*, on events of "particular relevance" to the *conjunto* and *(techno) banda* communities.[1]

> Tengo mi esposa y mis hijos que me
> los traje muy chicos, y se han olvidado
> ya de mi México querido, del nunca me
> olvido, y no puedo regresar.

> ¿De qué me sirve el dinero si yo
> soy como prisionero dentro de esta gran
> nación? Cuando me acuerdo hasta lloro
> aunque la jaula sea de oro, no deja de
> ser prisión.

> "¿Escúchame hijo, te gustaría que regresáramos
> a vivir en México?" "What you
> talkin' about, Dad? I don't wanna go back
> to Mexico. No way, Dad."

> Mis hijos no hablan conmigo. Otra
> idioma han aprendido y olvidado el
> español. Piensan como americanos.

Niegan que son mexicanos aunque
tengan mi color.

De mi trabajo a mi casa. Yo no sé lo que
me pasa aunque soy hombre de hogar.
Casi no salgo a la calle pues tengo miedo
que me hallen y me pueden deportar.

I have my wife and children whom I
brought at a very young age. They no
longer remember my beloved Mexico,
which I never forget and to which I can
never return.

What good is money if I am
like a prisoner in this great
nation? When I think about it, I
cry. Even if the cage is made of gold, it
doesn't make it less a prison.

(*Spoken*) "Listen, son, would you like to
return to live in Mexico?" "What you
talkin' about, Dad? I don't wanna go
back to Mexico. No way, Dad."

My children don't speak to me. They
have learned another language and
forgotten Spanish. They think like
Americans. They deny that they are
Mexican even though they have my
skin color.

From my job to my home. I don't know
what is happening to me. I'm a homebody.
I almost never go out to the street.
I'm afraid I'll be found and deported.[2]

These lyrics dramatize, as the anthropologist Leo Chávez suggests,
how the undocumented status of the worker and his family in the United
States "places limits on their incorporation into society" (1992, 158).
I hope they can serve as preamble for this book, a way of beginning to
explore the materially hybrid and often recalcitrant quality of literary
and (mass) cultural forms in the extended U.S.-Mexican borderlands:
hybrid because Los Tigres del Norte used Tex-Mex accordion music
and Spanish and English lyrics for their ballad; recalcitrant because their
hybrid verses deconstruct what the cultural theorist David Lloyd, in a
different context, has called "the monologic desire of cultural nation-

alism" (1994, 54). "Jaula de Oro" stands as a corrective to the xenophobic, nationalist, and racist "backlash" in the United States against the estimated four million undocumented workers, more than half residing in California.[3] To the undocumented troubadour-subject, the *jaula de oro* is simultaneously the golden state of California and what used to be called the American dream. Looking at his family's incorporation into U.S. society ("they no longer remember my beloved Mexico" and "my children don't speak to me [in Spanish]"), the Mexican father feels tensions everywhere in California, imprisoning him in both his private and his public spheres. The street, his job, and even his home places severe constraints on his movements. Everywhere, "this great nation" feels like a prison. A nightmarish culture of surveillance, a profound sense of fear and anxiety, pervades the undocumented worker's everyday life.

This feeling in postmodern California of a proliferation of "new repressions in space and movements"—as the urban historian Mike Davis finds in *City of Quartz*—is doubly felt by the undocumented Mexican worker and his family. By the 1990s, Davis asserts, an obsession "with the architectural placing of social boundaries ha[d] become a zeitgeist of urban restructuring, a master narrative in the emerging built environment" of our major cosmopolitan cities. While Los Tigres del Norte invoke this panopticon barrioscape in "Jaula de Oro," the wild vertiginous fear the undocumented worker expresses ("I don't know what is happening to me. . . . I almost never go out to the street. I'm afraid I'll be found and deported.") is clearly something more than a response to the jolts of postmodern culture, for his anxiety speaks to the continuing desire of the United States for "pure" national and cultural spaces and for what Davis apocalyptically calls "a hoary but still viable . . . plan for a law and order armageddon" (1990, 223).

The idea that undocumented workers and their children pose a problem (or a set of problems) is part and parcel of what Bill Hing, a Stanford University law professor, sees as "the worst anti-immigrant hysteria in U.S. history" (Chung and Le 1993, A15), surely an exaggeration, for the ethno-racial history of California and the United States has been characterized by what the multicultural historian Ronald Takaki calls rampant anti-immigrant "antagonisms" (1993, 7). Anti-immigrant racism today, however, assumes new forms and is articulated by postliberal and neoconservative politicians alike. In crisis-bound California, for instance, anti-immigrant scapegoating (largely directed against undocumented

Mexicans, Central Americans, and Asians) endures and is re-created by draconian proposals to stop what Governor Pete Wilson describes (in classic colonialist discourse terms) as "the flood of illegal immigration" (Kershner 1993, 1). Thus Democratic senator Dianne Feinstein calls for a dollar toll for crossing the borders with both Mexico and Canada, and Wilson urges Congress to pass a constitutional amendment to deny legal citizenship to children born in the United States to undocumented workers.[4]

Along with Los Tigres del Norte in "Jaula de Oro," I propose a different historical and (mass) cultural vision of what the Asian-American feminist cultural critic Shelley Sunn Wong calls the "American *Bildung*" (1994, 128). We do not see the golden nation-state as being invaded by so-called illegal aliens, corrupting and polluting pure cultural spaces beyond the borderlands. Nor do we accept the premise of those sociologists who stress the "pathological" side of the U.S.-Mexico border-crossing experience. Rather, our projects make space for an alternative narrative of what can now be called the ethno-racialized cultures of displacement—a recognition hinted at by the undocumented Mexican worker's vernacular assertion that he is irrevocably established in the United States: "It's been ten years since I crossed as a wetback."

Reading against the grain of the undocumented Mexican worker's deep and unreconstructed nostalgia for his *madre patria* (mother country)—he laments that his children "no longer remember" his "beloved Mexico that [he can] never forget"—we are able to wonder how fully cognizant Los Tigres del Norte were in creating a mass cultural form that by its very hybridized form and content constantly transgresses the North's monology of cultural nationalism. "Jaula de Oro," in my view, is recalcitrant to the material and aesthetic politics of cultural nationalism. A significant challenge to nationalist monology occurs in the *corrido* when the son answers the question put to him in Spanish by the father, "¿Escúchame hijo, te gustaría que regresáramos a vivir en Mexico?" (Listen, son, would you like to return to live in Mexico?) by responding in English, "What you talkin' about, Dad? I don't wanna go back to Mexico. No way, Dad." While the monolingual father despairs, the son's response in English materially hybridizes the *corrido*'s cultural critique of anti-immigrant feelings and literalizes the negative *way* of life in Silicon Valley. Moreover, it points to Los Tigres del Norte's own material hybrid formation in heteroglossic California, providing a renewed mass cultural ground for an alternative critique of the narrative of the nation. Hybridity, in this U.S. immigrant context, as the cultural critic Lisa Lowe theorizes in *Immigrant Acts,* "is not a natural or static category; it is a socially constructed . . . position, assumed for political reasons" (1996, 82).

Border Matters examines the nature of this new materially hybrid and cultural critique in the U.S.-Mexico borderlands, for there has not been any systematic investigation of the intercultural music produced by mass cultural intellectuals such as Los Tigres del Norte, Los Illegals, El Vez, (Kid) Frost, and Tish Hinojosa, or of the consequences of the cultural studies movement for U.S.-Mexico borderland theory, "culture studies," and literary production.

First carved out in the midst of U.S. imperialism by the Treaty of Guadalupe Hidalgo (1848) and the Gadsden Purchase (1853), the U.S.-Mexico borderlands have earned a reputation as a "third country," because our southern border is not simply Anglocentric on one side and Mexican on the other.[5] Although this "site," where the Third World implodes into the First, is a strip of land two thousand miles long and no more than twenty miles wide, some believe the U.S.-Mexico border extends all the way to Seattle. To "survive the borderlands"—as the feminist Gloria Anzaldúa (1987) suggests in her border-defying writings—is to become a dangerous "crossroads." A near-intercultural world unto itself, the U.S.-Mexico border is dominated by two foreign powers, in Washington, D.C., and Mexico City. The U.S.-Mexico border changes pesos into dollars, humans into undocumented workers, *cholos/as* (Chicano youth culture) into punks, people between cultures into people without culture.[6]

In response to these challenges and deterritorializations, *Border Matters* reconceives literary and cultural practices. What changes, for example, when American culture and literature are understood in terms of "migration" and not only immigration? "On which side of the border," asks the Mexican performance artist Guillermo Gómez-Peña, "is the avant-garde?" (1987, 1). "When will Gov. Pete Wilson, Senators Barbara Boxer and Dianne Feinstein and many other political pols in the state [of California] who rant about the immigration problem learn to dance the *quebradita?*" asks the U.S. Latino public intellectual Rubén Martínez (1994, 12). I explore these kinds of questions about modernity, postmodernity, and postcoloniality by bringing cultural studies in the U.S.-Mexico borderlands into dialogue with U.S. and British cultural studies. My aim is to encourage comparative intercultural research and theoretical work that moves us beyond the fragmentary knowledges juxtaposed by specialists in so-called interdisciplinary studies. I agree with the Latin American cultural theorist Néstor García Canclini that we need a transdisciplinary model more sensitive "to the opening of each discipline with the other" (1995, 204).

Part I of *Border Matters* focuses on the yet unwritten literary and cultural history of Chicano/a and Latin American social cultural "theorists" and postmodernist intellectuals such as Renato Rosaldo, Vicki Ruiz, George J. Sánchez, and Néstor García Canclini (chapter 1). It also examines the politics of modernist border culture in Américo Paredes's anti-imperialist literary productions *George Washington Gómez* (1990) and *Between Two Worlds* (1991) (chapter 2), the construction of borderland subjectivities in the poetry of José Montoya, Bernice Zamora, and Alberto Ríos (chapter 3), and the spatial postmodern contradictions in Arturo Islas's *Migrant Souls* (1990) and Carmen Lomas Garza's *Cuadros de familia/Family Pictures* of 1990 (chapter 4).

Part II begins with a discussion of the southern California texts of Helena María Viramontes, John Rechy, Los Illegals, and (Kid) Frost, among others (chapter 5). Stretching from the shanty *colonias* (districts) of Tijuana and San Diego to the surf and turf of Santa Barbara, this extended urban *frontera* is inhabited by a heterogeneous non-Anglo-American majority, tipping the ethnic scale away from what Mike Davis calls "WASP hegemony" toward "polyethnic diversity" (1990, 7). My view is that Viramontes's "The Cariboo Cafe" (1985), Rechy's *The Miraculous Day of Amalia Gómez* (1991), Los Illegals' "El Lay" (1983), and (Kid) Frost's *East Side Story* (1992) are more perceptive than writings by many theorists of urban postmodernism in representing the "urban hardening" of everyday life. Thus, countering the general postmodern art-culture system represented in mainline postmodernist studies, I suggest alternative border cultures, histories, and contexts. Culture is by nature heterogeneous and necessarily works through a realm of borders.

Here it seems appropriate to survey briefly the multiple institutional routes of the cultural studies movement in Britain and the United States with an eye toward establishing its "beginnings" and elucidating some of its current debates. For example, what do some of these cultural critics mean by the term *cultural studies*? According to Stuart Hall, one of the founding directors at the Centre for Contemporary Cultural Studies (CCCS) in Birmingham, England, cultural studies "was conceived as an intellectual intervention. It aimed to define and occupy a space" (1980, 16). Hall suggests that "the field in which this intervention was made had been initially charted in the 1950s. This earlier founding moment is but specified in terms of the originating texts, the 'original curriculum' of the field—Hoggart's *The Uses of Literacy,* Raymond Williams's *Culture and Society* and *The Long Revolution,* E. P. Thompson's critique of the latter and the example of related questions, worked in a more theoretical mode, in *The Making of the English Working Class*" (16).[7] For Hall, there are at least two ways of defining and understanding culture: (1) anthropologically, "as *cultural practices,*" and (2) more historically, "questioning anthropological meaning and interrogating it universally by means of the concepts of social formation, cultural power, domination and regulation, resistance and struggle" (27). As Richard Johnson (who succeeded Hall as CCCS's director in 1979) emphasizes in "What Is Cultural Studies Anyway?": "culture is neither autonomous nor an eternally determined field, but a site of social differences and struggles" (1987, 39).

British cultural studies, thus broadly defined, draws out and articulates the complex mediations and struggles between what Raymond Williams has called "culture" and "society." Moreover, throughout his career as a New Left theorist and an ethnic Welsh borderlands novelist, Williams analyzed the diverse historical "cluster of significations" given the word *culture.* As he writes in *Keywords,* it "is one of the two or three most complicated words in the English language" (1976 [1983 rev.], 87). Its history contains both elitist (Matthew Arnold and F. R. Leavis) formulations of culture associating it with the so-called superiority of Western traditions and more democratic connotations encompassing all symbolic activities in our everyday lives.

Fundamentally, "the idea of culture," Williams argues, "is a general reaction to a general and major change in the condition of our common life. Its basic element is its efforts at total qualitative assessment" (1958, 259). Williams completes his inquiry into the diverse significations associated with the word *culture* by concluding that it is crucial for students of cultural studies to combine cultural anthropology's reference to culture as "material production" with history's and literature's reference to culture as a "signifying or symbolic system" (1976 [1986 rev.], 91). Williams's summary definition of culture can help us to situate the broad transdisciplinary range of issues and meanings associated with cultural studies in Britain and the United States, for culture, he theorizes, represents "a whole way of [hegemonic] life [in struggle], material, intellectual, and spiritual" (16).

Following in this long British cultural studies tradition, the Americanists Cary Nelson, Paula Treichler, and Lawrence Grossberg argue that cultural studies—at present experiencing an "internationalist boom"—is "an interdisciplinary, transdisciplinary, and sometimes counterdisciplinary field that operates in the tension between its tendencies to embrace both a broad, anthropological and a more narrowly humanistic conception of culture." Cultural studies in Britain and the United States, they contend, is "committed to the study of the entire range of a society's art, beliefs, institutions, and communicative practices" (1992, 4).

This international success and proliferation of cultural studies, however, also brings what James Clifford calls "obvious dangers," particularly, he emphasizes, "of lost intellectual focus and political edge." While cultural studies emerged in Britain with Williams's and Hall's New Left interventions within and outside the academy, and though the cultural studies project was initially connected with adult education movements, the question becomes, has cultural studies in its travels from Birmingham to the United States "turn[ed] into" what Clifford calls "just another discipline (or transdiscipline)?" (1991, 1). Has cultural studies, in other words, become institutionalized in U.S. academies at the cost of its political edge?

Let me be briefly autobiographical to situate what I am about to say about the local history of the Center for Cultural Studies at the University of California at Santa Cruz. When I served on the center's steering committee, we attempted to link specific borders and diasporas—the U.S.-Mexican and the black Atlantic—as paradigms of intercultural crossing and mixing. Although those who founded the center at Santa Cruz in spring 1988 were not consciously thinking about the Birmingham CCCS when they began, they proposed, in the words of James Clifford, the founding director, "a center which would be visibly different from the many humanities centers around the country," for cultural studies "suggested a serious engagement with the social sciences and political arts" (1). Fortunately, the Center for Cultural Studies encouraged not only a Birmingham-like engagement with subcultural theory, feminism, and hegemony and its resistance but also a "homegrown" orientation for these interventions.

Over the past eight years, the Center for Cultural Studies has put together an ensemble of research clusters, workshops, publications, and visiting scholars including, among others, the British postcolonialists Stuart Hall, Paul Gilroy, and Isaac Julien; the Indian "subaltern studies" historians and novelists Ranajit Guha and Amitav Ghosh; and the Caribbean/Latin American cultural critics Edward Kamu Brathwaite and Néstor García Canclini. Under Clifford's directorship, the center focused on "comparative, transnational topics and problems" (1991, 1). More recently, the center has concentrated on what Clifford calls comparative treatments of intercultural "crossing as both traversing and mixing" (1992a, 1) and on encouraging collaborative work with the University of California Humanities Research Institute at Irvine on projects such as the "Minority Discourse" initiatives convened by Abdul JanMohamed, Valerie Smith, and Norma Alarcón.

All of these countertraditions have helped to catalyze the multiple trajectories in *Border Matters.* More specifically, Gilroy's *There Ain't No Black in the Union Jack* (1991) and *The Black Atlantic* (1993) have enabled me to argue that the culture of the U.S.-Mexico borderlands, like the black Atlantic diaspora culture, cannot be reduced to any nationally based "tradition."[8] As we will see in Viramontes's "The Cariboo Cafe" and Rechy's *The Miraculous Day of Amalia Gómez,* a South/North political culture of the Américas questions national, nationalistic, and what Gilroy calls "absolutist" paradigms of culture.

Thus envisaged, cultural studies—from 1960s Birmingham to 1990s Santa Cruz—is a tradition conjured, syncretized, and customized. As Grossberg suggests, cultural studies is an "alchemy"; its methodology is one of "bricolage"; and its "choice of practice . . . is pragmatic, strategic, and self-reflective" (Nelson, Treichler, and Grossberg 1992, 2). These traditions have led me to ask different questions: How do we tell other spatial stories? How do we tell other histories that are placed in local frames of awareness, on the one hand, and situated globally, geopolitically, on the other? The autoethnographic borderland "texts" by Luis Alberto Urrea, Rubén Martínez, and Richard Rodriguez (as well as by the writers and intellectuals discussed in Part I) may suggest different strategies for those interested in the positive practices associated with the international cultural studies movement, for *Border Matters* strives for a new comparative area of intercultural studies.

Chapter 6 continues to interrogate the productiveness and the limits of local and hemispheric mappings. Contradictory versions of transfrontier border culture appear in Urrea's *Across the Wire* (1993), a dizzying mix of travel writing, evangelism, and autoethnography; Martínez's *The Other Side* (1992), part *crónica* (chronicle) of youth culture and part travel narrative between Los Angeles, Mexico City, San Salvador, and Havana; and Rodriguez's *Days of Obligation* (1992), an argument against, as he says in the book's subtitle, his Mexican father's cultural and political values. Their autoethnographic writings are in many ways aligned with the deterritorializing gestures of borderland social science theorists such as Rosaldo, Sánchez, García Canclini, and Ruiz, who see in their postmodern ethnographies and in feminist theories of *la frontera* a representative liminal site for the postmodern condition.

If the book's first six chapters announce the postcontemporary coming of age of the U.S.-Mexico border as a paradigm of crossing, circulation, material mixing, and resistance, chapter 7, "Remapping American Cultural Studies," delves into an extended discussion of U.S.-Mexico border writing within the context of nineteenth-century U.S. cultures of imperialism. It provides another comparative focus by studying the uneven modernist writings of two chroniclers of Gilded Age Americanism, John Gregory Bourke and María Amparo Ruiz de Burton. Bourke, a soldier-anthropologist, in 1894 produced one of the first ethnographic studies of the U.S.-Mexico borderlands, an essay symptomatically entitled "The American Congo." If the force field of American border studies was hegemonically conceived by Bourke on the swirling countercurrents of the Rio Grande in South Texas in the American age of empire, Chicano/a cultural studies has had to contest Bourke's crude and violent mappings and representations of empire. Against Bourke's cultures of U.S. imperialism, I pose Ruiz de Burton's *The Squatter and the Don* (1885), a historical romance about Alta California and the American 1848.

In my attempt to suggest a historical and intercultural approach to U.S.-Mexico border writing and cultural studies, I use some terms and concepts that require additional defining. "*Transfrontera* contact zone" refers to the two-thousand-mile-long border between the United States and Mexico and to other geopolitical border zones, such as Raymond Williams's border zone between Wales and England. This zone is the social space of subaltern encounters, the Janus-faced border line in which peoples geopolitically forced to separate themselves now negotiate with one another and manufacture new relations, hybrid cultures, and multiple-voiced aesthetics. I borrow the term *contact zone* from Mary Louise Pratt's colonial discourse coinage, which owes much to sociolinguistics and improvised languages that develop among speakers of different native languages and in which the term is "synonymous with colonial frontier" (1992, 6). "*Transfrontera* contact zone" is an attempt to invoke the heterotopic forms of everyday life whose trajectories cross over and interact.

Another phrase that recurs throughout this work is "U.S.-Mexico border writing," by which I mean the writer's strategies of representation whereby *frontera* subjects such as Américo Paredes, John Rechy, and Helena Viramontes produce a theory of culture as resistance and struggle, not coherence and consensus. U.S.-Mexico border writing is a continuous encounter between two or more reference codes and tropes. As Guillermo Gómez-Peña suggests, "To understand [border writing] means to manage the greatest number of codes possible. For the non-border dweller, the 'here' (of the border) is a double 'there' (there is the 'there' of Tijuana and the 'there' of San Diego)" (1987, 2). Often, as with Paredes's literary writings, Los Tigres del Norte's *corridos,* or Gómez-Peña's performance videos, U.S.-Mexico border writing is bilingual and dialogic. My aim, however, is not to codify. Rather, I have sought to use U.S.-Mexico border writing as much to construct a non-Eurocentric perspective about cultural studies as to unify a rhetoric or stylistics of the border.

By examining the contact zones of the U.S.-Mexico border, the spaces where the nation either ends or begins, we can begin to problematize the notion that the nation is "naturally" there: these are spaces within which patronymic relationships take place. *Border Matters* challenges this stable, naturalized, and hegemonic status of the national by looking at the assumed equivalence we make between the national and the cultural. As I suggested earlier, the *conjunto* music of Los Tigres del Norte offers one important avenue for interrogating current national and international relationships, for cultural struggle in *corridos* such as "Jaula de Oro" is also a transnational struggle enacted between *patrimonios* (nations) as well as within nation-states. Their model of cultural studies, it bears emphasizing, queries the uneven power relations between national entities.

PART ONE

COMPARATIVE
INTERCULTURAL STUDIES

I

Cultural Theory in the
U.S.-Mexico Borderlands

I need to understand how a place on the map is also a place
in history.
  Adrienne Rich,
  "Notes toward a Politics of Location" (1986)

When politicians in the 1980s bemoaned the fact that America lost control of its borders with Mexico, they dreamed
up a lost age of mastery. In fact, from the Gulf of Mexico to
the Pacific Ocean, the [U.S.-]Mexico border was a social fiction that neither nature nor people in search of opportunity
observed. That proposition carried a pedigree of decades, if
not centuries.
  Patricia Nelson Limerick, *The Legacy of Conquest* (1987)

Cultural studies is loose in the world. Once located in an
embattled, somewhat legendary, program at the University
of Birmingham, cultural studies now seems to be all over
the map.
  James Clifford, "The Transit Lounge of Culture" (1991)

This mapping of cultural theory within the discourse of the U.S.-
Mexico borderlands is an invitation to literary scholars, historians,
cultural studies critics, anthropologists, feminists, mass culture critics, public interest lawyers, and antiracists to redraw the borders
between folklore and the counterdiscourses of marginality, between
"everyday" culture and "high" culture, and between "people with culture" and "people between culture." More broadly, it is a continua-
tion of the work in Chicano/a studies to have Chicanos/as perceived
as agents with culture—attributes that the dominant Anglocentric culture has largely denied to us because culture, they believe, lives somewhere else.[1]

Before moving from South Texas to teach in the Department of Comparative Ethnic Studies at the University of California at Berkeley, I lived in the center of the periphery, in the U.S.-Mexico borderlands, where the Rio Grande enters the Gulf of Mexico. A map of the lower Rio Grande border, from the mouth of the river "to the two Laredos," as Américo Paredes puts it, "shows a clustering of farming towns" and sprawling urban contact zones along both riverbanks, "with lonely gaps to the north and to the south" (1958, 7). In writing an earlier version of this chapter during the Columbus quincentennial, an occasion for a reconsideration of the effects of imperialism on culture, I tried, like Paredes, to spatialize on the map before me how this "periphery" was once the "center" of the imperial Spanish border province of Nuevo Santander, colonized in 1749 by José de Escandón to hold the line against English, French, and Anglo-American encroachment.[2] How can a map tell us how the U.S.-Mexico borderlands were once an ecological whole, with Mexico blending into the present-day southwestern American landscape? Can maps represent how, with independence in 1821, Mexico took over the Spanish borderlands only to have to fight off the United States in its quest to fulfill its manifest destiny? Can maps show how the Treaty of Guadalupe Hidalgo in 1848 added what Paredes calls "the final element to Rio Grande society, a border" (15), thus inaugurating a new phase of the U.S.-Mexico borderlands?

For years I have tried to piece together what it must have been like for Reyes and Carmelita Saldívar, my great-great-grandparents, to have been almost overnight "incorporated into the Union of the United States" (Treaty of Guadalupe Hidalgo, article 9). I try to imagine what it must have been like for them to improvise a new kind of cultural citizenship in the face of a hyperauthoritative treaty—a text—legitimizing U.S. empire, especially in justifying federal, state, and corporate ownership of former Nuevo Santander and Mexican lands. I try to envision explaining to them (using the legal scholar Patricia Williams's theory of the alchemy of race and rights) how the Treaty of Guadalupe Hidalgo (U.S. Supreme Court decisions notwithstanding) was meant to protect and enlarge the civil and property rights of Chicanos. I wonder whether it is more useful to argue (using Chicano/a activist arguments) that basic human rights guaranteed to Chicanos/as by the U.S. Constitution are no longer solely of a domestic character, for the treaty conferred local sovereign and global human rights that the United States simply refuses to acknowledge.[3]

In my childhood in Cameron County in South Texas, I saw the Texas-Mexico borderlands turn into an ecological wasteland, with more than ninety-three *maquiladoras* pouring out toxic waste and endangering life chances and life experiences on both sides of the border. As a result of these unregulated multinational factories (of General Motors, Quimica Fluor, PEMEX, among others), there have been in the last decade what the border journalist Ana Arana calls "a disturbingly high number of anencephalic births" (a rare disorder that leaves infants without a complete brain) in the Rio Grande Valley (1992, 20). At the other tip of the U.S.-Mexico border, nativist and white supremacist "Light Up the Border" campaigns in San Diego County have become the order of the day, and the INS with its doctrine of militarized low-intensity conflict has abused, shot, and incarcerated scores of brown border-crossers in what the international human rights group Americas Watch calls "inhumane detention facilities."[4]

While I grew up believing in the truth of precepts that were available to me—the reality of space, borders, and nations—I now locate myself within a zone of dangerous crossings with new "centralities" that challenge dominant national centers of identity and culture. In our subaltern U.S.-Mexico borderlands, the emergence of new "migrant" cultures shuffles the mainline U.S. *Bildung* of assimilation, acculturation, and the polyethnic state. In response to these challenges, this chapter reconceives postmodern and postcolonial cultural practices. What changes, for example, when culture is understood in terms of material hybridity, not purity? How is the imagined community of the nation—to use Benedict Anderson's (1983) terms—disrupted and customized by materially hybrid U.S.-Mexico borderland subjectivities?

I explore these kinds of questions by bringing cultural studies into dialogue with the complex black British diaspora culture orbits theorized by Stuart Hall, Paul Gilroy, and Kobena Mercer, among others, at the Birmingham Centre for Contemporary Cultural Studies. As the cultural critic Henry Louis Gates writes, "The Birmingham battle for making 'cultural politics' more than just a white thing quickly bumped into the conundrum of identity politics." Hall and Gilroy, Gates argues, "attempted to modulate old myths to meet new constituencies," opposing New Left Neolithic continuities created by Raymond Williams and E. P. Thompson "with the traditions that blacks who arrived in Britain since World War II brought with them" (1992, 26). My aim here is to continue making cultural politics more than just a "white thing" and to encourage comparative cultural research. For it is only when we add "color" to the formation of British and U.S. cultural studies that we can see, in Gilroy's words, that global radical practices in the 1950s and continuing in the present were "produced not spontaneously from internal and intrinsic 'English' [or 'American'] dynamics" but were "generated in a complex pattern of antagonistic relationships with the external, supra-national and imperial world for which the ideas of 'race,' nationality and national culture are the primary indices" (1992, 190).

Although in the next chapter I will study some of the key developments associated with the multiple modernist origins of Chicano/a cultural studies in the 1950s—for example, Paredes's attempts to represent the complex self-fashionings brought about by the bloody border conflict and to counter Anglocentric hegemony in border disputes—my purpose in what follows is not to write an institutional history. Rather, it is, first, to examine Renato Rosaldo's *Culture and Truth* for traces of its rich U.S.-Mexico borderland cultural theorizing and for its repositioning of the politics of postmodernism. Then I briefly analyze Vicki Ruiz's "The Rosa Guerrero Story," George J. Sánchez's *Becoming Mexican American,* and Néstor García Canclini's *Culturas híbridas* as examples of U.S.-Mexico border writing.

While we do not need yet another definition of what the postmodern or the postcolonial really is, it seems clear to me that U.S.-Mexico borderland sociocultural theorists such as Rosaldo, Ruiz, Sánchez, and García Canclini (as well as the writers from the human sciences discussed in the chapters that follow) are emphatically implicated in any attempt to map out the specificity of postcontemporary culture, history, literature, and society and thus to gauge this culture's distance from what might be called the culture of "high modernism."[5] As García Canclini characteristically writes, *la expansión urbana* (the urban expansion) in cosmopolitan sites such as Tijuana "intensifies cultural hybridity" (1990, 265). Put differently, postmodernism or postcolonialism in the inter-Américas context ought never to be viewed as a static and homogeneous phenomenon. As Walter Mignolo acutely puts it, "the postmodern and the postcolonial [in the Américas] are two faces of the same coin, locating imaginary constructions and loci of enunciations in different aspects of modernity, colonization, and imperial world orders" (n.d., 35). In any case, it seems clear to me that whereas modernism's border patrol once kept the barbarians out and safeguarded the culture within, there is now only liminal ground, which may prove fertile for some and slimy for others.[6]

Fundamentally, Rosaldo's *Culture and Truth* sets the postcontemporary agenda for cultural studies in the United States by demonstrating how the multiple concepts signified by the single word *culture* are more fluid than traditional anthropologists suggest. Conventionally, anthropologists think of other cultures as self-contained, bounded, homogeneous, and unchanging. Rosaldo, however, redefines culture as encompassing "the everyday and the esoteric, the mundane and the elevated, the ridiculous and the sublime. Neither high nor low, culture is all-pervasive" (1989, 26). Culture is postmodernist and postcolonial in Rosaldo's hands, for he attempts to negotiate forms of high social science art (Clifford Geertz, Victor Turner, and E. P. Thompson) with certain forms and genres of mass culture (*Miami Vice* and José Montoya's "El Louie") and the practices of everyday life.

One of the central aims of *Culture and Truth* is to wrest the concept of culture away from its elitist foundations and put it to use in terms of our everyday "lived experiences."[7] Contesting the antidemocratic narrowing of "culture" on many U.S. college campuses, Rosaldo complicates culture by repositioning it as a critical multicultural "borderland," for "our everyday lives are crisscrossed by border zones, pockets and eruptions of all kinds" (206). To counter the traditional Anglocentric uses of the term *culture,* he proposes two strategies. First, as I have already suggested, he defines culture as encompassing the "everyday," a definition that should help U.S. cultural studies focus on the lived experiences and struggles of people. Second, as Rosaldo contended most explicitly in his book's conclusion, the goal of our intellectual work in the 1990s and beyond ought to be "the education of our country's future generations." He asks, "How can we prepare students to enter the changing multicultural world of the coming century?" (218–219).

The title of Rosaldo's book consciously plays on the titles of two significant works in British culture studies—Matthew Arnold's *Culture and Anarchy* (1869) and Raymond Williams's *Culture and Society* (1958)— and anticipates Edward W. Said's *Culture and Imperialism* (1993). As is well known, Arnold sees "culture" as exclusively "high culture" and gives the West what Williams calls "a single watchword and a name" (1983, 114). Arnold's purpose in *Culture and Anarchy* is to

> recommend culture as the great help out of our present difficulties;
> culture being a pursuit of our total perfection by means of getting to

know, on all matters which most concern us, the best which has been
thought and said in the world; and, through this knowledge, turning
a stream of fresh and free thought upon our stock notions and habits,
which we now follow staunchly but mechanically, vainly imagining
that there is a virtue in following them staunchly which makes up for
the mischief of following them mechanically. (1869, viii)

To be sure, "culture" for Arnold is both study and ideology, and it is
related to the idea that without regulative norms, "the masses" become
pathologically violent.

Rosaldo, however, argues against Arnold's limited idea of culture and
aligns himself with Williams's materialist discussion of culture and society. Like Williams, Rosaldo argues against society's reduction to fixed
forms. In opposition to such frozen ideas as "worldview" and "false
consciousness," he (like Williams) examines the processes of ethno-racial
"structures of feeling," processes that are just emerging and not fully
articulated. Thus in his moving introduction, "Grief and a Headhunter's
Rage," as well as elsewhere in the book, he is interested in what Williams
has called "affective elements of consciousness and relationships; not
feelings against thought, but thought as felt and feeling as thought"
(1977, 132).

Throughout the first half of *Culture and Truth,* Rosaldo shows how
ethnographers are "positioned subjects," and he precisely demonstrates how their involvement of culture with what he calls "imperialist nostalgia" is itself a central fact of Western culture. Like Américo
Paredes and José E. Limón, he deliberately experiments with the traditional forms of ethnographic writing. In the chapter "The Erosion of
Classic Norms," for example, he playfully offers the reader what he
calls a "mythic tale about the birth of the anthropological concept of
culture and its embodiment in the classic ethnography" (1989, 30). Here
Rosaldo argues his position by writing in "talk story" the tall tale of
the Lone Ethnographer in search of his native. The emplotment of the
tale borders on the hilarious, for Rosaldo's Lone Ethnographer-Ranger
undergoes the rite of passage called "fieldwork," collecting his disin-
terested data in the hinterlands, and then returns home to write a "true
account of the culture" (30). For Rosaldo, however, "the sacred bundle the Lone Ethnographer handed to his successors includes a complicity with imperialism, a commitment to objectivism, and a belief in
monumentalism" (31).

In his now-famous "Imperialist Nostalgia" chapter, Rosaldo continues to decenter the forms of classic ethnographic writing by experimenting with avant-garde "montage" to show how travel writers and government officials such as Wilfred Turnbull, missionaries such as Sarah Graves, and ethnographers such as Michelle Rosaldo and he have displayed in their various writings on the Philippines the curious and paradoxical notion of imperialist nostalgia, the "phenomenon of people's longing for what they themselves have destroyed" (87). Missionaries, constabulary officers, and ethnographers, he argues, "all bore witness" and "participated . . . in the transformations taking place before our eyes" (87). Like Mary Louise Pratt, Rosaldo connects the "eye" of ethnography and travel writing with the "I" of imperialism.[8]

In the second half of *Culture and Truth*, Rosaldo both maps the Chicano tradition of cultural studies and becomes a major participant in it. His observations in the final chapters, "Changing Chicano Narratives" and "Border Crossings," mark the terminus of a line that stretches back to the interventions by Jovita González, Carlos E. Castañeda, George I. Sánchez, Arthur L. Campa, Américo Paredes, and Ernesto Galarza.[9] However, key writers in the postmodernist, postcolonialist, and Chicana feminist movement—Gloria Anzaldúa and Sandra Cisneros—also play a significant role in Rosaldo's reshaping of social analysis, for the narrative analyses of these U.S.-Mexico borderland writers "renew" what he calls "the anthropologist's search for meaning" (166).

In "Border Crossings," for example, Rosaldo offers a number of theoretical observations on "cultural visibility" and "cultural invisibility" in the social sciences. Here he recalls the advice of a mentor at Harvard University when he was contemplating doing his graduate fieldwork in the Philippines: "A teacher warned me that Filipinos are 'people without culture'" (197). Rosaldo, a borderland Chicano from Tucson, knew better: "[I] knew that the notion of 'people without culture,' or, with 'more' or 'less' culture than others, made no sense" (197). Throughout this chapter he "talks back" to his Harvard teacher and "objectivist" colleagues by showing how the traditional and normalizing anthropological practice of using the "detached observer" to make "ourselves" invisible to ourselves has been "debilitating" (198).

After considering the so-called people without culture in the Philippines and Mexico, he moves on to theorize about what he sees as the more dynamic category, "people between cultures" (198). A crucial research agenda for U.S. and global cultural studies opens up. *Culture and Truth* thus not only redefines and deconstructs the position of the "detached observer" in the social sciences, it brings new objects of study into focus, namely, "culture in the borderlands," for "human cultures" (in most metropolitan typifications) "are neither necessarily coherent nor always homogeneous" (207). For Rosaldo, border zones such as sexual orientation, gender, class, race, nationality, and age "should be regarded not only as analytically empty transitional zones but as sites of creative cultural production that require investigation" (208).

Rosaldo, of course, searches for portraits of the cultural border zones and eruptions in the mass media as well as in oppositional Chicano literary forms. For example, he encourages the reader to watch videotapes of *Miami Vice* to understand how the program, with its "white zoot suits, high tension mood music, and carefully chosen pastels," disguises itself as "affirmative action heaven, with blacks, Latinos, and whites all playing cops and robbers, vibrantly policing and trafficking drugs together" (212). According to him, *Miami Vice* plays out for American viewers how Latin American drugs are "invading" North America and how Latino drug traffickers are "infesting" middle-class white neighborhoods. To be sure, the edge of the U.S.-Mexico border is widening, but for him *Miami Vice* also informs middle-class Americans about the wave of immigrants from the South while it helps to explain the success of "new immigration" bills in Congress.

In addition to seeing the U.S.-Mexico border as the site of "spatial stereotypes," he understands it as a zone for ludic artistry. In a bold new reading of José Montoya's classic Chicano movement poem "El Louie," he characterizes the protagonist as postmodern before his time. Louie Rodriguez, he contends, "seeks out incongruity, unlikely juxtapositions [in American culture]: Cagney, El Charro Negro, Bogart, and Cruz Diablo." Louie is not only a tragic hero, as many Chicano critics have argued, but also a liminal Chicano character "playing the cat role, just playing." "El Louie" epitomizes the extended U.S.-Mexico borderlands as a culturally distinct space; it is at once a poem betwixt and between Chicano and Anglo-American cultural traditions and a work of art in which Montoya "celebrates polyphony in its polyglot text, and heterogeneity in making Anglo, Chicano, and Mexican elements move together in the dance of life" (216).

In common with the most stimulating new works in cultural anthropology, feminism, literary studies, and comparative ethnic studies, *Culture and Truth* is structurally innovative, highly personal, minimalist, and visionary in its claims based on wide scholarship. As the cultural critics Frances Mascia-Lees and Patricia Sharpe write, Rosaldo "not only advocates reflexivity and the use of narrative forms in social analysis, but laces his entire book with types of subjectivity he calls for": personal acts of bereavement, cultural critique of ethnic absolutism, and a renewed activism in the academy announced in the book's subtitle, *The Remaking of Social Analysis* (1992, 693). For this, Rosaldo's *Culture and Truth* especially commands the attention of workers in U.S. cultural studies.

With Rosaldo's interventions, the emergent Chicano/a cultural studies movement has focused on the strategies of racial formation and ethnicity in U.S.-Mexico border culture. Further, the writings of the historians Oscar J. Martínez and Mario T. García and the works of Arturo Islas, Alberto Ríos, John Rechy, and Carmen Lomas Garza, among others, have given Chicano/a cultural studies a cross-cultural comparative focus greater than the more positivistic social science field of "border studies" has conventionally had.[10] What Chicano/a cultural studies offers the loose group of tendencies, issues, and questions in the larger cultural studies orbits in Britain and the United States is the theorization of the U.S.-Mexico borderlands—literal, figurative, material, and militarized—and the deconstruction of the discourse of boundaries. Let me turn to the parallel developments in Chicana oral history and the new study of the *fronteriza* subjectivity of women.

In their edited collection, *Women on the U.S. Border,* the historian Vicki Ruiz and the sociologist Susan Tiano focus on new subjectivities on the U.S.-Mexico border. Offering insights into the lives of undocumented women coming to the United States as *solas* (single heads of households), of border women who work and organize themselves in the *maquiladoras* on the border, and of domestic workers who began to organize as early as 1933 in El Paso, Texas, and who have resisted the INS doctrine of low-intensity conflict, Ruiz and Tiano's anthology documents women's contributions to the material hybridization of culture on the border.

Ruiz's contribution to an emergent Chicano/a cultural studies is especially noteworthy. Using oral history (with its focus on popular culture) and stressing the lived experiences of everyday people, she attempts to let U.S.-Mexico border women represent themselves in the shaping of the historical and literary record. With its feminist emphasis on "subjectivity," Ruiz's oral history of Rosa Guerrero falls clearly within the sphere of Chicano/a cultural studies. As Ruiz puts it, "The personal-ization of the past brings vibrancy, sensitivity, and understanding of previous generations" (1987, 219). Through Rosa Guerrero, who grew up "brown" in El Paso during the decades following World War II, Ruiz reveals how, in their roles as teachers, performers, and spiritual leaders, women have created a new sense of "woman" that bears little resemblance "to the caricatures so prominent in popular and academic folklore" (213). With Guerrero's *testimonio* (testimony), Ruiz records how women are able to assert themselves politically in the face of the state institutions (such as schools) that codify subjects within the parameters established by the dominant group. Guerrero's recollection of how Chicana/o children were treated in the El Paso school system is particularly illuminating.

> I remember being punished for speaking Spanish. Nos daban coscorrones, pero coscorrones, o nos daban unas zuribandes con un board. Tenían un board of education por hablar español. Yo no entendía lo que decían, ni jota, ni jota. Pero por eso estoy cercana, y mi corazón y mi espíritu al programa bilingüe, porque sufrí unas cosas horribles. Yo no fuí la única; fueron miles de gentes que sufierion en Arizona, en Colorado, en Nuevo Mexico, en Texas, en California; que nos estereotipaban horriblemente. Don't you speak that ugly language, you are an American now, you Mexican child. They degraded us horribly, pero uno se hacía valer [but we asserted ourselves]. (226–227)

> [They'd hit us on the head but good, or they'd paddle us with what they called the board of education for speaking Spanish. I didn't understand what they were telling me, not one iota. That's why I'm so committed to the bilingual program, heart and soul, because I suffered horribly. I wasn't the only one. There were thousands of people who suffered in Arizona, in Colorado, in New Mexico, in Texas, in California; they stereotyped us horribly. . . .]

Ruiz's oral history is exemplary because it reconstructs the small details of everyday life (the site of all social struggle) on the U.S.-Mexico border and captures in an everyday, signifying vernacular the courage of border women such as Rosa Guerrero and their determination to assert themselves. More important, the construction of Guerrero's borderland consciousness allows us to begin to account for an undocumented area of subjectivity, what the historian Richard Johnson calls "structural shifts or major rearrangements of the self, especially in adult life" (1987, 69). In "What Is Cultural Studies Anyway?" Johnson distinguishes between subjectivity and consciousness. "Subjectivity," he writes, "includes the possibility . . . that some elements or impulses are subjectively active. . . . It focuses on the 'who I am' or, as important, the 'who we are' of culture." "Consciousness," in contrast, "embraces the notion of a consciousness of self as an active mental and moral self-production" (44). Rosa Guerrero's text thus engages the "subjective side of struggle, . . . [that] moment in subjective flux when social subjects . . . produce accounts of who they are, as conscious political agents" (69). Seen in this light, cultural studies is about the subjective forms we live by—the subjective side of social relations.

If the Chicana historian Vicki Ruiz ushers in a new project on U.S. Mexico border women's subjectivities, the urban historian George J. Sánchez's *Becoming Mexican American* (1993) emphasizes the materially hybrid interactions between ethno-racialization and identity among Mexican Americans, the largest immigrant group in California. Exploring the complex process whereby border-crossers from the South altered their self-orientation to that of "permanent residents" in *el norte* (the North) Sánchez's book rejects the traditional U.S. social science paradigm based on universalist teleology, moving from, say, the "primitive" to the modern condition. As the historian Philip J. Ethington suggests, *Becoming Mexican American* inaugurates for U.S. urban historiography "a borderlands framework that may at last answer the challenges that postmodernity poses to social science" (1996, 344).

Parts 1, 2, and 3 of *Becoming Mexican American* focus on what the author calls "crossing borders," "divided loyalties," and "ambivalent Americanism." Here he examines how, at the beginning of the twentieth century, Mexico experienced upheaval in the form of the Mexican Revolution (1910–1917), resulting in the diaspora of hundreds of thousands of Mexicans into Los Angeles. While Sánchez carefully traces the back-and-forth movements of the voluntary border crossings for these new Angelenos, he accurately records how the U.S. government's hegemonic immigration legislation made Mexican settlement in California a highly stressful experience. In 1917, for example, Congress passed a law placing, Sánchez writes, "substantial restrictions on European immigration and on those who entered from Mexico" (1993, 55). Other tactics in the 1920s were also used to limit Mexican immigration: a head tax of $8 was initiated at the border, and, later, a fee of $10 was required to secure a visa. All of this led to the joint effort by "local officials, the business community, and federal authorities in the Labor Department to set [repatriation] activities in motion" (214). In Los Angeles, Sánchez

argues, repatriation policies not only attempted to regulate border crossings from the South but also catalyzed a nativist discourse that defined
Mexicans and newly self-fashioned Mexican Americans (as well as
Asians) as ethno-racially impure "others." Thus, in the 1930s, Secre-
tary of Labor William Doak began demonizing Mexicans and Mexican
Americans in California in typical colonial discourse terms as some "four
hundred thousand illegal aliens" (quoted in Sánchez, 214), blaming them
for taking jobs away from "authentic" Americans at a time when the
United States was in a great economic depression. While Doak ordered
the Immigration Bureau to ferret out "these thousands," Sánchez notes,
the newly formed federal Border Patrol, which had less than forty agents,
was in no position to do so.

When repatriation failed, federal officials launched programs to teach
the border-crossers idealized versions of U.S. customs, practices, and
values. Although much effort was put into these so-called Americanization programs, the result, Sánchez happily suggests, was to instill in
the Mexican population of Los Angeles a new self-fashioned consciousness as ethno-racialized Americans. Sánchez's rich study describes
how Chicanos in Los Angeles at the turn of the twentieth century embodied what Rosaldo meant by his anthropological notion of "cultural in-
betweenness." By focusing on the Americanization programs that
developed after World War I and by exploring how Chicanos later used
the urbanized public space of consumer radio in Los Angeles to transculturate traditional *corridos* such as "El Lavaplatos" (The Dish-
washer), Sánchez convincingly shows how Mexican migrations into Los
Angeles rarely "uprooted all vestiges of one's native culture, but neither did Mexican culture remain unchanged in the United States" (272).

In contradistinction to Octavio Paz's protonationalist condemnation
of the Mexican-origin population of Los Angeles in *The Labyrinth of
Solitude,* Sánchez shows how the near-million Mexican residents were
neither "inauthentic Mexicans" nor "pathological." Rather, he writes
that these new Angelenos were "cultural bridges between two lands; in
fact, they had created a borderlands in the east-side barrios in which
cultural revival and re-creation were ever-present" (272). This was so
because the "back-and-forth nature of Mexican migration throughout
the twentieth century" (272) ensured a two-way traffic between the cultures of "el México profundo" (Batalla 1996) and the United States.

Becoming Mexican American deserves our attention not only because
of the way it fundamentally debunks Oscar Handlin's traditional

"uprooted" model of American urban "ethnogenesis" in Chicago and New York City but also because it spatially remaps what Shelley Sunn Wong calls the universal myth of the American *Bildung* (1994, 124), which situates Ellis Island as the central immigrant space in the nation. Sánchez's Los Angeles displaces the cultural and sociospatial myth of Ellis Island by presenting an alternative American *Bildung*. "Stand in the lobby of the transnational terminal at Los Angeles International Airport," he writes, "[and] witness the transformation of immigration adaptation to American society. Here in this airport, which has become the single largest port of entry for immigrants to this country, one sees continuous movement" (1993, 271). American identity for the Mexican-origin population of Los Angeles, for Sánchez, thus no longer means having a single patrimony, for the "continuous movement" between places characterizes a new transnational "becoming."

If the international cultural studies movement (as we saw in the introduction) is an ongoing discursive formation, with no simple origin, cultural theory in the U.S.-Mexico borderlands has charted itself in the multiple discourses of ethnography, feminist theories of subjectivity and oral history, urban studies and ethno-racial historical becoming, and the politics of postmodernism and postcolonialism. While it is clear that the global cultural studies movement has different histories, "different conjunctures and moments in the past" (Hall 1992), the cultural theory that we are studying here has "centered" itself in a particular way that might be called postmodern and postcolonial social analysis. Any examination of some of the key theoretical turns in cultural theory has to contend with García Canclini's *Culturas híbridas* (Cultural Hybridity).

If the British cultural studies project organized itself, as Hall writes, around "the moment of the disintegration of a certain kind of Marxism" (1992, 279), the postcolonial project of U.S.-Mexican borderland theory occurs at the very moment when interpretive anthropologists such as Rosaldo and García Canclini or social and urban historians such as Ruiz and Sánchez are providing accounts of other worlds "from the inside" and reflecting on the epistemological underpinnings of such work. If Rosaldo's, Ruiz's, and Sánchez's projects in the social sciences shift an emphasis from the attempt to construct a general theory of culture to a critical deconstruction of "objectivity" in ethnographic fieldwork and the politics of positionality and subjectivity, García Canclini's *Culturas híbridas* can be seen as emerging out of this particular U.S.-Mexico borderland theorizing of culture while at the same time positioning itself between theories of modernism, *lo popular,* and postmodernism.

If ours is an era of "postconditions," to use George E. Marcus and Michael M. J. Fischer's (1986) apt term, García Canclini's project is to show that the cultures of the U.S.-Mexico borderland need to be reconfigured and deterritorialized as these border-crossers (migrants from the "South" traveling to the *transfrontera* contact zones of the "North") fashion themselves in changing historical and geopolitical circumstances. García Canclini's experimental ethnography of the U.S.-Mexico borderlands thus requires the new narrative fragmentariness, he says, of the "videoclip," of hybrid cultures, and of our labyrinthine freeways. Moreover, the whole conception of the ethnographic "book" as a closed system must be respatialized, for, as he writes in the "Entrada" (Entrance), "quizá puede usarse este texto como una cuidad, a la que se ingresa por el camino de lo culto, el de lo popular o el do lo masivo. Adentro todo se mezcla, cada capítulo remite a los otros, y entonces ya no importa saber qué accesso se llegó" (perhaps we can use this text like a city, which we enter via the freeways of high culture, of popular culture, or of mass culture. On the inside everything is mixed together, every chapter refers to all the others, and as a result it is not important to know which road we traveled) (1990, 16).

One cannot help but notice the author's playful riffs (complete with urban, freeway, and car cultural tropes) in the introduction. These riffs, moreover, spill over into the book's organization, twenty-three autonomous chapters, each of which serves as a strategic narrative point—announced in the book's subtitle—of entry into and exit from the politics and aesthetics of modernity. As the cultural critic Jean Franco writes, *Culturas híbridas* "is packed with interesting data on contemporary painting, on new forms of popular culture such as the devils of Ocumicho, on the use of city scapes, monuments and museums, on mechanical reproduction, graffiti ('Yankees go home and take me with you'), comics, on Tijuana, on the way the public reacts to exhibitions of paintings by Picasso and Frida Kahlo" (1992, 136).

Amid the various "entrances" to *Culturas híbridas* lie García Canclini's attempts to situate Latin America's modernisms and postmodernisms. In fact, many of the chapters play with and explicate the uses and abuses of the signifier *modern*—including *modernism* proper, the less familiar *modernity,* and the Marxist *modernism*—in order not only to grasp the range of the problem in Mexico, Brazil, and Argentina but also to appreciate how differently Latin America and the Mexico-U.S. borderlands (specifically Tijuana–San Diego) have formed them. For instance, he writes, "¿Cómo hablar de posmodernidad desde el país donde insurge Sundero Luminoso, que tiene tanto de premoderno?" (How can we speak of postmodernism from a country [Peru] in which the Shining Path insurgents operate, which has much to do with the premodern?) (1990, 20).

Without doubt, the explanation of these terms in *Culturas híbridas* is not a "quick read." It takes up many of the middle chapters, registering the development of these terms in Latin America and recording the uneven construction observable between them. What García Canclini shows is how the various modernisms in Latin America—*modernismo* and *vanguardismo*—often either constituted violent reactions against global modernization (Pablo Neruda and Gabriel García Márquez) or replicated the values and tendencies of modernization by their own insistence on formal innovation and the processing of new aesthetics (Jorge Luis Borges and Octavio Paz).

If, as García Canclini suggests, modernism had something to do with the Enlightenment, with progress, and with rationality, he adds, "Queremos [también] entender por qué a uno de los promotores más sutiles de la modernidad en la literatura y el arte latinoamericanos [Octavio Paz] le fascina retornar a lo premoderno" (We [also] want to understand why one of the more subtle promoters of modernism in literature and art [Octavio Paz] returns so often to the premodern) (98). In other words, Latin American antimodernist modernists such as Borges and Paz often involved their projects in premodern visions. García Canclini concludes, however, that art in the U.S.-Mexico borderlands (and the Americas in general) can at present be theorized only as "hybrid," for art "en el presente . . . se reinserta en movimientos más amplios" (in the present . . . reinserts itself in the wider and new social movements) (125).

Latin America's modernisms and postmodernisms must therefore be seen as uniquely corresponding to an uneven development, or to what the author calls the central hypothesis of his book, namely, "hemos tenido un modernismo exuberante con una modernización deficiente" (we have had an exuberant modernism with a deficient modernization) (65). As a result of this unevenness, García Canclini writes, "lo que llamamos arte no es sólo lo que culmina en grandes obras, sino un espacio desde la sociedad realiza su producción visual" (what we call art is not only what culminates in great work, but a social space where society constructs its visual production) (228).

If modernism in Latin America thought of itself as an "exuberant" cultural production (albeit with "deficient" modernization), postmodernism in the U.S.-Mexico borderlands thinks of itself as an alternative and a renewal—disrupting and displacing years of long cultural ossification. In the next few pages, I consider García Canclini's rich theorizing of U.S.-Mexico border culture as an instance of postcolonial writing. My reading underscores several points of similarity with Rosaldo's theorizing of border zones. The aim is to suggest how "border theory" both challenges and complements the emergent authorities on the "postconditions" of our times.

In his book's final chapter, "Culturas híbridas, poderes oblicuos" (Hybrid Cultures, Oblique Powers), García Canclini grounds his study in the *transfrontera* urban space of Tijuana–San Diego. Like many towns along *la frontera,* Tijuana undergoes at the end of the nineteenth century a radical change from a cattle-ranching economy to an urban settlement. Moreover, as the geographer Lawrence A. Herzog notes, "at the turn of the century, the growth of Tijuana's northern neighbor, San Diego, would fuel the development of this border city" (1990, 95). In other words, as San Diego became a pre–Pacific Rim port and a U.S. naval base, demands for recreational and other services were created in Tijuana. Tourism, red-light districts, bar hopping, and the like emerged as the order of the day (see chapter 6).

According to Herzog, from 1950 to 1980 Tijuana's population grew from "65,346 to over 700,000 inhabitants" (107). García Canclini argues it is precisely this demographic explosion—*la expansión urbana*—that "intensifies cultural hybridity" (1990, 265). Of course, about two-thirds of this expansion was the result of exile and migrations from Latin America and the interiors of Mexico. "In-migrants to Tijuana," Herzog writes, "came from widely dispersed regions" (1990, 106). García Canclini suggests that as a result of this migration, we now have to talk about the fundamental changes generated by this urban mixing: "¿Cómo explicar que muchos cambios de pensamiento y gustos de la vida urbana coincidan con los del campesinado?" (How can we begin to explain that many of the changes in the thought and tastes of urban life coincide with those of the rural districts?) (1990, 265).

For the social theorist, this unblocking of aesthetic categories of all sorts (modernism, pop culture, and postmodernism) has to be theorized.

This is the purpose for García Canclini of *la frontera*—which he calls a "laboratory for postmodernism" (293)—where the various modernist culture rituals are daily disposed like rubbish (along with their formal values, now considered "elitist"). A playfulness of form—hybridity—can be seen, he suggests, in the various billboards and tourist relics catering to the urbanized youth masses.

To conclude our survey let us focus on two of several photographs García Canclini provides near the book's end. This new "fieldwork," not surprisingly, rejects the older and more traditional kind of ethnographic participant observation: "doing" the village, calling up informants, and so on. What the social scientist dramatizes in the photographs is a fieldwork with a difference, requiring the field-worker to live in the urban barrioscapes of Tijuana and learn to decipher the rich multicultural sign systems (in English and Spanish) of *la frontera*. The black-and-white photographs feature Tijuana in all its linguistic heteroglossia and postmodernity. One shows a giant billboard, setting for García Canclini Tijuana's servicing of an exploding transnational youth culture. Ads for rock music radio stations promoting "Rock en tu idioma" and alcoholic beverages such as Don Pancho's coffee liqueur selling an addiction to "enjoy the other choice"—such billboards, then, thematize concretely the hybrid, polyglot culture of the U.S.-Mexico borderlands. The other photograph shows two Anglo-American tourists riding zebras on the Avenida Revolución. They are accompanied by a young mestizo who helps them negotiate Tijuana's urban traffic. In the text García Canclini sardonically writes that in Tijuana these zebras are not what they seem to be: "En realidad, son burros pintadas" (In reality, they are painted burros) (300).

Of course, nowadays when we see pictures of painted burros masquerading as zebras García Canclini wants us to find ourselves exploring a whole new border culture of the image or the postmodern spectacle. This omnipresence of pastiche in *la frontera* is not incompatible with a certain style of border humor: for the social theorist it is at least compatible with original "First World" appetites for a society transformed into sheer images of itself and for pseudo-events and "spectacles." Appropriately enough, the U.S.-Mexico borderland's culture of the simulacrum comes to life precisely at a time of which the cultural theorist Fredric Jameson has observed "exchange value has been generalized to the point at which the very memory of use value is effaced" (1990, 18). This new temporal-spatial logic of the simulacrum has an

ethno-racialized underside, for white U.S. tourists from the North have
to cross the border into the South to experience what García Canclini
calls *lo primitivo,* the primitive (natives, *indio* cultures, zebras, etc.).

Anthropologists, James Clifford has recently written, "don't study in
villages, but rather in hospitals, labs, urban neighborhoods, tourist
hotels, the Getty Center" (1992c, 98). This trend in ethnographic practice (as García Canclini demonstrates in *Culturas híbridas*) challenges a
modernist configuration of the "primitive" object of fieldwork as racist,
romantic, archaic, simpleminded, and so on. But as self-reflexive as García Canclini consistently is in his rich study, one is struck by his apparent nostalgia in referring to Tijuana as "uno de los mayores laboratorios
de la posmodernidad" (one of the major laboratories of the postmodern)
(1990, 293). The language here sounds too "positivistic" and "scientific"
—for since Franz Boas's generation, as Clifford reminds us, the "field"
has always been a place of "controlled observation and scientific experimentation" (1992c, 98). At any rate, García Canclini forces us to ask
why only certain (positivistic) experiences count as fieldwork and at the
same time to rethink how the nation's historical patrimony no longer
means only having a city, a country, or a place, where everyone sharing
those spaces becomes "identical and interchangeable" (1990, 132).

Although pioneering cultural theory such as that of García Canclini
has provided insights into the reality of the U.S.-Mexico *transfrontera*
life in times of the "reconversion" of national economies guided by the
International Monetary Fund and, more recently, the North American
Free Trade Agreement (NAFTA), much more work in people's history,
Chicano/a "subcultures," and electronic mass-mediated culture (such
as *conjunto, technobanda,* punk, and rap) needs to be launched. Intellectual workers in the emergent Chicano/a cultural studies movement,
however, have yet to write the people's histories that, say, the British
cultural studies movement at the CCCS, under the directorship of Stuart Hall and Richard Johnson, has produced.[11] With the exception of
the work of scholars such as Rosa Linda Fregoso and Carl Gutiérrez-
Jones on film, of George Lipsitz, George Sánchez, and Steven Loza on
popular music and the postmodern poetics of place, of Rosaldo on television programs such as *Miami Vice,* of Sonia Saldívar-Hull on the *telenovela* and Chicana romance culture, and of José Limón on *curanderas*
(women healers), dance, and male working-class poetics, Chicano/a cultural studies has not yet pursued a focused study of Chicano/a mass
culture.[12]

If Chicano/a cultural studies is to flourish in the next century, it must begin to place a greater research emphasis on the ways in which our lived memory and popular culture are linked—on how the postmodernist shocks of electronic mass media create a crisis for "absolutist" paradigms of national culture and collective memory frames the production and reception of commercial culture. To paraphrase Jameson and Lipsitz, while new technologies certainly lend themselves to new forms of exploitation and oppression (colonizing our body as sites of capital accumulation), they also have utopian uses as new forms of resistance and struggle.[13]

Oral histories such as Ruiz's and the postmodernist cultural theories of Rosaldo, Sánchez, and García Canclini collectively challenge on the discursive level, irrespective of genre, the arbitrary deployment of boundaries, both as practiced by the INS and as professed from within the academy. Moreover, these borderland writers move cultural "theory" in and out of what Clifford calls "discrepant cosomopolitan" contexts.[14] What this means, then, is that Rosaldo's, Ruiz's, Sánchez's, and García Canclini's U.S.-Mexico border writing entails a new intercultural theory making sensitive to both local processes and global forces, such as Euro-imperialism, colonialism, patriarchy, and economic and political hegemonies. Thus envisaged, U.S.-Mexico border writing does not dichotomize the local and the global, for as Clifford argues, border cultures, like black diaspora cultures, "exist because of displacements, inter-cultural and trans-national crossings" (1992a, 4). As we will see, Américo-Paredes's, Arturo Islas's, and Carmen Lomas Garza's Texas, Alberto Ríos's Arizona, Helena Viramontes's and John Rechy's Los Angeles, Luis Alberto Urrea's, Rubén Martínez's, and Richard Rodriguez's Tijuana, John Gregory Bourke's "American Congo," and María Amparo Ruiz's Alta California offer us shifting and shifty versions of border culture.

2

Américo Paredes and Decolonization

One of the last models of "city and country" is the system we
know as imperialism.
  Raymond Williams, *The Country and the City* (1973)

Given the situation of the self-representation of multicultural
teaching of literature in the United States, it seems more
canny to stop (or start) with prospects for decolonization,
presumably a condition before post-coloniality (or postcolonialism) can be declared. As far as I can tell, . . . a general
condition of post-coloniality is a future anterior, something
that will have happened, if one concerned oneself with the
persistent crafty details of the calculus of decolonization.
  Gayatri Chakravorty Spivak,
  "Teaching for the Times" (1995)

Having examined some of the postmodernist sociocultural theory and
theorists of the U.S.-Mexican borderlands, we must reflect on earlier
modernist constructions of *la frontera* out of which proto-Chicano/a
culture and literature were produced. My fundamental premise is that
the dissident literature, folklore, and ethnography (from, say, the 1930s
to the present) produced by Chicanos/as should not be read as static
monocultural representations of history but as active influences within
and against what Walter Benn Michaels has called the "nativist modernism" of the United States (1995, 2). Viewing short stories, intercultural jests, novels, poetry, *décimas, corridos,* and ethnographies as, in
Hazel Carby's words, "weapons for social change" (1987, 95), cultural
criticism needs to study in detail how these artifacts shape U.S.-Mexico
borderlands culture and struggle.

  To begin analyzing a few of these issues, I dwell for the most part in
this chapter on the ethnographic and anti-imperialist literary work of
Américo Paredes, who was honored in 1989 by the National Endow-
ment for the Humanities as one of the first recipients of the Frankle
Prize for lifetime achievement in the arts and who in 1990 was one of

the first Chicano inductees in the Orden de Águila Azteca by the Mexican government for his contribution to the preservation of Mexican culture in the United States. For the purposes of this study, moreover, Paredes's modernist cultural work—"The Hammon and the Beans," *"With His Pistol in His Hand," George Washington Gómez,* and *Between Two Worlds*—has a more specific meaning as well.

As I have suggested elsewhere (1991a), Paredes's antidisciplinary Texas-Mexico border project underscores the ways in which the dominant Anglocentric discourse suppresses regional differences. In matters of cultural description, Paredes shows that what is striking (in this Anglocentric context) is the steady definition of certain areas as in this limited sense "regional," which can hold only if certain other locations are not discriminated in this way.[1] This discrimination is a function of centralization, a form of what Raymond Williams (1973a) has called the "city-country" opposition. It is clearly connected with the distinction between "metropolitan" (core) and "provincial" (peripheral) cultures, which became significant from the sixteenth century. Yet, as Williams has consistently argued, "this [discrimination] is no longer a distinction of areas and kinds of life; it is what is politely called in the academy a value-judgment but more accurately called an expression of hegemonic cultural dominance" (1983, 230).[2] Because Paredes's modernist cultural work represents the complex self-fashionings brought about by the bloody U.S.-Mexico borderland conflict, it also constitutes needed insights into the boundary disputes between and among academic disciplines as well as geographic territories. His bold deterritorializations thus serve both as tactical political strategies specifically designed to counter Anglocentric hegemony in border disputes and as transdisciplinary phantasms designed to transgress rigidly "border-patroled" discursive boundaries.

Seen in this light, Paredes occupies a significant position among U.S.-Mexico border intellectuals today.[3] No contemporary figures of the proto-Chicano/a movement generation have so extensive an oeuvre to their credit. In a working career of over forty years, Paredes has pursued his intellectual, creative, and critical concerns across a range that includes almost every majority and minority cultural form: enthnographies of the people of "Greater Mexico," literary criticism, analysis of *décimas* and *corridos,* collections of folktales, semantic inquiry, poetry, film scripts, the short story, and the novel.[4]

Yet until recently detailed discussion of Paredes's border-defying work has been almost nonexistent. And despite its increasing authority and influence in the field of Chicano/a cultural studies, there has so far been no attempt to analyze the work as a whole. The immense variety of Paredes's writing, which crosses academic boundaries and confounds disciplinary expectations, has no doubt contributed to this state of affairs, for, as the anthropologist Richard Bauman suggests, Paredes writes "in multiple voices. His scholarship is a richly textured expressive fabric, not at all confined to the standard expository prose and the we-they oppositions of conventional anthropological scholarship" (Paredes 1993, xxii).

In what follows, I begin by reading Paredes's work "backward," with a brief evaluation of his mature achievement in *"With His Pistol in His Hand"* and then moving to his early modernist narratives—a group of literary texts entitled "Border Country," stories such as "The Hammon and the Beans," and sections of *George Washington Gómez* that were written in the 1930s and 1940s and won first place in a literary contest sponsored by the *Dallas Times Herald* in 1952. Finally, I look at some intercultural poems Paredes wrote in the 1930s and collected in *Between Two Worlds*. While I am interested in showing a pattern of development, I especially want to underline what Paredes focused on from the very start: a critique of the cultures of U.S. imperialism.

The first scholarly overview appeared in 1986 in two groundbreaking essays, "Mexican Ballads, Chicano Epic" and "The Return of the Mexican Ballad," by José Limón.[5] Almost simultaneously Paredes himself addressed major definitions and representations of spatial materialism and the politics of geocultural identity, with the Arte Público publication of *George Washington Gómez,* a novel he started writing in 1936, completed in 1940, but did not publish until the exemplary postmodern year 1990. Thematizing the culture of conflict and empire along the border between the United States and Mexico, Paredes's modernist novel shows how the patterns of conflict since Polk's expansionist policies in the 1840s had become by the early twentieth century firmly set up in the "knowable communities" along the border (Williams 1973b, 14). In other words, Paredes dramatizes U.S.-Mexico border people and their social relationships in knowable and communicable ways.[6]

Perhaps more than anyone else's, Paredes's influence is profoundly felt in Chicano/a cultural studies. He has taught us especially that critical scholarship cannot be contained within the boundaries of the traditional university. In *"With His Pistol in His Hand"* (1958), *Folktales* of Mexico (1970), *A Texas-Mexican "Cancionero"* (1976), *George Washington Gómez* (1990), *Between Two Worlds* (1991), *Uncle Remus con Chile* (1992), and *The Hammon and the Beans and Other Stories* (1994), "border culture" is a term that transgresses various disciplines and theoretical boundaries: folklore, ethnography, musicology, history, and literary "theory."

With the publication of *Folklore and Culture* (1993), Paredes has continued to provide readers with a remarkable sample of his lifelong interest in the traffic in the borderland between cultural anthropology and cultural studies. While many of the essays in the volume are mainly rooted within the tradition of anthropological research ("The Folklore of Groups of Mexican Origin in the United States," "The Problem of Identity in a Changing Culture," and "On Ethnographic Work among Minority Groups"), the collection as a whole is thoroughly grounded in the details of everyday life and in what the author calls "the shock of cultures" (1993, 13). For Paredes, this culture of in-betweenness begins with "the bitter hatreds that developed" on the South Texas–Mexico border in the mid-1830s and "were diffused to other areas" of the two-thousand-mile line separating Mexico and the United States. As a result of the Treaty of Guadalupe Hidalgo in 1848, everyday life "from regional subcultures of Mexico" was transformed to "occupied" life within the United States (25).

No précis of Américo Paredes's scholarly U.S.-Mexico border writings would be complete without brief acknowledgment of their experimental (even wildly creative) quality.[7] As Limón persuasively argues, Paredes's *"With His Pistol in His Hand,"* like the *corrido* itself, involves "multiple voices, inversions, humor and irony," thus constituting "a [cultural] critique by way of an alternative model to the linear, hierarchical discourses in the service of advanced capitalism" (1992, 76). Likewise, the literary theorist Héctor Calderón writes that "although [*"With His Pistol in His Hand"*] is a result of academic scholarship, [originally] a doctoral thesis presented to the Department of English at the University of Texas at Austin in 1956, readers will be surprised by the self-reflexivity of its form" (1991, 15). *"With His Pistol in His Hand"* tells the story of the hegemonic border and the history of Paredes's ancestors in South Texas. Like many Chicano/a writers, Paredes declares that he is not an immigrant. Neither he nor his Nuevo Santander ancestors in the 1750s moved from the U.S.-Mexico borderlands; instead U.S. military aggression transformed the Rio Grande Valley in South Texas from what the historian David Montejano describes as fundamentally an organic class society (where a certain social order and relations made sense to a people) into a barbwired and segregated society.[8]

After discussing how the border was imposed on South Texas in the nineteenth century, Paredes focuses on how Chicanos at the beginning of the twentieth century used *corridos* to counter Anglocentric hegemony. As the literary scholar Ramón Saldívar puts it, "The nineteenth- and twentieth-century *corridos* served the symbolic function of empirical events (functioning as a substitute for history writing) and of creating counterfactual worlds of lived experience (functioning as a substitute for fiction writing)" (1990, 48). To be sure, Paredes sees his scholarly project as participating in the cultural conversations of the Southwest borderlands, where U.S.-Mexico border culture is a serious contest of codes and representations. More specifically, *"With His Pistol in His Hand"* inaugurates a Chicano artistic and intellectual response to the nativist modernist scholars of the 1930s and 1940s, such as Walter Prescott Webb and his followers, who represented in their texts a popular, romanticized history. At the same time, it must be emphasized that Paredes's book contests the nationalist and chauvinistic new interdisciplinary project of American studies. For Paredes, the consensus rhetoric of American studies with its emphasis on the motto *E pluribus unum* has to be negated and replaced with a more sophisticated sense of "culture" as a site of social struggle.[9]

To dramatize his sense of culture as a site of social contestation, Paredes's focus on *corridos,* we might say, is "antisubjectivist," because in ballads of border conflict like "El Corrido de Gregorio Cortez" he locates the sources of meaning, not in individual subjectivities, but in social relations, communication, and cultural politics. While the *corrido* certainly points to U.S.-Mexico border men such as Gregorio Cortez (who resisted arrest by Sheriff Morris and who defended himself "con la pistola en su mano"), the subject in this *corrido* is meant to stand not as an individual but as an epiclike construction of the South Texas society that interpellated him. As is well known, Cortez's fate, for Paredes, cannot be distinguished from communal fate.[10]

"With His Pistol in His Hand" concludes by mourning the "fall" of the *corrido* proper and its containment as a form of symbolic social resistance. "The period of 1836 to the late 1930's," Paredes writes, "embraces the life span of the corrido of the Lower Border." The Civil War, the English-speaking invasion of the borderlands, and the French

invasion of Mexico, however, "complicated the clash of peoples along the Border" (1958, 132). Nevertheless, if the *corrido* lost some of its evocative countercultural power in the 1930s with the rise of modernization and the agricultural revolution, the shock culture along the border in the 1950s and 1960s forced Paredes to see the emergent culture as a complex clash of "ethnos" (the chosen people) and "ethnikos" (outsiders). For he was now "aware that the cultural conflict [was] many-layered: the Mexican anywhere in Greater Mexico against the *gringo;* the Mexican on both sides of the Border against the *agringado;* the Texas-Mexican against the Mexican across the Rio Grande (*los del otro lado*); [and] the Mexican on both sides of the river against the Mexican from the central plateau" (1993, 14). Paredes first began to explore this "many-layered" cultural conflict along the U.S.-Mexico borderlands when he turned to writing another form of social resistance, the modernist Chicano novel.

While what Limón calls Paredes's "modern tragic sentiment" (1994, 85) and what Rosaldo sees as the author's "idealization of primordial patriarchy" (1989, 151) are certainly present in work such as *"With His Pistol in His Hand,"* the gendered transfigurations of the *corrido* hero and the decline of the utopian *corrido* epoch in South Texas are, in my view, the very subjects of Paredes's historical bildungsroman, *George Washington Gómez,* written during the Great Depression. Indeed, we can say without exaggeration that Paredes's modernist novel is precisely about the large and small dislocations in space that must occur before, at the novel's end, the hero George G. Gómez can completely assimilate. And that place is precisely located by Paredes at the center of competing local, national, and international interests, spanning the hemisphere. Formally, Paredes represents the Great Depression in South Texas—what he calls La Chilla (the Wailing)—as a structure of expansion and contraction. That is, he introduces the formal structure on which many of the novel's sections will be patterned, for he gives the reader a generalized view of the plight of Mexican-American men and women, followed by a closeup of his representative characters, García and Gómez. This formal literary pattern, of course, echoes the structural features of one of the most sensational modernist social protest novels of the period, John Steinbeck's *The Grapes of Wrath.*[11] Central to *George Washington Gómez,* then, is Paredes's preoccupation with geocultural identity, representation, and the politics of location.

George Washington Gómez (like many of the narratives that make up the collection "Border Country") is set in the midst of South Texas borderland conflict: the 1915 uprising by the seditionists *(los sediciosos)* from South Texas and northern Mexico and their thorough suppression by the U.S. Cavalry and the Texas Rangers. The uprising was inspired by the Plan de San Diego manifesto, which called for a coalition of Mexicans with (Amer) Indians, blacks, and Asians and the revolutionary creation of a Spanish-speaking republic of the Southwest. Led by the anarchists Luis de la Rosa and Aniceto Pizaña, the seditionists fought the "modernizing" dominant powers, including the U.S. Army, up and down the Rio Grande, burning bridges, derailing trains, and destroying irrigation pumping plants. According to David Montejano, "The conflict turned South Texas into a virtual war zone during 1915–1917. . . . Hundreds of people were killed, thousands were dislocated, and properties worth millions were destroyed" (1987, 117). Paredes's novel thus re-creates the bloody tone of life in the knowable community along the border in the first three decades of the twentieth century; more important for us, it shows how the seditionist revolt was a hybrid Mexican revolutionary/American anarchist product.[12] If the historian James A. Sandos is correct that the Plan de San Diego "has been denied a place of recognition among the great political Plans of the Mexican Revolution, and it has earned no place in the history of working-class radicalism [in the United States]," Paredes's *George Washington Gómez,* we might say, recovers and dramatizes a revolutionary struggle in the U.S.-Mexico borderlands that, in Sandos's apt words, "has been orphaned, abandoned by the practice of writing national histories that stop at national boundaries" (1992, 172).

Brownsville, Texas, the site of numerous incidents of cultural resistance, is represented by the author as "Jonesville-On-the-Grande," a place under occupation by the conquering U.S. Army based at "Fort Jones." *George Washington Gómez* thus specifically sets itself in the period just after the last great resistance by Texas Mexicans on the border seeking to regain land lost by their parents and grandparents to Anglo-Americans and their Texas Rangers.

George Washington Gómez begins with the birth of a new type of border hero in the midst of these "border troubles." The protagonist's father, Gumersindo, along with an Anglo doctor, makes his way through mesquite and Texas Ranger roadblocks to aid María in the birth of their third child. "A good Mexican," Gumersindo is determined from the start to raise a son named after "the great North American . . . who was a general and fought the soldiers of the king" (1990, 16). But why does Paredes trace his hero's cultural genealogy to the leader of both revolutionary and republican America? Does he want to suggest that his character's rhetoric of descent (simultaneously a rhetoric of ascent and consent) is central to the dynamics of cohesion in America? Will his brown hero's future lead a new republic replete with mythic past and "manifest" destiny? Materially hybrid and heteroglot, *George Washington Gómez* reexamines—ironically as the title suggests—the decline of the *corrido*'s heroic age and the rise of ethnogenesis on the border. Anticipating Stuart Hall's notion of cultural identity "as a production . . . always in process, and always constituted within, not outside, representation" (1990, 222), Paredes, in near-Zizekian fashion, suggests that your name becomes you because you retroactively become what you are named.

Like José Martí's cultural deconstruction in "Nuestra América" (Our America) (1891) of the name *America*, Paredes begins the novel by thematizing the ritual naming of Gumersindo and María's son: "[María] looked at him tenderly. And what shall we name him? she wondered aloud" (1990, 16). In response to her question, her husband, mother, and brother all suggest names, each symbolic of the alternative possibilities for the hero's "manifest" destiny: Crisósforo, a "grandiose" name, is offered by the boy's proud father but is quickly ridiculed by the signifying Feliciano as sounding too ridiculously close to the Spanish word *fósforo*. Next the grandmother offers a safe Catholic name, José Ángel, but she is quickly overruled by Gumersindo's blunt "Ángel! . . . It would ruin him for life." Names alluding to Mexican and Chicano revolutionaries, Venustiano Carranza and "Cleto" Pizaña, and even the father's own name, Gumersindo, are momentarily considered but surprisingly dismissed. María finally settles the ritual process: "'I would like my son.' . . . She faltered and reddened. 'I would like him to have a great man's name. Because he's going to grow up to be a great man who will help his people'" (16). Searching for the names of "great men" that the *norteamericanos* had produced over the years, Gumersindo thinks out loud: "I remember Wachinton. Jorge Wachinton." Unable to pronounce the foreigner's name, the grandmother hilariously calls out "Guálinto." And thus the hero is named. This hybrid clash of geocultural identities, of course, will be the very ground for the larger cultural clashes in the novel, jolting the narrative in what Ramón Saldívar calls "decidedly unforeseeable patterns" (1995, 325).

"Born a foreigner in his native land" and "fated to a life controlled by others" (1990, 15), George Washington (Guálinto) Gómez's Americanization will be fraught with contradiction. In ideological terms, what Paredes offers us in his Mexicotexan bildungsroman is an ongoing thematization of the child's traditional organic community and the forces of the new dominant culture. Life in the border site of Jonesville-On-the-Grande is made concrete in the opening chapters by the brutal suppression of Chicanos by the Texas Rangers, by Pizaña and de la Rosa's violent armed retaliations against the gringos, and by the symbolic competing names of the hero: Guálinto (an Amerindian-sounding name like Cuahútemoc) and George Washington.

When Gumersindo is gunned down by the Rangers, he makes his brother-in-law Feliciano promise him "never to tell his son" how he died at the hands of the *rinches,* for he "wanted his son to have no hatred in his heart" (31). While raised by Feliciano and María to be "a leader of his people," Guálinto acculturates through stages, acquiring through his schoolteachers "an Angloamerican self" (147). Although he is able to negotiate his proliferating modernist subject positions quite well and eventually realizes that there is not "one single Guálinto Gómez" (147), at the novel's end Paredes's protagonist graduates from high school; attends the University of Texas; marries a white ethnographer, Ellen Dell (whose father was once a Ranger); legally changes his name to George G. Gómez; and becomes a "spy" for the U.S. Army during World War II. Claiming that he is a lawyer for a multinational plant that is expanding in the global borderlands, he returns to South Texas as a first lieutenant in counterintelligence whose new job is "border security." Yet it is precisely at this stage in the hero's construction of a solid bourgeois and modernist identity that we realize Paredes's cultural deconstruction. For his recommendation in the narrative is not to solve the crisis of the hero's identity politics but to proliferate and intensify the crisis by having George's "I" dissimulated through a recurring fantasy and daydream.

> He would imagine he was living in his great-grandfather's time, when the Americans first began to encroach on the northern provinces of the new Republic of Mexico. Reacting against the central government's inefficiency and corruption, he would organize *rancheros* into a fighting militia. . . . He would discover the revolver before Samuel Colt, as well as the hand grenade and a modern style of portable mortar. In his daydream he built a modern arms factory at Laredo, doing it all in great

detail, until he had an enormous, well-trained army that included Irishmen and escaped American Negro slaves. Finally, he would defeat not only the army of the United States but its navy as well. He would reconquer all the territory west of the Mississippi River and recover Florida as well.

At that point he would end up with a feeling of emptiness, of futility. . . . He always awoke with a feeling of irritation. Why? he would ask himself. Why do I keep on fighting battles that were won and lost a long time ago? Lost and won by me too? They have no meaning now. (282)

The above passage is neither the best nor the worst of Paredes's text. Rather, it shows dramatically the many complicated pressures working within the novel. The nuanced consciousness of Anglocentric expansionism into the borderlands, beginning with the Texas Wars of Independence in 1835–1836 and continuing with Polk's chauvinist war with Mexico in 1846–1848, is a necessary accompaniment. At the same time, there is the remarkable critique of Mexican party politics and the corrupt presidency of Antonio López de Santa Anna that inevitably played a decisive role during the war. As the historian Richard Griswold del Castillo points out, the struggle between various groups produced "chronic instability" that made it impossible for Mexican forces to match up against U.S. forces (1990, 6–7). If global imperialism, as Edward Said notes, can be "said to have begun in the late 1870's, with the scramble for Africa" (1990, 70), Paredes's novel suggests that the homemade American kind began earlier. The importance of the period 1835–1848 for Guálinto, of course, is that it marks the emergence of U.S. empire. Additionally, 1848 has a particular meaning for him not only because Mexico had been defeated (yielding Texas, California, and New Mexico as spoils) and the Oregon Territory appropriated but also because U.S. imperialism had created a group of second-class citizens within the belly of the beast.

These considerations provide a fascinating expanded dimension to *George Washington Gómez,* for a good deal more can be said about what Amy Kaplan (1990) has called the double discourse of U.S. imperialism— nationhood and manhood—and how Paredes's novel can provide access to the repressed political context of American imperialism. While Guálinto's conscious connections are to people and places in South Texas, his latent dreamwork reveals that there are *other* connections of which he has faint glimmerings but which nonetheless demand his attention, particularly his plan to build an "arms factory" at Laredo and to put together "an enormous army that included Irishmen and escaped American Negro slaves." Like the small group of Whig party members who opposed the 1846 war, Guálinto suspects that the war itself was a plot to strengthen the position of the slave owners. In other words, Polk used the war as an opportunity to expand the slavocracy. It is hardly surprising, therefore, that Guálinto dreams of armed solidarity with escaped African-American slaves.

If the feminist philosopher Judith Butler (using the psychoanalytic work of Jean Laplanche and J. B. Pontalis) is correct that there is "no subject who has a fantasy, but only fantasy as the scene of the subject's fragmentation" (1990, 110), Paredes demonstrates in this scene how the political "phantasmatic" of the U.S.-Mexico borderlands continually haunts and contests the borders that circumscribe George's construction of a stable identity. What are the possibilities for social change in the face of capitalist hegemony whose powers of co-optation are so great that they manage to turn desire against itself?

With George G. Gómez we are far removed from the utopian collective concerns of border heroes like Gregorio Cortez. Paredes, however, in re-creating the "border troubles" in his narrative sets the stage for the Chicano novel some thirty years before the so-called Chicano Renaissance of letters in the 1960s. Moreover, his focus on *corridos* and on folklore and musical performance in his numerous writings forces us to look at folklore and popular culture as equally powerful, creative, and influential areas of counterdiscourse. Paredes, indeed, dwells in his scholarly and creative writings on the role of folklore as an instrument of the culture of conflict; folklore undertakes struggle itself in the forms of songs, legends, jests and jokes, and *dichos* (proverbs).

As Richard Bauman suggests, Paredes's "work is an exemplary vindication of that premise on which the best of folklore and anthropology is built: that a deep, detailed, nuanced understanding of the local will inspire a more global vision" (1993, xii). Thus, in a wonderful scene near the novel's end, young Guálinto relishes his mestizo/a working-class culture by dancing to the local accordion-driven *conjunto* music of South Texas. "The music," Paredes writes, "was a fast shrieking polka, played so fast that the time was barely recognizable. The men streamed in and took the girls out on the floor, where they danced furiously in a hop-step-skip fashion. The little house trembled on the slender foundations to the scraping and stomping" (1990, 242). Here Paredes dramatizes that, for Chicanos, *norteño* music is synonymous with a vernacular working-class consciousness. In Guálinto's embrace of *conjunto*, he subtly shows how his hero's place (late in the novel) was with his local mestizo/a working class—"not the Spaniards like the Osunas" (247). In the novel, *conjunto* polka music becomes a political ideology by stressing local characteristics, by representing vernacular music, and by confirming everywhere the multiple dynamics of Chicano/a identity and nonidentity.[13]

Paredes's modernist novel specifically relates, among other things, the encounter of the ethnographic field-worker with the native inhabitants of South Texas. In other words, Paredes begins to open up the question of how cultural analysis constitutes its objects—societies, traditions, knowable communities, subjectivities, and so on. Near the novel's end, Paredes deconstructs the ethnographic encounter in South Texas by sardonically describing the nativist modernist and culture collector K. Hank Harvey.

> He was considered the foremost of authorities on the Mexicans of Texas. Hank Harvey had been born in New York City some sixty years before. He had gone to grade school there and then worked in a delicatessen to make some money so he could come down to his dreamland, Texas.
> . . . After he had come to Texas with only a few years of schooling, he resolved to become an authority on Texas history and folklore. In a few years he had read every book there was on the early history of Texas, it was said, and his fellow Texans accepted him as the Historical Oracle of the State. There was a slight hitch, it is true. Most early history books were written in Spanish, and K. Hank didn't know the language. However, nobody mentioned this, and it didn't detract from Harvey's glory. (271)

The best part of this passage is Paredes's demystification of the authority of the executive historical ethnographer and opening to discussion, in James Clifford's words, "ethnography's hierarchy and the complex negotiation of discourses in power-charged, unequal situations" (1992c, 100). Paredes shakes things up by representing Harvey as a monological scholar incapable of fully inscribing his "native" subjects. Eventually Harvey learns a "few words of Spanish which he introduced into all of his later writings, somewhat indiscriminately." His fame as a historian and folklorist grows "too big even for the vast Texas," and soon he becomes a "national and then an international figure" (1990, 271).

Paredes's wry description of Harvey, however, becomes full of anger, for Harvey's scholarly project occurs alongside a peculiar sense of mission— what used to be called the white man's burden.

> K. Hank Harvey filled a very urgent need; men like him were badly in demand in Texas. They were needed to point out the local color, and in the process make the general public see that starving Mexicans were not an ugly, pitiful sight but something very picturesque and quaint, something tourists from the North would pay to come and see. By this same process bloody murders became charming adventure stories, and men one would have considered uncouth and ignorant became true originals. (271–272)

For Paredes, what has come to be called the Spanish borderlands by ethnographic historians such as K. Hank Harvey is in fact what the anthropologist James A. Boon calls a fiction, an imperialist historical formation, a mystification, "a shifting paradox," and an ongoing mistranslation (1990, ix). To be sure, Harvey functions in the novel as a symbol for nativist modern scholars such as Charles F. Lummis (*The Land of Poco Tiempo*) and J. Frank Dobie (*Tongues of the Monte*), who claimed to have "discovered" and invented the Spanish Southwest for the Anglo-American popular readership. As Héctor Calderón writes, "In a span of eleven years, from 1891 to 1900, Lummis published eleven books, changing what was a physical and cultural desert into a land internationally known for its seductive natural and cultural attractions" (1991, 3). Dobie, like Lummis, was instrumental in constructing disciplinary folklore societies in the Southwest and was the first to teach a course on the culture of the Southwest at the University of Texas at Austin. As Dobie officially and characteristically bragged to others, "I can speak Mexican fluently and read Spanish easily, though I am tardy in writing Spanish. However, with a very little effort I could handle the Spanish language in any capacity. I know the Mexican genius. I am an expert rider and a good shot" (quoted in Limón 1994, 64). Paredes thus pegs the Harveys of the Southwest as representing the "Mexicans of South Texas" in the mode of what Rosaldo (1989) has called imperialist nostalgia, that longing on the part of imperialist agents such as missionaries, ethnographers, and government officials for the indigenous forms of life that they often had a hand in destroying. In this discourse, Paredes describes the Spanish borderlands as the site where men like Harvey can be real authorities, where they can lament the closing of the frontier.

When Harvey is invited by the local white administrators to give the keynote address at Guálinto's graduation from Jonesville High, Paredes's hero along with the majority of Chicanos in the audience "shift nervously in their seats" as they listen to the speaker's discourse on empire: "We're here to honor this bunch of fine young people, citizens of this great state of Texas, who are going out into the world. May they never forget the names of Sam Houston, James Bowie, and Davey Crockett. May they remember the Alamo wherever they go." Oblivious to the fact that for his brown audience, history really hurts, he ends his tale of empire by saying, "Whenever our forefathers rose on their hindlegs and demanded independence . . . , when they arose with a mighty shout and forever erased Mexican cruelty and tyranny from the fair land, when they defeated bloody Santa Anna and his murderous cohorts at the heroic battle of San Jacinto, they set an example which younger, weaker generations would do well to follow. Girls and boys, I give you the world; it is at your feet as young Americans" (274).

At a time when a well-financed and increasingly powerful group of intellectuals and journalists is attempting to reverse the democratic processes that have lately made the university more representative, Paredes's critique of U.S. empire, white supremacy, and nativist modernism requires special attention.

Behind the title of Paredes's novel lurks the haunting cultural symbology of George Washington, who in his Farewell Address of September 17, 1796, proclaimed, "The name of American must always exalt [your] just pride . . . more than any appellation derived from local discriminations. With slight shades of difference, you have the same Religion, Manners, Habits, and political principles" (quoted in Bercovitch 1991, xv). For Américo Paredes, however, "the name of American" is an interpretive fiction. Doing the work of the dominant culture, Washington's address, like the rest of the American literary canon, interprets away differences among the religions, manners, habits, and political principles of the people from "Our America." As the literary theorist Sacvan Bercovitch provocatively suggests, "the name of American worked not only to displace the very real (and deepening) differences within the country, but equally—within the country's reigning liberal constituency—to display differences of all kinds as proof of a victorious pluralism" (1991, xv). Paredes thus presents a counterdiscourse to the homemade nativist discourses of U.S. imperialism: he articulates the experiences, the aspirations, and the vision of a people under occupation.

What distinguishes Paredes from his Anglocentric modernist contemporaries is not his intellectual or aesthetic judgment but the extraordinary depth of his understanding of the dynamics of empire. His
cultural work written in the 1930s and 1940s shares with that of other
U.S. writers of color (W. E. B. Du Bois, Jovita González, Richard
Wright, Zora Neale Hurston, among others) a desire to produce what
Paul Gilroy (1993) calls a counterculture of modernity. At the same time,
Paredes's work belongs to a whole globalized movement of socially
"minoritized" writers (James Joyce and Franz Kafka) who helped to
devise a new vocabulary within which to grasp not only complex ethno-
racial structures of feeling but also what Raymond Williams has
described as "the unprecedented social forms of the industrial city"
(1989, 32). Paredes's *George Washington Gómez* asks, among other
things: How did the U.S. cultures of imperialism affect modernist writers along the U.S.-Mexico border? Did the age of U.S. imperialism also
create (antinativist) modernists who raged against present-day life
under empire?

As in *George Washington Gómez,* much of the action of Paredes's
modernist short story "The Hammon and the Beans" (written around
1939) takes place on the city streets of Jonesville, Texas, near Fort Jones.
Here the narrator recalls young Chonita pleading daily and bargaining
with U.S. soldiers for their leftover food. Impelled by military occupation and economic dislocation, Chonita, "a scrawny girl of nine" (1994,
6), carves out a path for her impoverished existence, by no means an
easy task. Throughout the story the lives of the border characters are
interrupted, disturbed, and ritualized by the "routine" of Fort Jones:
"At six sharp the flag was raised on the parade grounds to the cackling
of the bugles, and the field piece thundered out a salute. The sound of
the shot bounced away through the morning mist until its echoes worked
their way into every corner of town" (3). Paredes's very sentences express
the militarization of life for the conquered subalterns and how daily
they struggled, "we and the post, side by side with the wire fence in
between" (5).

Paredes focuses on what living under military occupation means to
the subaltern, for it is knowable and communicable. The schoolchildren, of course, respect Fort Jones because they have to, but they also
find the "distant men in the khaki uniforms" fascinating: "At six . . .
we went to watch [them] through the high wire fence that divided the
post from the town. Sometimes we joined in the ceremony, standing at

salute. . . . But at other times we stuck out our tongues and jeered at the soldiers. Perhaps the night before we had hung at the edges of a group of old men and listened to tales about Aniceto Pizaña and the 'border troubles' as the paper still called them" (4).

In straightforward language Paredes represents how a dominant culture remains dominant. He shows how it orders everyday life with its ceremonies and military music, and even how it seems in the process to filter everything out—other cultures, ethno-racial people, other classes. Simultaneously, Paredes highlights how the forms of power and authority are subverted in the countertales told by the old men about border fighters and through the taunts of Chicano schoolchildren. Interestingly, the real creative work of cultural resistance comes from the fort's margins.

Every evening Chonita (who lives in a one-room shack rented to her parents by the narrator's family) walks from the barrio to the fort's "mess halls and [presses] her nose against the screens and [watches] the soldiers eat" (5). She is amazed at the soldiers' "food-stuffed mouths" and mesmerized by their coarse dinner banter: "Hey bud, pass the coffee!" "Give me the ham! Yeah, give me the beans" (5). When Chonita is shooed away by the cooks, who give "her packages with things to eat," she returns home not only a victorious breadwinner but also a vernacular border poet-in-the-making, for she expertly mimics the utterances of the soldiers. Although the majority of the subaltern schoolchildren who attend the English-speaking schools poke fun at her, Chonita's bicultural vernacular has a deeper folk meaning. By freely expressing herself in a new border Spanglish ("Give me the hammon and the beans!"), Chonita unwittingly signifies on the educated schoolchildren's supposed superiority. Her poetic transculturation of the English word *ham* and the Spanish word *jamón* into the Spanglish construction *hammon* smuggles into the modernist story an ethno-racial folk belief among Chicanos that eating too much ham, bacon, or side beef makes people stupid and flatulent.

The narrator and the schoolchildren, however, are largely unaware of this intercultural border jest, and they eventually lose track of the barrio girl. One day, when the narrator becomes ill, he overhears the doctor tell his parents that poor Chonita has died. When asked by the narrator's father what she died from, the doctor, "looking out toward the lights of Fort Jones," responds angrily, "Pneumonia, flu, malnutrition, worms, the evil eye. . . . What the hell difference does it make?" (7).

The doctor's answer as he gazes toward the lights of the dominating Fort Jones says everything. He then juxtaposes his present-day twentieth-century U.S. empire with the "classical" empires of the past: "In classical times they did things better. Take Troy, for instance. After they stormed the city they grabbed the babies by the heels and dashed them against the walls" (9). This measuring of the present against classical cultures of imperialism is really beside the point, for infanticide, whether classical or modern, is still infanticide.

Paredes ends his story with the narrator, sick in bed, hearing "the cold voice of the bugle, gliding in and out of the dark like something that couldn't find its way back to wherever it had been" (9). Hearing the Fort Jones bugle, the narrator thinks about Chonita and mourns. Chonita's bicultural yell "Bring me the hammon and the beans!" and the narrator's tears are their socially symbolic responses to the cultures of U.S. imperialism. But for Paredes they are more than that. It is the modern questions in "The Hammon and the Beans" that matter: Why is U.S. military domination so brutal for the subaltern? Why does the Fort Jones bugle make the young narrator "feel that [he] was so alone in the world" (5)? What are the appropriate responses to the catastrophes of U.S. empire? "The Hammon and the Beans," like *George Washington Gómez,* is Paredes's modernist attempt to see the whole of dominated everyday life in South Texas—how modernizing Fort Jones in itself disturbs, divides, and rules the lives of both young and old.

From this perspective Paredes is a writer who belongs to an inter-American tradition not usually considered his, that of the "decolonialist" intellectual bringing before the reader's eyes the upheaval of an anti-imperialist imagination in the U.S.-Mexico borderlands. If this is not a customary way of seeing Paredes's modernist cultural work, his poetry written during the 1930s and 1940s—published in *Between Two Worlds* (1991)—can shed light on a lyrical poet caught between the world of *corridos* and *sonnetos.* As Ramón Saldívar suggests, *Between Two Worlds* could perhaps be called the historical bridge between the modern and the postmodern, "represent[ing] the bifurcated, interstitial, indeed one might say *differential,* quality of the kind of writing that has come to be called 'border writing'" (1993, 55).

Without doubt the theme of liberation emerges in this volume, a strong theme that is already present in the works of Paredes's inter-American contemporaries such as Langston Hughes, Aimé Césaire, Nicolás Guillén, and Luisa Espinel.[14] This modernist resistance literature, of course,

developed quite consciously out of a desire to distance the "native" intellectual from the European and (more recently) the Anglo-American master. Let me hasten to add that if there is something more graspable that
ties Paredes to the imagination of anti-imperialist writing, it is the representation in many of his poems of "spatial geographical violence" (what
Edward Said simply calls another name for imperialism) through which
the South Texas–Mexico borderlands are charted, explored, mapped out,
and brought under the Anglocentric empire's control. As Paredes suggests in his explicitly vernacular poem "The Mexican-Texan," written
to protest the state of Texas's centennial celebration in 1935, "He no
gotta country, he no gotta flag / He no gotta voice / all got is the
han' / To work like the burro; he no gotta lan'" (1991, 26–27). For Paredes, the history of the South Texas borderlands is inaugurated by the
loss of local place, whose geocultural identity must be searched.

Many of the poems, therefore, attempt to map and to invent a territorial space that derives historically from the deprivations of the present. This border poetry, we might say, is explicitly *cartographic*,
anticipating the postmodern geographies of space dramatized in the
deterritorialized border writings of Alberto Ríos, Arturo Islas, Carmen
Lomas Garza, and John Rechy (see chapters 4 and 5).[15] Among the many
striking examples of this cartographic mapping is the poem entitled "The
Rio Grande."

> I was born beside your waters,
> and since very young I knew
> That my soul had hidden currents
> That my soul resembled you.
>
> .   .   .   .
> We shall wander through the country
> Where your banks in green are clad,
> Past the shanties of rancheros
> By the ruins of old Bagdad. (15–16)

With the Rio Grande's "swirls" and "countercurrents," with its contested territoriality, there comes in the poem a whole set of assertions,
recoveries, and devastated locations and "ruins" and "shanties"—all
quite literally flowing on this poetically projected riverscape, wandering down "by the margin of the sea" (16). Certainly Paredes's allusion
to the "ruins of old Bagdad" signals his concern with the colonial past
of South Texas, evoking the "orientalized" mystery of crumbled empires
and the emergence of new ones.

If Paredes's *Between Two Worlds* participates in producing a modernist poetry of decolonization, in insisting on historical alternatives to the cultures of U.S. imperialism (he indeed searches for a more congenial revolutionary history in Nicaragua in the poem "A César Augusto Sandino"), his volume also anticipates the changing U.S.-Mexico borderland subjectivities implicit in the poetry of the Chicano movement, reconstructing a new narrative and, more important, interweaving vernacular "folkloric" verse such as the *copla, décima, son,* and *danzón* with the "high art" sonnet. As one reads Paredes's poetry of the early 1930s, there is an uncanny resemblance to the engagement and inter-American project of creating a poetry with "color," as the Cuban poet Nicolás Guillén sardonically put it in his famous prologue to *Sóngoro cosongo* (1931).

While many of the poems not only demonstrate the young poet's debt to Guillén and Hughes (Paredes's long onomatopoeic work, "Africa," with its obsession with drums easily could have come straight out of Guillén's *Motivos de son*), the poetry also owes much to the *modernista* poetics of Rubén Darío. A representative early poem is entitled "Aguafuerte estival."

El sol de la tarde, cual viejo lascivo
acaricia su cuerpo
con luz moribundo—ella exhala un suspiro
Frente al gran espejo.

Sus ojos confusos
no miran de lleno
su cuerpo desnudo,

muslos sonrosados,
caderas redondas
y seno elevado
tiemblan como
una llama perdida
entre rojas tinieblas.

Y por el campo de sus ojos
pasan en estampida
los centauros. (71)

The afternoon sun, like a lascivious man / caresses your body / with dying light—she exhales a sigh / in front of the grand mirror. Your confused eyes / do not see / your nude body / pink thighs / round hips / elevated bosoms / trembling like / a lost flame / among reddish darkness. / And in the field of your eyes / the centaurs stampede.

The mature author of "Border Country" and *"With His Pistol in His Hand"* is nowhere to be found in these adolescent verses. The one local note is the passing reference to the South Texas "sol de la tarde." The woman in the poem, moreover, is a construction of commonplaces that probably goes as far back as Petrarch. "Aguafuerte estival," in this light, thematizes the poet's debt to its well-known patriarchal conception of "woman."

Using "Aguafuerte estival" as a marker for Paredes's poetry, let us study another poem, "Flute Song."

> Why was I ever born
> Heir to a people's sorrow
> Wishing this day were done
> And yet fearful for the morrow.
>
> Why was I ever born
> Proud of my southern race,
> If I must seek my sun
> In an Anglo-Saxon face.
>
> Wail, wail, oh flutes your dismal tune,
> The agony of our new birth;
> Better perhaps had I never known
> That you lived upon the earth. (24)

Although there are affinities between this poem and the previous one (both rely heavily on a constellation of literary commonplaces), "Flute Song" highlights the persistence of an antithetical geocultural and political space in which the "southern race" "must seek my sun"—in the "Anglo-Saxon" North.[16] In reading poems such as "Flute Song" and "The Rio Grande" next to narratives such as "Border Country" and *George Washington Gómez,* one feels not just the existential disappointments of life brought on by the cultures of U.S. imperialism but also a painful beauty that spreads over the landscape of the U.S.-Mexico borderlands.

Many of the poems, additionally, attempt to focus on the poet's and his people's genealogy. Paredes's "Moonlight on the Rio Grande" even attempts to transculturate his verse by injecting into its very rhythms and structures an ethno-racialized and working-class ancestry.[17]

> The moon is so bright it dazzles me
> To look her in the eye,
> She lies like a round, bright pebble

On the dark-blue velvet sky,
She hangs like a giant pebble
In the star-encrusted sky.

The Rio Grande is bent and brown
And slow, like an aged peon,
But silver the lazy wavelets
Which the bright moon shines upon,
As bright as the little silver bells
On the round hat of a peon. (28)

The transculturation of the Rio Grande into a "bent and brown . . .
peon" entails important alterations in the rest of the poems, for once
Paredes replaces conventional poetic topoi from the Western canon with
South Texas–Mexico border ones, his verses begin to acquire a profoundly creative and hybrid dimension. Thus the vernacular musical
verses, such as "Coplas," "Tango Negro," "Guitarreros," and "Bo-
leros," together with his modernist poems dramatize the apparent poetic
"betweenness" announced in the title of the book.

    Without doubt, the role of music in the poems discussed above makes
them perfectly compatible with Paredes's more renowned vernacular
poetry, foreshadowing his mature interests in U.S.-Mexico border
music (the *décima* and the *corrido*) and folklore. If anything, my focus
on the poems in the anti-imperialist *Between Two Worlds* demonstrates
that the young poet's "Flute Song" and "Moonlight on the Rio Grande"
border on being modernist "ethno-racial" verses of decolonization.

    For these reasons, my favorite founding texts for my own version of
intercultural studies in the U.S.-Mexico borderlands are Paredes's
splendid series of spatial decolonialist discourses. Throughout his multifaceted career he has never doubted the value of the intellectual tools
given to him by the academy. But he takes the literary and scholarly
instruments he has been given and turns them against the disciplinary
rigidities of the academic, official cultural, and hegemonic mainstream.
Paredes, by far one of the most commanding figures in proto-Chicano/a
studies, in his modernist work consistently insists on social relations,
connections, and complex affinities—crossing the border-patrolled
boundaries between discourses and cultures alike.

3

Changing Borderland Subjectivities

Is there a connection between the folkloric tradition of the U.S.-Mexico border *corrido* and expressions of Chicano/a poetry? Do these connections thematize generations, traditions, and countertraditions? Do they convey deterritorializations? Marta E. Sánchez (1980), Ramón Saldívar (1990), Teresa McKenna (1991), José E. Limón (1992), Carl Gutiérrez-Jones (1995b), and Rafael Pérez-Torres (1995) have provided historically pertinent, critical interpretive answers to some of these questions in their readings of Chicano/a literary production.[1] Their theoretical works, moreover, offer solutions to the failure in earlier formalist, archetypal, and also (post)structuralist theories to locate the contexts of the literary work specifically in relation to gendered, juridical-cultural, oral-linguistic-semiotic, and formal differences. In this chapter I want to supplement this "negative dialectical" (Adorno 1973) project by outlining the possibility for a U.S.-Mexico borderlands study of Chicano/a subjectivity represented in some poetry and by offering a representative précis of postcontemporary Chicano/a poetic practices, based on social theory and ethnocultural methodology.

THE *CORRIDO* AS SOCIAL TEXT

At the outset of such a Chicano/a poetic history, we have the early poetry of José Montoya, one of the most highly regarded Chicano barrio artists and postcontemporary poets. Better known to the Chicano community as one of the founders of the Royal Chicano Art Front (RCAF), he is also more often thought of by commentators as exclusively a Chicano movement poet than as a visual artist, cultural critic, and *corrido* and blues singer. Unfortunately, this tendency to view him as a barriologist and only incidentally as a producer of socially symbolic texts prevailed among various early observers of Chicano literature. The few scholarly writings concerning Montoya's literary texts elucidate little of the historical, formal, and ideological dimensions of his work.[2] I have two goals

57

here: to provide a brief introduction to Montoya's early poetry and to articulate a critical perspective that comes from an examination of his poem "Los Vatos." Although Montoya, who was born in Escaboza, New Mexico, in 1932, had been producing short stories and poetry since adolescence, it was not until 1969 that his work was published. Even a quick reading of Montoya's early poems gives the impression of a new, Chicano sensibility: namely, its power to dramatize otherness and to bring readers into electrifying contact with social forms wholly different from Anglocentric ones.

Montoya gave nearly all of his early poems to the Chicano academicians Herminio Ríos and Octavio I. Romano in the late 1960s for their volume, *El Espejo / The Mirror* (1969). I use the term "early poems" here to refer to the poems collected in this first anthology of Chicano literature. Although little is known of the occasions for these poems, one thing is certain: one can see in them the emergence of a major Chicano poet offering a counterpoetics of aesthetic resistance and cultural critique. Despite the relatively small number of poems in the 1969 collection, some of Montoya's major themes are already evident. Most of the early poems, in one way or another, are elegies, some deploring the harsh treatment of farmworkers ("La Jefita"), others lamenting a lack of Chicano rebelliousness ("Lazy Skin"), and still others questioning the anxiety of influence in American literature ("Pobre Viejo Walt Whitman"). In poem after poem the speaker recounts the incidents in his life that led him to epiphanies about the self, revelations that mediate between social phenomena and what may be called private facts. Furthermore, phrases such as "numb sorrow," "dull pain," and "soft moans of relief" are used throughout the collection to depict a world of daily drudgery and social struggle. In addition to its analysis of the private, existential Chicano/a subject, Montoya's early work reveals the collective Chicano character types, dramatic situations, and paradigms that recur in his later work, *El Sol y los de Abajo and Other R.C.A.F. Poems* (1972) and *In Formation: 20 Years of Joda* (1992). The characters who dominate his world from the start are the speaker-protagonists, who assume such guises as a young Chicano farmworker ("Lazy Skin" and "Resonant Valley"), a *corrido* producer-singer ("Los Vatos"), and *un madre sufrida*, who in the early poems is sometimes simply the speaker's mother portrayed as a sufferer of endless labor and barrio violence. Montoya's early poems, in short, disclose to themselves a culturalist and historical Chicano subject. In the process, moreover, they explain the criteria that establish and generate a socially disciplined U.S.-Mexico border-land paradigm. Montoya envisions his poems as an attempt to decen-ter a monolingual, Anglocentric literary tradition and to recenter an ethnopoetic Chicano practice that Américo Paredes (as we saw in chap-ter 2) theorized in the late 1950s and early 1960s.[3]

Properly considered, Montoya's early poems reveal themselves to be a representation of dialectical thought and composition. Ideologically and, even more, psychologically, Montoya is a Chicano radical, an expe-rienced *veterano* of the "pachuco" epoch. His subject in "Los Vatos" is a pachuco. Pachucos, as the dramatist Luis Valdez has taught us, were young Chicanos who flaunted the zoot suit in the late 1930s and 1940s. They came to national attention in June 1943 when U.S. military men attacked them on the streets of Los Angeles in what are now known as the zoot suit riots.[4] Montoya's work creates out of the pachuco a model of social resistance to assimilation into U.S. society and a "dialectic of difference" (Saldívar 1990) from traditional Mexican views such as those espoused by Octavio Paz, who claims in *The Labyrinth of Solitude* that pachucos were inauthentic Mexicans.

It may well be that Montoya is most arresting as a Chicano poet not only when he dramatizes the poetic formulations of Chicano protest and history but also when he displays their equivalents in poetic form. Both Chicano and U.S.-Mexico border history are announced in the very rhythms and structures of his running lines, in the *corrido*-like form he employs and customizes. As he has indicated, in this way language and form are liberated from what he regards as the imperialism of Anglo-centric forms and thought. In this light "Los Vatos" is a paradigm for the unalien Chicano.[5] It is realist and observationist in its rhetoric, as though the singer-poet were telling us what he had seen and experienced during the pachuco epoch, guitar and pen in hand.

Montoya's precision of observed detail explains something about the surface meaning of his poetry: on a certain level, he is a realist, an observer of the concrete intracommunity actualities of Fresno, Fowler, Sanger, and Sacramento, California. He not only conducts a reading of the pachuco consciousness and its effects on a Chicano family, he also investigates and transforms the model of narration implicit in the *cor-rido*. In "Los Vatos," Montoya's *corrido*-like form dramatizes the fun-damental themes and essential topoi (the commonplaces) that will inform his later and more renowned poetry: the contrasting aspects of Chicano barrio life—family and innocence, on the one hand; street life, blindness, and senseless violence, on the other. This opposition, of course, is depicted in socially symbolic terms. I quote from most of the poem.

> They came to get him at three o'clock
> On a Sunday afternoon that summer of '48.
> Five of them and a guitar in a blue '37 chevy. . . .
> Two got down soothing long sleek hair,
> Hidden eyes squinting behind green tinted tea-timers. . . .
> Benny watched them from the window of the tiny bedroom.
> His sister of the huge, slanting eyes—eyes that
> Surely witnessed in another time, in another land now
> Foreign, Moctezuma slain—played on the bed; life being
> Still good to her at that age. But Benny felt sorry for
> Himself by feeling sorry for her. He felt a numb sorrow
> For many things—and he felt anger.
> His brain, his stomach, his feet—all of him—was not himself at all and he
> could stand outside and look in. He was at once a rock and a lump of jello,
> Something—a thing but not himself.
> This he could see and not understand fully, but everything that was
> happening was happening, somehow.
> "The boys!" called his mother, and her innocence made lacerations on his
> torpid mind. "Benito, the guys Want you, ven! Cuidado, and don't stay out
> late!" She warned, in false concern. Benny is a good boy!
> He walked past her without seeing her and in his thoughts, illusive like a
> moth, the incredible notion to crawl into her and the chance to be born
> again passed before him. But the street and the heat and the guys waited.
> Like all the other times of camaraderie of long ago before last night's
> dance had changed all that. And now a mask went forth strutting a brave
> deathwalk.
> A clouded mind half-knowing, aware only of the hot sun's leaping flames
> bounding off the Fresno street.
> He was consumed by a wall of heat and he managed to utter, "here?"
> then the mercury burst!
> And he felt a red-hot wire—or was it a piece of ice?
> Pass across his belly and he expired a soft moan of relief
> Then his breath was cut short from behind—Then again
> And again. (Montoya 1969, 186–187)

To understand the process of textuality and establish criteria by which we can discover and define the nature of the Chicano/a subject, we must begin by examining the social form that transforms experience, perception, and narration into materials of a socially symbolic act. "Los Vatos" can be seen as a complex of heteroglot signs that dramatizes the worldview and historical sense of a particular ethno-racial group, class,

and culture, reducing years of experience into a constellation of significant metaphors. "Los Vatos," moreover, through its conscious *corrido*-
like form, recapitulates the pachuco experience in its relation to "racial
formation" (Omi and Winant 1994) and reduces both experience and
vision to a paradigm. That is, Montoya's self-conscious reference to the
corrido as a social and historical form evokes in Chicano readers a sense
of the U.S.-Mexico borderland and Southwest life struggle inherent in
the *corrido* and all but compels belief in the sociopoetic vision of reality implicit in it. "Los Vatos" thus can be read as an intellectual or artistic social text that bridges the gap between the world of mind and the
world of real affairs, between past and present, between desire and
action. It draws on a historically and ideologically specific U.S.-Mexico
border form and on the content of individual and collective experience,
structures it, and develops from it imperatives for aesthetic resistance
and cultural critique.

The nature of the *corrido* as form and content is social and revolutionary, drawing heavily on the deepest levels of what Fredric Jameson
(1981) has called "the political unconscious," defining relationships
between the temporal and the eternal. The *corrido,* as Paredes has taught
us, is sung by Chicanos who live throughout the U.S.-Mexico borderlands in the southwestern United States. Its function is to reconcile individual experience into a collective identity. According to Paredes,
corridos that "sing the feats of the first Mexican-American rebels against
the North American government" came into existence at the end of the
1850s (1979, 13). An uprising led by Juan Nepomuceno Cortina in 1859
in South Texas, for instance, was celebrated in various border *corridos,*
of which we still have fragments. From the *corridos* of Cortina and others, this Chicano paradigm establishes the laws of folk narrative that
give the Chicano images life.[6] *Corridos* appear to be built of three structural elements: a hero or protagonist, with whom the Chicano or Mexican audience is presumed to identify in some way; a world in which
the hero acts and is acted on by antagonistic, often Anglocentric forces,
which is presumably a reflection of the audience's conception of the
world; and an oral narrative, in which the interaction of the protagonist and the world is described. Specifically, the hero, as Paredes tells
us, "is always a Mexican whose rights or self-respect are trampled upon
by North American authority" (1979, 13).

What is significant about the *corrido* as social text is that we are
always left with images of the hero-subject and the world that enable

us to identify with (and thus enter) the world of sociopoetic or subaltern myth; and as "Los Vatos" suggests, the *corrido* can change through time and accommodate new Chicano perceptions and experiences. (Years later Montoya would, in fact, compose and sing a *corrido* entitled "Los Huelguistas" [The Strikers] for his Trio Casindio and the Royal Chicano Air Force debut album, *Chicano Music All Day*.) This ability to adapt is certainly true of Montoya's poetic song. Benny and his pachuco world can be readily abstracted as "images," which may in turn evoke for us the whole history of the U.S.-Mexico border *corrido*. Montoya's vision of the pachuco experience, though open to the social, psychological, and ideological forces of American society in late capitalism, is related to nineteenth-century Mexican-American perceptions and histories and the *corrido*'s implicit theory of social critique through its fixity of form. His radical alteration of subject and barrio may be seen as marking the point at which a new epoch of ethno-racial history, culture, and ideology can be said to begin.

Lest I be misunderstood as championing Montoya's poem as an unnuanced example of resistance literature, let me reiterate that "Los Vatos" signals a profound transformation of U.S.-Mexico borderland subjectivity. If the *corrido* proper (as María Herrera-Sobek, Paredes, and Limón have brilliantly demonstrated) displaced the Spanish *romance* both aesthetically and thematically when it traveled from Spain to Nuestra América's borderlands, it is not surprising that the form undergoes a sea change as it travels from South Texas to the wild San Joaquin Valley of California. Although it is indisputable that "Los Vatos" thematizes what Limón calls a "world of intracommunity violence" (1992, 108), it does not follow from this that the poem is "diminished as [a] sociopolitical statement" (107). Rather, Montoya's "Los Vatos" can be seen as participating in a kind of "organic" barrio cultural conversation fomenting a cultural strategy for aesthetic resistance and cultural critique. As Antonio Gramsci would certainly have pointed out, a radical analysis of California barrio life (as represented by "Los Vatos") can only acquire social force if it is embodied in a new form and an alternative experiential vision—in this case, of the meaninglessness of intracommunity barrio violence.

A study of Chicano/a poetry must therefore begin with an attempt to define at least some of the cultural paradigms that have emerged from the historical experience of the U.S.-Mexico contact zone. Montoya's early poetry establishes his importance in the recentering of Chicano perception and experience in formal, unalien paradigms. Given the strength of the *corrido* paradigm in the Chicano experience, it is surprising that subsequent postcontemporary Chicano/a poets (with the exception of popular culture artists such as Los Tigres del Norte, Trio Casindio, and Tish Hinojosa) have not looked to it consciously or unconsciously for structuration and content. I am not suggesting that other paradigms are not social in nature, but I am suggesting that the *corrido* is one of the central sociopoetic Chicano folk and mass culture paradigms.[7] I do not intend to trace a complete history of Chicano/a poetic forms in the remainder of the chapter; however, I would like to sketch a brief outline of other negating Chicano/a poems and comment on their importance to an emerging subaltern U.S. poetics. Let me stress that I offer here simply a tentative model of a possible radical Chicano/a hermeneutic practice.

BERNICE ZAMORA AND THE CHICANA SUBJECT

I begin this section with the self-evident claim that conventional social theory is not often concerned with the ethnopoetic or borderland feminist consciousness of the historically situated author or reader of a text. This failure of social theory to deal with individuals, ethno-racial groups, and texts on the margins can be corrected by accommodating U.S.-Mexico border feminist poetic theory in its concept of a private and collective subject.

The Chicana feminist project has received attention from, among others, Marta Sánchez, Norma Alarcón, Chela Sandoval, Alvina Quintana, Sonia Saldívar-Hull, and Cordelia Candelaria.[8] I should like to add to their recent formulations on the construction of the Chicana subject by commenting on Bernice Zamora's *Restless Serpents* (1976), her first book of poems. *Restless Serpents* is an ambitious work that proposes a radical and complex critique of Western male power in social, cultural, psychoanalytic, and literary discourse. Zamora's critique derives from her interest in Third World literature, Third World movements, and ethno-racial feminism and from her diverse background: assistant professor of English and American literature at Santa Clara University, single parent of two daughters, and author of several studies on Chicano literature, as well as guest editor of several issues of *De Colores,* a journal of Chicano thought and culture.

The metaphor of the restless serpent—it appears explicitly in at least two of Zamora's poems and implicitly throughout her book—coils and recoils the reader's praxis of transformation. Her work is a swerving from reference to reference, from intertextual, extratextual, and inter-sexual codes that break through the constraints of "capitalist appro-priations," to use Gilles Deleuze and Félix Guattari's phrase (1977). Indeed, the serpents are venomous beasts that can only be soothed by desiring machinic verse, "strokes more devastating than devastation arrived" (Zamora 1976, 74). As Juan Bruce-Novoa puts it, "Zamora's poetry like those serpents fascinates: they are inscrutable signs of life and death in beautiful form, capable of demonic possession" (1977, 153). My hypothesis for Chicano/a borderlands poetics is this: Zamora's restless serpents and sexually charged figures of speech can function as revolutionary investments of desire, capable of exploding the structures of patriarchal society. Her erotic art, moreover, is a concrete answer to the question of how our hybrid divisions and desires can deploy their forces within the social, political, and literary domains.

We begin our consideration of Zamora's ethno-racial feminist project by looking at her apparently unproblematic short poem, "So Not to Be Mottled":

You insult me
When you say I'm
Schizophrenic.
My divisions are
Infinite. (1976, 50)

First, the Chicana subject is to be seen within a rhetorical (i.e., tropo-logical), social, and schizoanalytical context.[9] We must account for the ways readers process these different levels of a text. In a heuristic read-ing of Zamora's poem we can start by comprehending the linguistic signs in a primarily referential manner. But immediately we run into prob-lems. At the mimetic level the poem can say one thing and mean another. Furthermore, we are at times faced with bizarre signs or contradictory results when we interpret in an exclusively referential way. Hence we must seek another level of reading—a dialectical interpretation with-out necessary teleological synthesis. Zamora's poem is certainly a text that on the surface does not pose extreme difficulties for the reader. The speaker in the poem, presumably a woman, rebukes another person, presumably a man, for calling her a schizophrenic. The first part of the poem is clear enough. But why is the speaker insulted when the man calls her schizophrenic, for at the same time she claims to transcend conventional schizophrenia? The speaker says, "*My* divisions are / Infinite." This rhetorical logic at the tropological level calls out for a hermeneutic reading, but the poem provides no clear indication of what semantic transformation is appropriate.

Blocked within our mimetic reading, we must consider Zamora's poem from a broader frame of reference: her ethno-racial feminist perspective. Zamora's textual supraschizophrenia can thus become a clue to our secondary level of reading. Throughout *Restless Serpents,* Bernice Zamora wishes to explode our traditional notions of socially constructed human genders. She does this primarily by making our sexual and cultural silences speak through her verse. She also examines the limits of sexuality and desire, which are never static entities. As Marta Sánchez has pointed out, Zamora's poems dramatize "what men have not permitted women to say, or what men themselves have not said" (1980, 55). Zamora's world, in other words, is a world "within limits / Fixed by a law / which is not ours" (1976, 17).

Definitions of the Chicano/a subject are imposed on us by outsiders: God, government, schools, churches, and so on. In our prisonhouse of sexual and erotic codes we love each other, for "we have in common / the experience of love" (17). Zamora herself is a product of this highly repressive world. Colorado, her home state, and the rest of the Southwest have been conquered and colonized by Anglo-American males, priests representing the Catholic Church, and traditionally conservative Chicano males. *Restless Serpents,* therefore, necessarily dramatizes a world of violence, sexually repressed silence, and productive erotic desire. In this larger frame of reference, Zamora's poem takes as object of study conventional psychoanalytic discourse and interpretation. Her text, we might say, is an expansion of two psychoanalytic opposites: the one male centered and Oedipal in origin (a tale of neurosis); the other, a tale or allegory of an anti-Oedipal, ethno-racial feminist tradition. "So Not to Be Mottled" covers the whole blotching and streaking of the subject, for it materially hybridizes rather than neuroticizes.

Zamora's poems in *Restless Serpents* are desiring technologies; she stores up her treasure so as to create an immediate explosion. Put differently, the speaker in *Restless Serpents* in general and in "So Not to

Be Mottled" in particular knows how to scramble the codes of the self, how to cause erotic flows to circulate, and how to construct material hybridity. Zamora's poetic ethno-racial feminist project desires to destroy the illusion of the ego, guilt, law, limits, and Western repression. Its expansion of the Chicana/o subject employs a vision of infinite division of the self. In this regard, Zamora's project suggests a montage of desiring machines, a "mottling" Chicana exercise dramatizing a rhetoric of fragmentation that extracts from the text its social and revolutionary forces.

ALBERTO RÍOS'S U.S.-MEXICO BORDER BAROQUE

As a kind of working conclusion on the making of the Chicano/a subject, let me offer some speculative remarks about the Chicano/a subject, the critical U.S.-Mexico border, and what Alejo Carpentier called *lo barroco americano* (the American baroque), that is, "decorative elements that completely fill the space of . . . all available space" (1995, 93). With Ríos's *Whispering to Fool the Wind* (1982), his first full-length book, Chicano poetry begins to perform its negating and differentiating dialectics in new, "baroque" ways. Born in Nogales, Arizona, Ríos expresses that ideology of our bicultural (Mexican and American) vision by which postcontemporary Chicano/a writers from Montoya to Zamora have sought to convey their radical sense of otherness, the culture shocks of the modern Southwest in late capitalism. In Ríos's work, the social realism of the border *corrido* is mixed with *lo barroco* of the Américas to create a Chicano phantasmatic, mediating between higher and lower worlds. In each of Ríos's well-wrought poems, his texts can be seen to be setting up a network of edges or borders into which the reader is lured with a determinate promise of comprehension.

The critical boundaries outlined in *Whispering to Fool the Wind* are self/other, prose/poetry, adulthood/childhood, life/death, reality/marvelous reality, and United States/Mexico—all binary oppositions that call out for critical deconstruction. Most of the poems in fact focus on the liminal geographic spaces of Chicano border towns such as Nogales, often bordering on two worlds, two languages, two cultures, and two literary traditions—Latin American and North American. It is just such a differential border baroque that Ríos seeks to effect through his verse. In poem after poem words come from a relative's wrinkles ("Nani") or from mouths piped up from the dead: "I am a man / who has served ants with the attitude / of a waiter, who has made each smile as only / an ant who is fat can, and they liked me best / but there is nothing left" (42). His best poem in *Whispering to Fool the Wind* is "El Molino Rojo," in which he leaves behind the "real" and enters a world of the "not real." On the surface "El Molino Rojo" is a story of Cuate, Robles, Indio, Chapo, and Missy, old men who each day must come to a wooden building housing a bar named El Molino Rojo. Daily, they must make conversation, drink pulque, and play pool. But one of the men, Chapo, is dead. Thus the whole poem has a phantasmatic quality as the characters try to interpret Chapo's words.

> Chapo is the youngest who died two years ago
> but still must come here
> because he has nowhere else
> and no one.
> He is always popular
> telling the jokes of a drunk
> sometimes in a girl's voice,
> silly, but only out of habit.
> He no longer drinks and each is glad,
> they've been telling him for so long.
> A shudder comes over him:
> misfortune is near.
> No one listens to him
> because he is dead,
> but each man thinks,
> *what can he mean.* (45)

A deep-rooted Mexican and Chicano belief in the life of the dead is thus imaginatively dramatized. What distinguishes the dead is their desire to communicate, live, and love. They had once all lived "in this country," "in one small town." They had loved, struggled, joked, and brawled together, but in death as in life they remain locked in the same routines and illusions. Robles, for instance, eternally frowns, "sits only in one place," the place he fought for; Cuate, a "fat twin," still tries "to recall his own childhood / the bugs, the smell of anise / of mint in the side garden after watering / the smell of wet sand in the wash / in his feet / on his legs." And Indio, who shines shoes in the barbershop like his black friends, is "permanently bruised," confident that "he will live for centuries because he deserves to." Missy comes to the bar "because he is the owner"; he wants to tell his friends to leave, and he desperately wishes to go "with them somewhere else." But their illusions and struggles are destructive. When Missy's wife dies, Missy spends his years trying to collect "money from those who had none," gazing at the broken pool table, "but he can't do anything to fix it." "El Molino Rojo," of course, can be taken as a socially symbolic barrioscape, the place of *los de abajo*—the underdogs. Though the characters are from the subaltern, this is not only a poem about domination. Ríos plunges deeper into the "real" that Chicanos live by. Thus Indio, "proud and a man," Cuate, always "betting," and Robles, always "fighting," cherish their illusions, their arms around each other's shoulders. Only the myths and the present absences live on when they die. "El Molino Rojo" is the center of the Chicano barrioscape. Ríos thus shows a U.S.-Mexico border town coming to an end without an end. The poem stands as an emblem of the phantasmatic in general and of what Jameson has described in *The Political Unconscious* as "the worldness of the world" manifesting itself "to itself . . . when the landscape seems charged with alien meanings" (1981, 134–135).

If Ríos's poetry is a kind of magic realist storytelling, then his short story cycle, *The Iguana Killer* (1984), is a kind of U.S.-Mexico border baroque poetry. Written for what the author calls a "young adult audience," the stories explore the liminal world of childhood and the border town of Nogales, Arizona/Sonora. In the title story, "The Iguana Killer," young Sapito uses the baseball bat his grandmother sends him from south of the U.S.-Mexico border to become the greatest iguana killer in Mexico. "Pato" is a tale about a fat boy who "smells bad." Although most of the young adult stories are rather straightforwardly narrated, "The Way Spaghetti Feels" and "The Birthday of Mrs. Piñeda" border on the metafictional and magic realist impulse in postmodernist fiction.

In "The Way Spaghetti Feels," written from a young woman's point of view, Ríos has a black Angus cow serve as a post office for young Maricela and a shy pen pal. "The Birthday of Mrs. Piñeda," the most lyrical story in the collection, is primarily about a husband's attempt to control his wife's discourse and domestic space. At the story's end the husband finally allows his wife to tell her *cuento de nunca acabar,* her story without an end: "Mariquita Piñeda began her story on her birthday, and it went on and on, further, through the night and pushed a shoulder against lunch time of the next day" (119). *The Iguana Killer* thus engages the problems of intersecting and competing borders, both literary and territorial, often interrupting the genre limitations of the very tales themselves.

But it is in his haunting narcorealist story, "The Child," that he thematizes the U.S.-Mexico border line, delineating a geopolitical space of low-intensity conflict. The most important border signifiers in this tale are those of anonymous narcodrug dealers and police officers from the South, but equally dramatic are the unreported middle-class drug addictions in the North. Within this contested space along the U.S.-Mexico border two Mexican women, Mrs. Sandoval and Mrs. García, dressed in black, leave the city of Guaymas one Wednesday morning, crossing the Sonora highways on their way to Nogales to attend a family funeral on *el otro lado* (the other side). For its start, "The Child" inscribes its tropes of border crossing by accentuating what Paredes has described as the U.S.-Mexico border's "continuous mutual influence moving in both directions" (1993, 6). In other words, the story binds the *México profundo* in the South to the *México de afuera* in the North through the informal circuits of exchange by families on both sides of the border. Ríos expresses this cultural and familial circulation as a form of "gift-giving," for the women brought "tortillas, sweet bread, sugar, all gifts" for their relatives in the United States (1984, 12).

Once on the bus "hurtl[ing] them" *al norte*, the women attempt to pass the time by looking out the window or by "fan[ning] themselves" with newspapers and magazines that they read "many times" on their journey (13). Across the aisle from them a thin man sits next to a sleeping "little boy" with a blanket around his head. When the curious Mrs. García inquires about the boy's condition, the thin man (who moves "like an ostrich") reassures her by saying that they are traveling north "to see a doctor, a specialist in Nogales, maybe Tucson" (14). The conversation ends in polite silence when the señora asks the man if he has tried folk remedies: "Did you try giving him some *yerba buena* tea? . . . Did you try honey and lemon? Maybe with a little bit of tequila? That always helps" (14–15).

When the bus stops in Hermosillo, Mrs. García refreshes herself with an *agua de manzana* (apple juice) at El Yaquí restaurant and orders a glass of ice water for the sick child, left sleeping on the bus. When they return to the bus and attempt to awaken the child, Mrs. García screams out, "Oh, Oh, my God! This child is dead" (19).

After teasing the reader with a meandering border-crossing narrative on the road, Rios reveals the lurid truth: "The child was dead. It had been dead for a long time. That is true. But it had also been operated on. The boy's insides had been cleaned out and replaced with bags [of dope]. . . . Then the boy was sewn up again, put into clothes" (21). Ríos deliberately interrupts the playful world of the young adult genre by radically experimenting with its form and content. Disrupting the pleasure principle of the young adult *cuento* (story) cycle, "The Child" constructs an alternative vision of the U.S.-Mexico border reality principle, where children and women are not only the genre's protagonists but also victims of what we now call the war on drugs. Read in this light, "The Child" accentuates what Mary Patricia Brady describes as "the depths" of narcodrug trafficking along the U.S.-Mexico *frontera*, "transform[ing] the quotidian practices" of everyday life (1996, 268).

In Ríos's *Five Indiscretions* (1985) nearly every poem is about desire, sexuality, and religion, and nearly every poem deals with the socially constructed boundaries between men and women. Most of the poems in this book achieve a level of excellence not far below the peak moments found in *Whispering to Fool the Wind*. No Chicano poet writing today is a more exquisite—a more fastidiously deliberate—technician than Ríos. His work is always lavishly multilayered, and the most abiding quality is its poetic brilliance. In part 1, the poems are written from a woman's perspective. Here he juxtaposes poems about desire, religion, and violence. In "Prayers to the Dangerous," for instance, the poet is able to bring two central concerns, eros and spirituality, into clear focus.

> Pretty girls go walking away to prayers.
> What they pray for, C-shaped, is not so different:
> homemade waffles, omelettes all filled with mushrooms.
> But in the omelettes
> one girl thinks of fire: in the hands, and eyelids
> as they drooped, that halfway excruciation
> coming from a moment without a name yet,
> pressing and pressing. (11)

In the title poem, "Five Indiscretions," he continues with his earlier practice of writing meandering, sad poems about a woman whose "power" was "never once making love to a man" (26). In part 2, Ríos shifts his focus from a feminine world to the masculine U.S.-Mexico border subcultural world with characters like El Santo the wrestler and Reies the boxer. In perhaps the most hyperbolic poem, "On January 5, 1984, El Santo the Wrestler Died, Possibly," his male protagonist is so fierce and tenacious even in death, it is claimed, that he would "get angry, get up, and come back after them. / That way for which he was famous" (51). But it is in "Combing My Hair in the Hall," an autobiographical poem, that Ríos returns to his obsessive artistic U.S.-Mexico borderland theme, the "third language" invented in Nogales by an English-speaking mestizo and a Spanish-speaking grandmother.

> Then she spoke with her woman's hands
> only, no words left, then only her smell
> which had once been warm, tortillas,
> or like sugar breads just made.
> In the half-words of our other language,
> in the language of the new world
> of which she had had time to show me
> only half, I tried to speak to her. (84)

To be sure, the protagonists in Ríos's work live with their grace, wit, and hybrid language improvisations. Their worlds are fraught with betweenness and unpredictability, yet they have enormous gifts for understanding "the half-words of our other language."

In this chapter I have traced the changing subjectivities in Chicano/a poetics from 1969 to 1985. From representative examples of José Montoya's, Bernice Zamora's, and Alberto Ríos's poetry and short stories, I argue that Chicano/a poetics must necessarily include a negative dialectical, formal, social, sexual, and differential perspective of Chicano discourse and culture. A Chicano/a poetics, moreover, must include some characterization of border culture, and that characterization, in turn, must be derived from sets of texts in which Chicano/a culture is manifest. It is possible, but not easy.

I have taken Chicano/a literary production seriously, and I have tried to follow Herbert Marcuse's (1969) claim that ethno-racialized folks are inherently radicalized by their socially marginalized and constricted position in the United States. Unless we can relate the struggle of U.S.-Mexico people against exploitation in the past, we shall not fully understand our own present and so will be less able to change it. Chicano/a poetics must not be an alternative technique for deconstructing-interpreting texts.[10] Instead, it must be part of our liberation from tokenism, condescension, racism, and oppression, and that is why it is well worth pursuing.

4

The Production of Space by
Arturo Islas and Carmen Lomas Garza

A whole history remains to be written of *spaces*—which
would at the same time be the history of *powers* (both of
these terms in the plural)—from the great strategies of
geopolitics to the little tactics of the habitat.
            Michel Foucault, "Of Other Spaces" (1987)

Every society—and hence every mode of production with its
subvariants— . . . produces a space, its own space.
            Henri Lefebvre, *The Production of Space* (1991)

How can we begin to situate and map U.S.-Mexico border spaces without privileging political and cultural "centers"? How do we characterize non-Eurocentered transfrontier identifications? Is there any getting
around a local / global opposition that, in James Clifford's formulation,
"*either* favors some version of globalism self-defined as progressive, modern, and historically dynamic *or* favors a localism rooted (not routed)
in place, tradition, culture, or ethnicity conceived in an absolutist mode"
(1992a, 10; his emphasis)? If, as we have seen, Renato Rosaldo, Vicki
Ruiz, George Sánchez, Néstor García Canclini, and Américo Paredes
theorize that U.S.-Mexico border cultures are historically constructed
spaces of intercultural crossings *between* global and local alternatives,
Arturo Islas's *Migrant Souls* (1990) and Carmen Lomas Garza's
Cuadros de familia / Family Pictures (1990) explore how Chicano/a identities are entangled with social spaces: parlors, writing rooms, hospital
rooms, *curandera* rooms, barrio *casitas* (houses), *ferias* (fairs), and the
U.S.-Mexico borderlands. In other words, their migrations between the
local and the global constitute a new cultural dominant in Nuestra
América's borders.

If one of the most significant features of postmodern narratives is
their attempt to negotiate topospatial forms of high art with certain forms

and genres of mass culture and the practices of everyday life, Islas's *Migrant Souls* exploits this impulse. He brings together the impact of classic Puritan rhetoric on our culture—what Sacvan Bercovitch (1975), among others, calls the shaping influence of religious or quasi-religious symbols of society (book 1 is appropriately entitled "Flight into Egypt")—with references to the 1950s through the mambo, doo-wop, Elvis, Greta Garbo's face, and mass culture magazines such as *Popular Romance.*[1]

MIGRATORY SPACE

Migrant Souls focuses on Josie Salazar and her gay cousin, Miguel Chico, with extended meditations on Jesús María (the emergent matriarch after Moma Chona's death), Gabriel (a priest and Miguel Chico's brother), and Sancho Salazar (Josie's father). The novel is composed of two parts, "Flight into Egypt" and "Feliz Navidad." The first part explores Josie's and Miguel's everyday life in Del Sapo, Texas, and simultaneously cognitively maps their shifting border identifications in Texas and California. "Feliz Navidad" sets its narrative clock to what the narrator calls the "annual ritual of hypocrisy," when the Angel family gathers for their Christmas Eve reunion. Originally entitled *A Perfectly Happy Family,* the novel does its cultural work by defining itself against what Roberto Cantú calls "biblical metaphors originally associated with deliverance" (1992, 151)—as so much of subaltern literature and culture presently is.

Through this negative Christian symbology, Islas explores the social constructs that define compulsory heterosexual hegemony in the U.S.-Mexico borderlands. As in *The Rain God* (1984), ethno-racial oppositions in *Migrant Souls* between Chicano and "Spanish" (the so-called *gente de razón*) identifications in members of the same Chicano/a family create a dramatized hierarchy of power—thus positioning certain Angel family members (Josie, Miguel Chico, Sancho, and Serena) as inferior to the passing *gente decentes,* or decent people (Mama Chona, Jesús María, Dick), in Del Sapo. The cultural work of *Migrant Souls* is to radically critique the bourgeois ethno-racial manners and heterosexual pretensions of the Angel family.

In February 1991, almost one year after Islas published *Migrant Souls,* he died from complications from AIDS at his home on the Stanford University campus. Born in El Paso on May 24, 1938, Islas attended public schools in the U.S.-Mexico borderlands and enrolled at Stanford in 1956. He graduated as an English major (with a French minor) in 1960 and was accepted into the Stanford Ph.D. program in English. After completing his Ph.D. coursework, Islas worked for several years as a writing instructor at the Veterans Administration Hospital in Menlo Park, California. In 1967 he returned to Stanford where he passed his Ph.D. oral examination and finished his elegantly written dissertation (under the direction of Wallace Stegner) on the Jewish-American novelist Hortense Calisher.

In 1971 Islas was appointed assistant professor of English at Stanford University. He began writing what was to become *The Rain God,* a novel that meticulously and poetically re-creates the topography along the U.S.-Mexico borderlands and the social, gender, and sexual relations of its people. So considered, *The Rain God*—awarded the 1986 Southwest Book Award for fiction by the Texas Border Regional Library Association—is a sweeping and richly textured narrative of the heroic, moving, and magical story of Mama Chona (the puritanical matriarch of the Angel clan) and her migrations north from Mexico, her children's and grandchildren's claiming of America, and their lusts, passions, and desires. In his subsequent novels, *Migrant Souls* and *La Mollie and the King of Tears,* published in 1996, Islas continued to weave the genealogies and fates of his mestizo/a characters in interconnected stories.

If one great motif of Islas's life and fiction is the "migration out," from the local to the transnational, an equally powerful counterdiscourse is the notion of "return." "I return often to my parents' home now," Islas wrote in one of his last published essays, "—you can go home again and again after and if you are willing to grow up—and to that southwestern desert country where the light has a clarity that stuns and where one is closer to the sky than anywhere else on earth" (1990a, 3).

Highly bicultured, Islas incarnated the very ideals of the border-crossing intellectual, equally at home in the San Francisco Bay Area or Cuidad Juárez, easily moving from the North into the South and vice versa. Fluent in three languages and literary traditions (English, Spanish, and French), Islas legitimately laid claim to the critical cosmopolitan tradition of novelists like Henry James, William Faulkner, Marcel Proust, and Gabriel García Márquez. He often focused on their works in his popular undergraduate classes and evoked them in his writing as models for cultural and literary practice. Additionally, one of his most successful courses at Stanford, one he called "American Lives," juxtaposed readings in critical multicultural American autobiography (Cherríe Moraga, Gloria Anzaldúa, and Maxine Hong Kingston) with his students' attempts to reconstruct their own lives.

Islas's success, even celebrity, as a "local color" novelist recently has been accompanied by a more global recognition. In *The Buried Mirror* (1992) the Latin American novelist and critic Carlos Fuentes points to Islas's novels as exemplary of the "boom" in U.S. Latino/a literature—an emergent transnational writing. Islas's fiction, Fuentes suggests, joins a hybrid tradition going from Juan Ruiz's *El Libro de buen amor* to the dizzying postmodernist jolts of Gabriel García Márquez's *El General en su laberinto*. Fuentes is absolutely right in noting that Islas's importance rests, in no small part, on how he involved himself in U.S.-Mexico hybrid aesthetics with meditations on questions of culture and identity. But *The Rain God* and its companion novel, *Migrant Souls*,[2] in my view, manage to encompass some five hundred years of U.S.-Mexico border space and time, of the geography, history, and psychology of *la frontera*. The more cosmopolitan Islas gets, the more local he becomes and vice versa—a paradox he himself captured eloquently in the title of his second novel, *Migrant Souls*. And it is this spatial contradiction that I explore here. How can these two opposite spaces—a two-thousand-mile-long and twenty-mile-wide U.S.-Mexican border and the celestial space of reified souls—feed into and out of each other in this work?[3]

To begin my case for a "topospatial" analysis of Islas's *Migrant Souls*, I intend to respond briefly to an objection to a reading of the novel that emphasizes space over temporality. *Migrant Souls*, an opponent to our topospatial reading might argue, may have plenty of interesting things to say about space, place, "in-betweenness," and geography, but these are in the long run supplementary to its real concerns, which are psychology, the knowable past, and family history. Miguel Chico himself, one of the central consciousnesses of the book (his cousin Josie Salazar is the other), the traditional argument might claim, is a psychological novelist "writing his dissertation on Henry James" (1990b, 181), not any sort of U.S.-Mexico geographer; and the very structure of the book is historical, not spatial, consisting of a series of flashbacks to Miguel Chico's and Josie's early adulthood (book 1) and Miguel Chico's ritualistic bouts of alcoholism during Christmas Eve festivities at his parents' home in Del Sapo (book 2).

The local historicizing in the novel is indeed dramatized when Islas describes how Josie, Serena, and "their cousins watched Mama Chona live to be more than one hundred years old" (47). To be sure, family history is its explicit theme. *Migrant Souls* is packed with histories, hegemonic, legendary, mythic, personal, and alternative. These include the placid family history that Mama Chona kept for the Angel clan ("those sacred objects that bound her and her family to the Angel traditions: an enormous and worn wooden chest, its leather straps frayed and hanging useless front and back, which she told them contained the documents and relics that proved that the Angels had descended from castles in Spain; a very chipped statue of Jesus, almost twenty inches high, the right index finger repaired and pointing to His Sacred Heart; and the imposing framed photograph of her husband" [10]); the official Thanksgiving history Josie and Serena learned in the public schools in 1947 and their reciting from Longfellow's canonical "Hiawatha" (22) or the different deportation *historias,* such as that of "Benito Cruz . . . who had been picked up three times already, detained at the border for hours, and then released with the warning that he was to carry his identification papers at all times" (23); and the oral communal history that is Rudy's recitation of family genealogy ("This was Mexico before it was the land of liberty and equality for some. And before that it was Indian territory. They knew how to live in it. So where are we? . . . We're on the border between a land that has forgotten us and another land that doesn't understand us" [165]). All these voices, vernacular styles, and forms, all these uneven histories, struggle for predominance in the novel.

All this is true of *Migrant Souls.* It is a profoundly nuanced family history, and thus far the objection to a topospatial analysis of the novel might seem to be on target. Such an analysis, however, does not have to conceive of space and time as sharp opposites, so that insisting that *Migrant Souls* is marked with historicity does not have to undermine my claim that it is simultaneously spatial. I will address these issues below, but for now let me suggest that *Migrant Souls* does aim to identify a "repressive" space for the *gente decente* of Del Sapo, a spatial fetishism that sets in when history, race, gender, and sexuality are repressed, customized, perverted, performed, and erased from the scene.

In a representative passage early in the novel Islas reflects on the sophomoric games Josie and Miguel Chico played on the Angel family. Once a month they sent anonymous cards to the relatives informing them of their "remote" and "fated" lives in what they called "the

Order of Saint Wretched": "Sitting on the [piano] bench in the perpetual twilight of their aunt's parlor, Miguel Chico felt trapped. If he joined his cousin in the fun, the crow at the back of his neck would dig more deeply into his brain. If he told his aunt the truth, both she and Josie would be angry with him and the hummingbirds would eat away at his heart" (60). It is important to emphasize the force with which Islas uses the word *trapped* in this scene. Space—the little tactics of the aunt's parlor, a "perpetual twilight"—is a "bad" space, a space that never ends, space as betwixt and between, space as harboring ideology. Such spatial fetishism is not a quality of the Del Sapo borderlands space, since the U.S.-Mexico border from 1848 to the present has been used and abused as use and surplus value. Rather, for Islas, it is a social way of seeing, an alienated consciousness in Del Sapo, Texas.

The other relatives' rooms that Miguel Chico visits in Del Sapo are no less repressive, often producing "eerie" (233), "otherworldly" (240), and "solitary" (168) sensibilities. One of the central episodes near the novel's end in book 2 is Miguel Chico's dealings with his aunt Jesús María (a minor character flatly described in *The Rain God* as a "religious fanatic"). While rooms, porches, parlors, kitchens, and barrio *casitas* continue to preoccupy Islas and his central consciousness, Miguel Chico, Islas the antiromantic novelist enjoys exaggerating Jesús María's flights from the everyday world to the spiritual: "after her husband's abrupt death, which she took personally, Jesús María began to enjoy her solitude. Its silence was a daily, if not glowing, visitation she had not desired or expected, and she found herself in a state of fearful wonder gliding from one room to another like a nun in an empty convent" (168–169). Rooms, even Jesús María's magical rooms in her "red brick house in the old part of town near the Cathedral" (166), are "empty" spaces such as those a nun might find in a solitary convent. Alienated, empty, solitary rooms point to what this novel is centrally about, for *Migrant Souls'* project might be summed up as an effort to spatialize good and bad geopolitics and the suffocating habitats of compulsory heterosexuality across the extended borderlands of Texas and California, leading Miguel Chico to note "the medieval atmosphere of Del Sapo," which "was enough to drive any sensitive person quite mad." "In some places," say, California, he continues, "there at least, the world wasn't divided into the saints and the sinners" (123).

Given the interactions between the strategies of U.S.-Mexico geopolitics and the little tactics of the habitat in *Migrant Souls,* arguments overemphasizing "historicity" and "temporality" over *frontera* topospatiality are not so much incorrect as merely incomplete. To better situate the concept of topospatiality in this chapter, I now wish to briefly discuss some theories of space by Juan Bruce-Novoa, Kristin Ross, and Henri Lefebvre as a way of locating my reading of Islas's and Lomas Garza's texts as profound explorations of U.S.-Mexico border geography.

We owe the notion of a predominance of space in Chicano/a literature to Juan Bruce-Novoa's 1974 essay, "The Space of Chicano Literature." What the Chicano theorist stresses is the relationship between discontinuity and continuity, time and space: "Discontinuity is the social order, founded on work and time, the concept of the individual which rigidly defines us as separate from others. Continuity includes those spaces in which human individuality is violated and depersonalized, resulting in the dissolution of the normal order, the interruption of temporal flow and the unity of all particular beings in spatial simultaneity" (1990, 95).

In effect, Bruce-Novoa calls for a new kind of literary space in Chicano/a literary studies, for "literature," he argues, "becomes a space for responding to chaos" (96). While he is rightly to be credited for resisting the Euromodernist fascinations with the rhetoric of temporality, my hesitation with his nuanced thesis in "The Space of Chicano Literature" is that it assumes the epistemological, phenomenological, and anthropological priority of language (literature) over social space. The preexistence of an empty space is simply taken as a given, and only the space of (Chicano/a) writing is dealt with as something that must be created.[4]

More fundamental to my analysis of U.S.-Mexico border space is Kristin Ross's splendid *The Emergence of Social Space,* for she is one of the first to redeem the idea of space from arcane aesthetic reifications— showing us that nothing can be more political than the way objects, territories, and regions are spatially distributed. "Within traditional Marxism," Ross explains, "a preoccupation with spatial categories was taken as the mark of 'spatial fetishism,' a wrong-thinking conceptualizing of space as an autonomous determinant. . . . But space, as a social fact or as an instance of society, is always political and strategic" (1988, 9). Ross's emphasis on social space does more than correct the "imbalance" in traditional Marxist "historical materialism"; her book also acknowledges how the Paris Commune in 1871 was a jolting transformation of everyday life, especially the seizing and reconstructing of a place, a city, a sector of the nation-state by the masses.

Standing behind Ross's magisterial reading of the spatial and anti-hierarchical events of May 1871 is Henri Lefebvre, the Marxist philosopher who, through the events of May 1968 in France, came to recognize the significance of urban conditions of daily life as central to revolutionary sentiments and politics. In *The Production of Space* Lefebvre calls for a new kind of spatial imagination capable of confronting the past in new ways involving the body, the city, the cosmos, the political and libidinal economies. For our purposes in conceptualizing a topospatial analysis, Lefebvre's work can help to ground the idea of nations and their borderlands in more concrete terms.

While most people, Lefebvre argues, define the nation "as a sort of substance" that springs up from a territory with natural borders, thus justifying "both the bourgeoisie's national state and its general attitude" by promoting nationalism as "natural and eternal truths," other theorists of the modern nation "maintain that the nation is an ideological construct" or a cultural artifact (1991, 111). For Lefebvre, both of these views are unsatisfactory because "the nation is . . . scarcely more than a fiction projected by the bourgeoisie onto its own historical conditions and origins." Against these views, what he calls "abstract internationalisms," Lefebvre insists that the nation is "a focused space embodying a hierarchy of centres (commercial centres for the most part, but also religious ones, cultural ones, and so on) and a main centre—i.e. the national capital." Fundamentally, then, the nation implies imperial violence, "a political power controlling and exploiting the resources of the market . . . in order to maintain and further its rule" (112).

The aim of these topospatial readings, it bears some repeating, is to show the profound interaction of space and history, geography and psychology, nationhood and imperialism, and to define space as not just a "setting" but as a formative presence throughout. Any serious historicist reading of *Migrant Souls* would have to claim that the novel is full of uneven histories, but then what offers to supersede all these is—as the title suggests—the megaspace of hemispheric migration and the micromapping of rooms, parlors, and kitchens. The most striking history of spaces in the book is the author's chilling distance, explicitly established, from the tall tales of the American immigrant experience. Instead of "immigrant" individuals and families making their way toward Americanization on their own, Islas portrays collective strategies by women, men, and children of what Renato Rosaldo calls "passing up" (1992b, 5), or resistance to assimilation.

Instead of open markets, free competition, and equal opportunity in the United States, Islas reveals unequal gender and sexual positioning in family units and different ethno-racial groups. Instead of a univocal class consciousness or a *raza unida* (united race), Islas exposes alliances between compulsory heterosexuality and religion and between capital and labor against immigrant and migrant laws. All of this is stated straightforwardly by the central consciousness, Miguel Chico, through his key words *migration* and *border crossing:* "The Rio Grande— shallow, muddy, ugly in those places where the bridge spanned it—was a constant disappointment and hardly a symbol of the promised land to families like Mama Chona's. They had not sailed across an ocean or ridden in wagons and trains across half a continent in search of a new life. They were migrant, not immigrant, souls" (1990b, 41). Islas's U.S.-Mexico border imagination, as the literary critic Antonio Márquez writes, is partially thematized for us "by placing Miguel Chico in relation to family history, the Angel family in relation to Mexicano-Chicano/a history, and the novels in relation to an historical imagination that strips off layers of time and memory to disclose the unsaid, the repressed history hidden under the weight of ignorance, propriety, or shame" (1994, 10–11). Islas more significantly in this passage displaces the northeastern American *Bildung* of Ellis Island with that of the Angels' South-North border-crossing story.

Although Islas does not exclude the willing acculturation of the majority of the Angel clan (Mama Chona, Eduviges, and Ricardo), he daringly portrays a variety of chosen options, including the possible "transculturation" of the U.S.-Mexico borderlands. As one of the younger members of the Angel family hyperbolically puts it during a ritual Christmas party, "The truth is . . . we don't know who we are because we don't know where we are. . . . Just like our souls are between heaven and earth, so are we in between two countries completely different from each other. We are Children of the Border" (1990b, 164–165).

Readers will no doubt be struck by Islas's affirmation of the Angels' dependence on hemispheric and global events and conditions, for migration in this light is just another name for the international labor market. In short, the revisions of accepted national wisdom about our dream of a "melting pot" or the more recent imagined communities of ethnic pluralism turn around these two basic issues in *Migrant Souls:* the global economy of migration and the critique of the social science assimilation paradigm, which in the United States proposes a linear progression of immigrant / migrant cultures toward a monological American national character.[5]

At the same time, Islas is brutally frank in the novel about the lack of real border crossings between Anglos and Chicanos in Del Sapo during the 1940s and 1950s, for the border zones between the ethno-races remain fixed by tradition. In this context of nativist white supremacy, the ethno-races in Texas comprise segregated worlds, each bent on maintaining a racial absolutism that is reminiscent of what Rosaldo calls "the nation-state's determination" (1992b, 4) to produce homogeneity at all costs. Yet what is innovative in Islas's intervention in his novel's discourse of the ethno-race problematic is his devastating commentary on the effects of five hundred years of crime in the Américas, that of native "populocide." In the novel's first pages, Josie's mother bluntly mouths the dominant (both Hispanic and Anglo-American) culture's views about Amerindians: "She's simply acting like an Indian. . . . Everyone knows they don't talk and can't answer politely when someone asks a question" (1990b, 5).

Islas's analysis of ethno-racial formation in *Migrant Souls,* of course, has to be located in relation to the speaker, Eduviges Angel, for the author's critique derives not from the mestizo/a culture in general but from the Angels' snobbish classification of themselves as *la gente decente* in Del Sapo. Later in the novel, Islas defines *la gente decente* in rather explicit terms: "Manuel and Ricardo knew that the phrase 'decent people' meant middle-class Catholics" (201). As Rosaldo puts it, "Ascent into the category of decent people . . . often involves the deliberate concealment of personal history and past identity. Concerted efforts to pass (one passes up, not down) reveal both the existence of a social boundary and personal insecurities about a lifetime of negotiating which side of the line one stands on" (1984, 5).

Just as in *The Rain God,* the Angels in *Migrant Souls* emblematize dominant Spanish and conservative Chicano social and racial pretensions at the expense of Amerindian sensibilities. Mama Chona and her sister Jesús María construct these rigid ethno-racial ideologies in the family, namely, a coherent set of values, representations, and beliefs, and they alone condemn or condone their family's values and morals. Mama Chona, it is explained to the reader, lightened her skin color and rose from the migrant lower classes to *la gente decente* through marriage and baptism: "Encarnación Olmeca, or Mama Chona as she

instructed them to call her—may have had Indian origins her maiden
name suggested, but she married Jesús Angel. By this act, as well as her
baptism into the Church of Rome, Mama Chona felt herself and her
children to be elevated into civilization for all time" (1990b, 8).

To the history of hemispheric migration, the reader must add the
global cosmology underwritten by Judeo-Christian and Meso-
Amerindian symbology. As Miguel Chico stresses, Mama Chona's
maiden name, Encarnación Olmeca, splendidly combines European and
Amerindian traditions; her name as well as her Amerindian complex-
ion, however, are erased in her grand scheme to make the Angels part
of *la gente decente*. Ethno-racial shifts, then, like the many shifts in class
described in *Migrant Souls,* are what Rosaldo calls "strategies"—from
the rituals of baptism and marrying up to the violent scolding of daughters for failing to conform to mythic class aspirations (1992b, 6).

Migrant, not immigrant, spaces, then, are the terrain of known practices and operations in the novel. In the book's concern with both large
and small spaces and power, we can see a quest for synthesis, the kind
of brief, precarious poses that a bold muralist and a miniature portrait
painter might combine. Typically, in *Migrant Souls,* the spatial poetics
revolve around not only hemispheric migrations but also rooms that
are disturbing spaces within spaces. It is my view that a map of spaces—
an architecture of rooms—rather than a history proper is the central
aim of the novel, though it is certainly not the case that this mapping
cancels history.

I now want to explore some of the novel's major spatial structures
of feeling and to further demonstrate the interactions between space
and social relations, which were initially worked out six years earlier
in Islas's *The Rain God* and later fully developed in *Migrant Souls.* In
Islas's first installment of the Angel saga, an intense physical feel for
rooms—parlors, sickrooms, hospital operating rooms, and writing
rooms—was already characteristic of his developing spatial poetics. Late
in *The Rain God,* for example, when the convalescent Miguel Chico
cannot sleep because of a recurring nightmare about beasts, blood, and
feces, he leaves the bedroom and sits in the writing room "at his desk
and record[s] the details of the dream. He needed very much to make
peace with his dead, to prepare a feast for them so that they would stop
haunting him. He would feed them words and make his candied skulls
out of paper" (1984, 160). As the cultural critic Rosaura Sánchez writes,

At her deathbed Mama Chona entrusts the family to Miguel Chico, a burden that he rejects yet still bears. Many years later the grandson would still be looking for a way to stop being haunted by the dead. The novel itself is ultimately the answer; it assumes the form of a collective confession, an act of exorcism, a ritual within which the writer is both confessor and collective sinner. . . . The novel deals then with a need to exteriorize the private sphere, the family circle from which the character is estranged. (1991, 119)

In other words, space—the central consciousness's writing room—informs the U.S.-Mexico border writer's desire to take stock of the past. But the room of rooms in *The Rain God,* that whose structure of feeling the topospatial reader must be able to come to terms with, is not the writing room or the study but the closet, that literal and figural room which dominates the novel's opening pages: "In the closet Miguel Chico hugged his mother's clothes in terror. The familiar odor in the darkness kept him company and faintly reassured him" (1984, 17). Assuredly, the closet is a space of taboo for the young boy, perhaps the space of a "primal scene" and of the boy's family romance of Oedipal proportions.

Yet in the end it is migration acts, rather than Oedipal primal scenes, immobility, and death, that gather force until they begin to carry Miguel Chico out of the bleakest of all the hidden spaces—what Islas calls "the gate of [Miguel Chico's] secret territory" (120). Thus the central contrast between Miguel Chico in *The Rain God* and in *Migrant Souls* is substantially a spatial one. Initially inhabiting the space of what the literary critic Eve Kosofsky Sedgwick calls the "epistemology of the closet" (1990), Miguel Chico's trajectories diverge. The most fraught encounters in which Miguel Chico is involved in *Migrant Souls* are those out of the closet and in the rooms of his relatives during the Christmas holidays. One notable episode near the book's end begins with Miguel Chico negotiating his way through Ricardo's den where the *familia* is eating tamales and slices of turkey, proceeding to talk with his brother Gabriel, and ending in one of the bedrooms where the brothers can be alone—a spatial trajectory from the family circle to the private confessional sphere that helps him, paradoxically, to return to the family sphere: "Let him go in love," Gabriel advises the solitary brother.

But we should not equate Miguel Chico exclusively with privacy or enclosed "secret territories." For *Migrant Souls* is also fascinated by the historical journeys and territorial structures the Angels make as they

move across the border, north from Mexico, during the Mexican Revolution and the little habitats the men and women set up in their barrio *casitas*. Home for Sancho, one of Miguel Chico's uncles, is literally
an expanded architecture: "In the privacy of the garage he had con-
verted into a den for himself" (1990, 115), he entangles and disentan-
gles the divisions between the private and the semioutside space. But
"home" for Sancho also includes the brilliant space of the U.S.-Mexico
borderlands, where he literally finds himself "in the mountains and lakes
of northern Chihuahua. In that wild country . . . his Indian blood came
to life and made him feel at home with land and sky" (4). The "eerie"
and "secret" territories of Miguel Chico, I want to suggest, are com-
plemented by Sancho's other spaces.

In the Ernesto Galarza commemorative lecture delivered at Stanford
University in 1990 entitled "At the Bridge, on the Border, Migrants and
Immigrants," Islas characteristically described his intense feelings for
border matters and liminal, transnational spaces, the major preoccu-
pations of his writings and teachings:

> In my experience, the two-thousand-mile-long Mexican–United States
> Border has a cultural identity that is unique. That condition, that land-
> scape and its people, are what I write about in my fictions. . . . Like
> some of my characters, I often find myself on the bridge between cul-
> tures, between languages, between sexes, between religions, between
> my profession as teacher and my vocation as writer, between two dif-
> ferent and equally compelling ways of looking agape at this world.
> (1990a, 3)

With this feminist-inspired "bridge" consciousness, we pass from dis-
interested academic analysis to the materially hybrid and "betweenness"
spatial obsession of other U.S.-Mexico borderland intellectuals such as
Anzaldúa, Viramontes, and Rechy (see chapter 6). History is thus structured "at the bridge, on the border," and the interaction of bridges and
borders produces a distinctive kind of social space, where "a wide river,
mostly dry except when thunderstorms create flashfloods, separates it
[the United States] from Mexico. Heavy traffic flows from one side of
the river to the other, and from the air, national boundaries and differences are indistinguishable" (Islas 1984, 113).

U.S.-Mexico border space in this context of nation and narration is
in the end Janus-faced, and the movement between "outside" and
"inside" must necessarily always be a process of hybridity, incorporating
migrant souls in relation to the body politic, generating other spaces

and sites of meaning, and producing new border spaces of political antagonism and unpredictable forces for political representation.

DOMESTIC SPACE IN LOMAS GARZA'S *CUADROS DE FAMILIA / FAMILY PICTURES*

If Arturo Islas is a poet of the room of rooms, the closet, the distinctive South Texas *monito* paintings (depicting cartoonlike figures) by Carmen Lomas Garza reveal her to be a poet of rooms with a difference, for she rearticulates domestic and geopolitical spaces. Of primary importance among the emerging spatial poetics of the U.S.-Mexico *frontera* is Lomas Garza's collection of fourteen paintings visualized and narrated from the perspective of the young Chicana artist Carmen. Like Sandra Cisneros's *The House on Mango Street* (1985), Lomas Garza's *Cuadros de familia / Family Pictures* (1990) represents a childhood vision, the complex predicaments of gendered social space. In addition to suggesting a return to visual "storytelling" (one of the main features of the postmodern) within her community of Kingsville, Texas, Lomas Garza's work emphasizes the crisis heterotopias for Chicanas—what Amalia Mesa-Bains calls the aesthetics of the *domesticana* (1991, 132).[6] In other words, what characterizes Lomas Garza's spatial poetics is not minimalism and camp sensibility but the rather different aesthetics of abundance, her embellishments of home altars, *cumpleaños fiestas* (birthday celebrations), *tamaladas* (tamale-making gatherings), and *curandera* ritual practices. Her materially hybrid and heteroglot *códice* (codex) thus helps to establish in Chicana painting what has become over the course of the 1980s and into the 1990s the project for narratives by Chicanas, what Ramón Saldívar described as "a clear-sighted recognition of the unavoidably mutual overdetermination of the categories of race and class with that of gender in any attempted positioning of the Chicana subject" (1990, 182).

La feria en Reynosa (The Fair in Reynosa), the lead painting in the collection, places the child Carmen immediately in the sweeping geopolitics of the U.S.-Mexico borderlands, in the barrio arts and crafts fairs in Reynosa, Mexico. Like Islas's border crossings and Chicana bridge consciousness in *The Rain God* and *Migrant Souls,* Lomas Garza grounds these images in the folkloric and topographic social spaces of the heterotopic *feria.* As the artist's own work wonderfully shows, this hybrid painting relies on popular border art forms such as *papel pica-*

do (paper cut-outs) that she learned to appreciate from the border crafts-people and artisans depicted.

As Lomas Garza straightforwardly put it, "Vinierion artesanos y artistas de todo Mexico. Había mucho puertos que vendían comida y artesanías" (Artists and entertainers came from all over Mexico. There were many booths with food and crafts). Let me hasten to add that the central preoccupation of *La feria en Reynosa* is the nostalgic, even idyllic relationships of daughters and fathers and daughters and family, for as the painter remarks, "Pinté a un padre comprando tacos y al resto de la familia sentada a la mesa. La niñita pequeña es la preferida de su papá, y por eso es que él la permite acompañarlo" (I painted a father buying tacos and the rest of the family sitting down at the table. The little girl is the father's favorite, and that's why she gets to tag along with him) (1990, 4). The other paintings allegorically emblematize the daughter's spatial relationships with her father, mother, grandparents, aunts, and brothers and sisters in mainly utopian moments and simultaneously document her emerging spatial understanding of the nature of the domestic economy in its geopolitical and private spheres.

Situated against the alienating and solitary rooms of *Migrant Souls*, fixed in the "perpetual twilight" of *la gente decente* in Del Sapo, Lomas Garza's rooms (described below) focus on the practices of everyday life and open up the interiorized spaces of the border *casitas* deep in South Texas. As she puts it in her moving essay "A Piece of My Heart," "I felt that I had to start [my paintings] with my earliest recollections of my life and validate each event or incident by depicting it in a visual format. I needed to re-celebrate each special event or re-examine each unusual happening" (1991, 13). *Tamalada* (fig. 2), a "special family happening," shows something rather different from Islas's maligned and imprisoning social spaces. Here Lomas Garza takes us to her parent's kitchen, where the family is making tamales. The entire family is depicted in the unalienated sexual division of labor, for in the painter's household *todos ayudan* (everybody helps) (1990, 22).

Given the evocative power of these utopian family representations, it may seem odd to discuss two paintings in which young Carmen does and does not appear and which, unlike the other paintings in Lomas Garza's book, tackle phantasmatic rural social spaces with wit, grace, and an understated border humor. Yet the paintings *Para la cena* (For Dinner; fig. 3) and *Conejo* (Rabbit; fig. 4) represent an allegory of the unsolved problems of family romance and the sexual division of labor.

Figure 2.   Carmen Lomas Garza, *Tamalada,* 1988, oil, 24 × 32 inches. Courtesy of the artist.

Despite these vast themes, which encompass the gendered and political unconscious in South Texas, the paintings are small, with abundantly well-crafted details and stunning facial expressions, thus giving the effect that Islas strived for in his fiction—the effect of a miniature version of the haunting works by Rufino Tamayo and Frida Kahlo. The topics of the paintings—undomesticated food and ritual violence—are recorded in Carmen's younger brother's *susto* (fright): he spills his snowcone. *Para la cena,* however, owes much to the rich, understated border humor of South Texas, for it suffuses Lomas Garza's phantasmatic texts, even if children (the book's presumed audience) seem to confuse the painter's wit and humor with purely literal depiction. As a contribution to this dual recognition—the phantasmatic and border humor—we can do no better than to hear the painter's testimony about the work: "[Arturo] estaba tan sorprendido por lo que veía que se le empezó a derramar su raspa. . . . Yo sabía que mis abuelos criaban gallinas, pero no había sabido antes cómo era que las gallinas se convertían en sopa" ([Arturo]

Figure 3. Carmen Lomas Garza, *Para la cena*, 1985, oil, 24 × 32 inches.
Courtesy of the artist.

was so stunned by the scene that he started to spill his snowcone. . . .
I knew my grandparents had always raised chickens, but I never knew
how the chickens got to be soup) (8). Two aspects of her grandparents'
barrio space interested Lomas Garza particularly—first, that their
backyard, like most in South Texas, contained a *gallinero* (chicken coop);
and second, that Arturo's and her own idealized conception of chicken
soup suggests the Freudian reality principle.

In *Conejo*, Lomas Garza gives us another extraordinary reexami-
nation of the phantasmatic in barrio life, for the young Carmen (who
is usually positioned in the margins of the paintings) is entirely absent
from the kitchen space (it is her younger sister, Margie, who plays on
the kitchen floor). Carmen instead views the ritual practice of the grandfather preparing fresh rabbit for dinner from her grandparents' bedroom. Yet the painting itself (and Arturo's surprise and wonder)
cannot gloss over the rift between the sexual division of labor and U.S.-
Mexico border culture, even though the book as a whole attempts to
capture what Arturo Islas demanded of Chicano/a narrative, that it

Figure 4. Carmen Lomas Garza, *Conejo*, 1987, gouache, 11 × 14 inches. Courtesy of the artist.

give expression to the rich communal family life of Chicano border culture (Islas 1975).

While in the series as a whole Lomas Garza (un)wittingly divides U.S.-Mexico border culture into the grandmother making tortillas and the grandfather dressing rabbits for dinner, she nevertheless distances herself in significant ways in the last painting, *Camas para soñar* (Beds for Dreaming), from the traditional dialectics of gendered and sexual social space. To begin with, compared with most of the other paintings in the book, this canvas directly focuses on the spatial relationships between mother and daughter. The effect is to concentrate on the young girl's mother, for "mi madre fue la que me inspiró a ser artista" (my mother was the one who inspired me to be an artist) (1990, 30). Nevertheless, the net effect of the painting, the picture as window—the painter's mother is shown from outside the house trapped in the domestic sphere while her daughters are up on the roof on a beautiful cloudy night talking about the stars and constellations—is to demonstrate the mother's daily sacrifice for her daughters' artistic imaginations. The organization of U.S.-Mexico border culture in *Cuadros de familia / Family Pictures* is patriarchal and hierarchical.

The problems of domestic space and of women's subjectivity come to the fore in Lomas Garza's splendid *Camas para soñar* and in her hybrid codex. Simultaneously, she forces the viewer to gaze upon the plane between reality and imagination, between external and internal worlds—what André Breton called the visual pleasure of windows. "It is impossible," Breton writes, "to consider a picture as anything but a window. . . . I can enjoy an enormous spectacle" (1972, 1–2).

But what are we to make of the painter's hybrid use of the genre of children's literature and the Amerindian *códice* to tell her autobiography and to construct fresh definitions of the culture of resistance? Lomas Garza forces us to see that while the children's *cuentos* cycle rarely merit serious attention in the academy, the form's very marginality, as Pratt (1981) has suggested in a different context, enables it to become a site for other spaces, for radical experimentation, and allows it to include women and children as protagonists. Marginal genres such as Lomas Garza's *Cuadros de familia / Family Pictures* thus become the site of political innovation and cultural creativity.[7] As a self-consciously visual intervention in postcontemporary storytelling, Lomas Garza's *códice* scripts a course for Chicanas that sharply resists the erasure of the *domesticana* spaces in U.S.-Mexico border culture. Moreover, she replenishes the void that has remained in Amerindian art since the original *códices* were burned by the invading Spanish army and the colonial administrators. Prior to the arrival of the Europeans in Mexico in the sixteenth century, the pictorial narratives of Mixtec, Maya, and Aztec *códices* drew what the art historian Marcos Tranquilino-Sánchez has called "the political histories, cosmologies, religions, and scientific and medical knowledge-power and practices of those . . . Amerindian societies. That vast indigenous knowledge was destroyed by zealous European evangelism in massive burnings that left a conquered people" bereft "of their power, dreams, and identity" (1992, 3).

What we have been concerned with in this chapter is the production of U.S.-Mexico border space in the work of Arturo Islas and Carmen Lomas Garza, even though this space is neither a subject nor an object but—in Lefebvre's terms—"a social reality," or better still, "a set of relations and forms" (1991, 116). If the neoconservatives have been eager to attack critical multiculturalism for its egocentric sensibility of "inclusiveness," as Bruce Robbins notes (1992, 170), my aim has been to suggest that U.S.-Mexico border writing does not merely extend the canon but radically reframes and topospatially reconceptualizes what it means to be "worldly," "cosmopolitan," and "regional." As we will see in the next two chapters, which explore the extended borderlands of southern California and northern Mexico (especially San Diego, Tijuana, and Los Angeles), U.S.-Mexico border writing, at its best, attempts to account for representational space and the representation of space, their interrelationships and their links with social practice.

PART TWO

EL OTRO LADO /
THE OTHER SIDE

5

On the Bad Edge of *La Frontera*

> Where the transmission of "national" traditions was once the
> major theme of world literature, perhaps we can now suggest
> that transnational histories of migrants, the colonized, or
> political refugees—these border and frontier conditions—may
> be the terrains of world literature.
>
> Homi Bhabha, "The World and the Home" (1992)

In an influential manifesto published in *La Línea Quebrada* (The Broken Line) in 1986, Guillermo Gómez-Peña theorizes the *transfrontera* urban galaxy of San Diego and Tijuana as a new social space filled with multicultural symbologies sent out in polyglot codes (Spanish, English, *caló*, and Spanglish).[1] Though perhaps too steeped in poststructuralist playfulness (at the expense of critical multicultural work), Gómez-Peña's tract nevertheless hits on one of the central truths of our extended U.S.-Mexico border culture: the *frontera* culture, stretching from the shanty barrios of Tijuana and San Diego to the rich surf and turf of Santa Barbara (dominated by the megaspace of Los Angeles in the middle), is an enormous "desiring machine."[2] Starting from Deleuze and Guattari's famous concept of the machine in their *Anti-Oedipus* (1977), Gómez-Peña envisions a radical rereading of the U.S.-Mexico border as a conjunction of desiring machines. Such a notion of the *frontera* as a desiring machine with flows and interruptions, crossings and deportations, liminal transitions and reaggregations, is fundamental to my reading of the extended U.S.-Mexico borderland cultural texts of Los Angeles, for it will permit us to travel along different routes and paths other than the sunshine / noir and black / white master dialectics thematized in Davis's *City of Quartz* (1990).

The two-thousand-mile-long U.S.-Mexico border, without doubt, produces millions of undocumented workers from Central America and Mexico who are essential to the economic machines of North American agriculture, tourism, and industry. The U.S.-Mexico border thus produces not only masses of agricultural farmworkers, low-tech laborers (mostly women), dishwashers, gardeners, and maids but also a military machine of low-intensity conflict: INS helicopters, Border Patrol agents with infrared camera equipment used to track and capture the border-crossers from the South, and detention centers and jails designed to protect the Anglocentric minority in California who fear and even loathe these scores of *indocumentados*. Moreover, this desiring machine also comprises an enormous bureaucratic, political, cultural, and legal machine of *coyotes* (border-crossing guides for hire), *pollos* (pursued undocumented border-crossers), *fayuqueros* (food peddlers), *sacadineros* (border swindlers), *cholos/as,* notary publics, public interest lawyers, public health workers, and a huge "juridical-administrative-therapeutic state apparatus" (JAT)—to use Nancy Fraser's unruly coinage (1989, 154).[3]

What matters for us is that the U.S.-Mexico border machine constructs the subject-positions exclusively for the benefit of the North American JAT machine: juridically, it positions the migrant border-crossers vis-à-vis the U.S. legal system by denying them their human rights and by designating them "illegal aliens"; administratively, the migrant border-crossers who desire amnesty must petition a bureaucratic institution created under the 1986 Immigration Reform and Control Act (IRCA) to receive identification papers (including a social security card); and, finally, therapeutically, migrant border-crossers in their shantytowns in canyons throughout California have to grapple with various county health departments and Environmental Health Services offices. For instance, at one shantytown called El Valle Verde (Green Valley) in San Diego County, the Environmental Health Services director shut down the migrant border-crosser's camp "for violations dealing with lack of potable water for drinking, building-code violations, [and] fecal material on the ground" (quoted in Chávez 1992, 108).

This analysis of the U.S.-Mexico border as a juridical-administrative-therapeutic state apparatus allows us to see that migrant border-crossers from the South into the North are largely disempowered by the denial of cultural and legal citizenship.[4] The JAT border machine, moreover, positions its subjects in ways that dehumanize them. It often personalizes them as "illegal aliens," "cases," "dirty," "amoral," and "disease-ridden," and so militates against their collective identity. As Fraser says about the JAT welfare system, this border machine "imposes monological, administrative definitions of situation and need and so preempts dialogically achieved self-definition and self-determination"

(1989, 155). To be sure, these are *interpreted* identities and needs that are fashioned for migrant border-crossers. Further, these interpretations are highly political and therefore subject to dispute. In what follows, I analyze the social texts of Helena María Viramontes, John Rechy, Los Illegals, and (Kid) Frost as liminal culture critiques and analyses of the interpreted identities and needs of Latinas/os in California, for they have been more accurate and politically perceptive than mainline postmodern realists and urban planners in representing what Mike Davis calls "the programmed hardening of the urban surface" in the extended *frontera* of southern California (1990, 223).

If "all machines have their mastercodes," as the literary theorist Antonio Benítez-Rojo has suggested in a different context (1992, 17), what are the codebooks for the cultural machines of these U.S.-Mexico border writers? What networks of subcodes unite these autonomous works of art? What are the central rituals, ceremonies, and ideologies in the texts of the *transfrontera* contact zone? And finally, what are the benefits of examining U.S.-Mexico border texts as cultural practices with institutional implications for cultural and critical legal studies?

UNDOCUMENTED CROSSINGS

To begin to answer some of these questions, let us examine a liminal short story, "The Cariboo Cafe," from *The Moths and Other Stories* (1985) by Helena María Viramontes, coordinator of the Los Angeles Latino/a Writers Association and former literary editor of *XhismeArte* magazine. I emphasize Viramontes's institutional grounding as a former coordinator and editor in Los Angeles because it is an unsettling fact that all too often U.S. Latino/a writers are omitted from intellectual surveys and literary histories. Even sympathetic, New Left surveys, such as Davis's superb *City of Quartz,* that explore the role played by waves of migrations of intellectuals to Los Angeles—from Charles F. Lummis and Theodor Adorno to Ornette Coleman and the gangster rap group NWA—schematize intellectual history in exclusively racialized black and white terms or in linear East and West global mappings.[5] Like the scores of brown maids and gardeners with their brooms and blowers working all over California, isn't it time that we sweep away once and for all this Manichaean construction? Might not a sweeping, even crude, transnational South-North mapping (using the interpretive power of liminality) be more appropriate?

Viramontes's richly provocative "The Cariboo Cafe" has elicited rigorous ideological, Chicana feminist, and semiotic, gendered readings by literary critics such as Sonia Saldívar-Hull, Barbara Harlow, and Debra Castillo, who convincingly portray it as a local Chicana feminist text with "an internationalist agenda" (Saldívar-Hull 1990, 193), as "a site of confrontation between popular and official interpretations of the historical narrative" (Harlow 1991, 152), or as a "tortured dystopia" (Castillo 1992, 94). My view, however, is that there has not been enough attention to the diverse manifestations of "liminality" in the story, or to the explicitly migrant border-crossing phenomena of the "unhomely" that, in Victor Turner's terms, fall "betwixt and between the positions assigned and arrayed by law, custom, convention, and ceremonial" (1969, 95). Using insights from anthropologists such as Turner, I propose less to elaborate a manifesto of U.S.-Mexico border liminality than to use the interpretive force of this concept to tell us something about Viramontes's "The Cariboo Cafe" and the rites of passage migrant border-crossers from the South into the North generally share.

Anthropological discussion of migrant border-crossers as "liminals" can be said to begin with Leo Chávez's experimental ethnography, *Shadowed Lives* (1992), in which he describes migrant border crossing as a "transitional" phase in the three-step process of ritual initiation. Relying and elaborating on Arnold Van Gennep's *Rites of Passage* ([1909] 1960) and Turner's *The Ritual Process* (1969), Chávez traces the interstitial stages migrant border-crossers from both Mexico and Central America make in their journeys to the U.S.-Mexico borderlands. While Chávez, perhaps, overemphasizes "the transition people undergo as they leave the migrant life and instead settle in the United States" (1992, 4), we could extend his sensitive reading of liminality by adding a synchronic dimension as Turner suggested. For Turner, "liminality should be looked upon not only as a transition between states but as a state in itself, for there exist individuals, groups, or social categories for which the 'liminal' moment turns into a permanent condition" (Pérez Firmat 1986, xiii–xiv).

A liminal reading of Viramontes's "The Cariboo Cafe" thematizing the ritual process thus would emphasize both Van Gennep's and Chávez's temporal, processual view with Turner's topospatial supplementation. Liminality in Viramontes's hands, as Turner himself said, is "a semantic molecule with many components" (1969, 103). Seen in this light, "The Cariboo Cafe" is built on a series of multiple border cross-ings and multilayered transitions that an undocumented migrant wash-erwoman undergoes as she moves from the South into the North. Foremost among the transitions thematized in Viramontes's story are the washerwoman's actual border crossings, for crossing both the *fron-tera sur* (southern border) in Central America and the U.S.-Mexico bor-der without documentation is what Chávez sees as the "monumental event" (1992, 4) in the lives of many migrant border-crossers.[6]

Like many undocumented migrants, Viramontes's washerwoman gathers resources and funding from her family and extended commu-nity (her nephew Tavo sells his car to send her the money for a bus ticket to Juárez, Mexico), for crossing the border with its *coyotes, sacadineros,* and *fayuqueros* is a very costly undertaking. Fundamentally, "The Cari-boo Cafe" allegorizes hemispheric South-North border crossing in terms anthropologists such as Chávez see as emblematic of undocumented bor-der-crossers in general: "a territorial passage that marks the transition from one way of life to another" (4). As an exemplary border-crossing tale, then, we can initially map "The Cariboo Cafe" in Chávez's tem-poral, ritualistic terms: it moves (in a nonlinear narrative) through the interstitial phases of separation, liminality, and (deadly) reincorpora-tion. Let met hasten to add that throughout her disjunctive narrative Viramontes privileges the everyday experiences (the rituals of separa-tion and liminality) the washerwoman must face as she travels from her appointments with legal authorities in Central America (guerrillas have "disappeared" her five-year-old son) to the actual border crossings and to her final search (together with two undocumented Mexican migrant children, Sonya and Macky) for sanctuary at the Cariboo Cafe. The cafe sign symbolically reads "oo Cafe," for "the paint's peeled off" except for the "two o's" (Viramontes 1985, 64).[7] In other words, whereas anthropologists such as Chávez see the U.S.-Mexico border "limen" as threshold, for Viramontes it is a lived socially symbolic space.

But why does Viramontes represent the U.S.-Mexico border limen in "The Cariboo Cafe" as position and not as threshold? The reasons for this are complex, but one is that the washerwoman, like the major-ity of undocumented migrants in the United States, never acquires what Chávez calls the "links of incorporation—secure employment, family formation, the establishment of credit, capital accumulation, compe-tency in English" that will allow her to come into full cultural and legal citizenship (1992, 5). Not surprisingly, the washerwoman in the story remains a "marginal" character, crudely described by the Anglo-American manager/cook of the "zero zero" cafe in the following terms: "short," "bad news," "street," "round face," "burnt toast color," "black hair that hangs like straight rope" (1985, 65). Given the racist synecdochic view of undocumented migrant border-crossers as "otherness machines" (Suleri 1989, 105), forever blocked from attaining full cultural and legal citizenship, why did the Central American washerwoman migrate to the U.S.-Mexico borderlands? What narrative strategies did Viramontes use to represent the washerwoman's shifting and shifty migrations?

The first question is easier to answer than the second. While the majority of undocumented border-crossers from Mexico migrate to the United States out of a desire for economic mobility (often doing so for generations and thus seeing migration as family history),[8] migration from Central America, as Chávez emphasizes, is a relatively recent phenomenon, closely related to the Reagan-Bush war machine that supported the contras in El Salvador, Nicaragua, and Guatemala. Viramontes's washerwoman migrates from her unnamed pueblo in Central America to escape from the political war waged against Amerindians and mestizos/as and, more phantasmatically, given her posttraumatic stress syndrome, to continue searching among the "unhomely" for her five-year-old son.

> These four walls are no longer my house, the earth beneath it, no longer my home. Weeds have replaced all good crops. The irrigation ditches are clodded with bodies. No matter where we turn . . . we try to live . . . under the rule of men who rape women, then rip their bellies. . . . [T]hese men are babes farted out from the Devil's ass. (1985, 71)

Displaced by civil war, defeated by debilitating patriarchy, and deranged by the murder of her son, the washerwoman migrates, in stages, to the extended U.S. *frontera* to flee from guerrilla activity. Once across the U.S.-Mexico border, she will work "illegally" at jobs that, for the most part, legal Americans disdain: "The machines, their speed and dust," she says, "make me ill. But I can clean. I clean toilets, dump trash cans, sweep. Disinfect the sinks" (72).

These multiple border-crossing rites of passage are not narrated in a traditional realist fashion. Rather, Viramontes's story is scrambled in three separate sections, with each narrating the shifting, interstitial experiences of the washerwoman and the two undocumented Mexican children. The decentered aesthetic structure of Viramontes's text has elicited rigorous attention from literary critics. Saldívar-Hull, for example, suggests that Viramontes "crafts a fractured narrative to reflect the disorientation that the immigrant workers feel when they are subjected to life in a country that controls their labor but does not value their existence as human beings" (1990, 223). Likewise, Harlow elegantly argues that the political content of Viramontes's text merges (in strong dialectical fashion) with the tale's aesthetic form: "Much as these refugees transgress national boundaries, victims of political persecution who by their very international mobility challenge the ideology of national borders and its agenda of depoliticization in the interest of hegemony, so too the story refuses to respect the boundaries and conventions of literary critical time and space and their disciplining of plot genre" (1991, 152). For Saldívar-Hull and Harlow, Viramontes's "The Cariboo Cafe" challenges both the arbitrariness of the nation-state's borders and the institutionalized mobilizations of literary conventions such as plot structure, space, and time.

Castillo presents a diametrically opposed reading of Viramontes's experimental narrative—a narrative bereft of traditional transitions between sections and without markers indicating breaks and shifts in time and place. For Castillo, "the story presents itself as a colonialist narrative that is obviously, unambiguously, at least doubly (more accurately, multiply) voiced" (1992, 79). The challenge of "The Cariboo Cafe" for Viramontes, as Castillo sees it, is rather complicated. On the one hand, Viramontes must "giv[e] voice to the silent refugees, as well as to such minimally articulate people as the other urban dwellers"; on the other, she must further "balance" in the story "two very different constituencies: those who read, who speak, who enjoy freedom of speech, and those who are illiterate, who dare not speak." In short, donning the class-conditioned 1960s perspective of a Sartrean reader, Castillo criticizes Viramontes's experimental aesthetics as follows: "The Sartrean critic might legitimately address the propriety of [Viramontes] writing a complex work in English about (and partially for) people who cannot speak, much less read, even the simplest phrase" (80).

Although it is not entirely clear why Castillo questions the propriety of Viramontes's experimental aesthetic practices (perhaps she desires an orderly realist tale done in the various appropriate *telenovela* [soap opera] Spanish languages and styles), she does succeed in posing one of the text's central questions: "Who speaks . . . in this story? What is his/her language, sex, age . . . ?" (80). Provocatively, Castillo answers that "readers alternately [speak]. . . . We, who speak for them, who give voice to their unexpressed longings, their inchoate thoughts, their emptied selves" necessarily speak from the dominant perspective of what Castillo (quoting de Certeau) calls "a primarily repressive" and "learned culture" (81). Castillo then suggests that our reading practices are mobilizations, for "ours is a police action: separating out the voices, bringing law and order, soliciting confessions" (82).

Given the transgressive border crossings (both aesthetic and political) in "The Cariboo Cafe," isn't there a possibility for a noninstrumentalized view of the nature of Chicana resistance literature, reading practices, cultural critique, and philosophical and literary production? Might not Adorno's aesthetic philosophy of nonidentity and negative dialectics be more appropriate than a 1960s Sartrean philosophy of engagement? "Adorno," Fredric Jameson writes, "was surely not the philosopher of the thirties . . . ; nor the philosopher of the fifties; nor even the thinker of the sixties—those are called Sartre and Marcuse; and I have said that . . . his old-fashioned dialectical discourse was incompatible with the seventies. But there is some chance that he may turn out to have been the analyst of our own [postmodernist] period" (1991, 5).

Perhaps there should be nothing scandalous in reading Viramontes's autonomous "The Cariboo Cafe" in Adornean aesthetic and political terms, for both writers shared more than addresses in Los Angeles. (Adorno, we might recall, like scores of Central Europe's most celebrated intellectuals, sought political sanctuary in Los Angeles during the fascist terror.) As Mike Davis notes, it was in "Los Angeles where Adorno and Horkheimer accumulated their 'data,' [and] the exiles . . . allowed their image of first sight to become its own myth: Los Angeles as the crystal ball of capitalism's future" (1990, 48). Though ignorant, of course, of what Davis calls "the peculiar historical dialectic that had shaped Southern California" (48), Adorno's rousing critique of Hollywood, North American consumerism, the "Culture Industry," and so on clearly allies him with Viramontes's cultural critique of the harrowing underside of the glossy Los Angeles postmodernist culture. In other words, for Viramontes the postmodern such as it is in Los Angeles is a fully planned strategy, the social and psychic effects of which are historical dislocation and cultural relocation.

Further, Adorno's conception of the experimental work of art as something radically different might allow us to view Viramontes's narrative practices in terms other than Sartre's philosophy of engagement. To begin with, the work of art, as Adorno stressed in his *Aesthetic Theory,* "obeys immanent laws which are related to those that prevail in the society outside. Social forces of production and social relations of production return in the very form of the work." Briefly stated, for Adorno, "the most authentic works of art are those that give themselves over to their historical raw materials without reservation and without any pretense to floating above it somewhere" (quoted in Jameson 1991, 187). Foreshadowing Fredric Jameson's well-known notion of the political unconscious, Adorno theorizes the work of art as "unconsciously the historiography of [its] own epoch." Thus envisaged, "The Cariboo Cafe" does not offer Sartrean engagement or even Brechtean praxis, for "praxis," Adorno writes, "does not lie in the effects of the work of art, but rather [is] encapsulated in its truth content" (quoted in Jameson 1991, 188). This means, then, that the complex aesthetic experiences contained in Viramontes's text always lead us back to history—to the history of undocumented migrant border crossing, to the history of postmodernism in Los Angeles, and to the constellation of class contradictions from which the work of art emerged. It would therefore be justifiable to say that if Viramontes's text leads us back to history, this means in Adornean terms that for works of art the "nonidentical" is society.

The vital relationship of Viramontes's experimental border aesthetics to her political thinking about culture in Los Angeles involves more than the content of her views on undocumented border-crossers; as Saldívar-Hull and Harlow have suggested, it also lies significantly in the fractured form of the story itself. The phantasmatic story of the Central American washerwoman crossing multiple borders to search for her son leads her to two undocumented Mexican children, Sonya and Macky, with whom she establishes a new transnational family.[9] Multiple border zones thus crisscross in the tale, allowing us to begin a complicated rereading involving historical, political, and cultural simultaneity in the Américas.

If disjunctive separation, liminality, and reaggregation are the central cultural rituals performed in "The Cariboo Cafe," then it is hardly surprising that rhetorically and tropologically Viramontes relies heavily on prolepsis (flash-forward) and analepsis (flashback) to structure the tale. It begins in medias res with a near-omniscient narrator situating the realities of migrant border-crossing separation: "They arrived in the secrecy of the night, as displaced people often do, stopping over for a week, a month, eventually staying a lifetime" (1985, 61). From the very beginning, liminality is thematized not as a temporary condition of the displaced but as a permanent social reality.

Given that both of Macky and Sonya's parents work (undocumented workers are rarely on welfare),[10] the children are instructed to follow three simple rules in their urban galaxy: "never talk to strangers"; avoid the "polie," for the police are "La Migra in disguise"; and "keep your key with you at all times—the four walls of the apartment were the only protection against the street" (61). But Sonya, the young *indocumentada,* loses her apartment key. Unable to find their way to a baby-sitter's house, Sonya and Macky begin their harrowing encounter with the unhomely's urban galaxy, what Viramontes lyrically describes as "a maze of alleys and dead ends, the long, abandoned warehouses shadowing any light[;] . . . boarded up boxcars [and] rows of rusted rails" (63). Looming across the shadowed barrioscape, "like a beacon light," the children see the double zero cafe sign.

Without any traditional transitional markers, section two tells in the working-class (albeit bigoted) vernacular of an Anglo-American cook the lurid story of the unhomely's experiences at the Cariboo Cafe, especially those of the washerwoman, Sonya, and Macky. Situated in the midst of garment warehouse factories where many of the undocumented border-crossers labor, the zero zero cafe functions as a sanctuary from the mean streets of Los Angeles. On an initial reading, however, it is not at all clear how the brave, new transnational family—the washerwoman, Sonya, and Macky—met, or why they are now together at the cafe. All we know is reflected through the crude nativist testimonial narrative of the manager: "I'm standing behind the counter staring at the short woman. Already I know that she's bad news because she looks street to me. . . . Funny thing, but I didn't see the two kids 'till I got to the booth. All of a sudden I see the big eyes looking over the table's edge at me. It shook me up" (65–66).

Viramontes, of course, shakes things up a bit more by describing another of the unhomely's predicament of culture, Paulie's overdose at the cafe. He "O.D.'s" in the cafe's "crapper; vomit and shit are all over . . . the fuckin' walls" (67). Not surprisingly, the immense U.S.-Mexico border machine shifts into high gear: "Cops," the cook says, are "looking up my ass for stash," and later on "green vans roll up across the street. . . . I see all these illegals running out of the factory to hide [and] three of them run[ning] into the Cariboo" (67). Section two ends with the cook saying, "I was all confused" (68).

Having moved through separation and liminality in the first sections, Viramontes's denouement (section three) provides readers with what we may call a phantasmatic folktale of (deadly) reincorporation. Slipping in and out of stream-of-consciousness shellshock, the narrator explains, "For you see, they took Geraldo. By mistake, of course. It was my fault. I shouldn't have sent him out to fetch me a mango" (68). Eventually the washerwoman fills in the gaps left by the earlier sections: when Geraldo failed to return, she is hurled into the spatiality-time of night: "the darkness becomes a serpent tongue, swallowing us whole. It is the night of La Llorona" (68).

With this reference to La Llorona, readers can begin to make sense of the tale's freakish entanglements. Using and revising the legend of La Llorona to produce cultural simultaneity in the Américas (uniting Central American and North American borderland history), Viramontes allows us also to hear the deep stirrings of the unhomely wailing woman. Capturing the shared legacy of five hundred years of Spanish conquest and resistance, the legend of La Llorona creeps into the zero zero place of Chicana/o fiction: "The cook huddles behind the counter, frightened, trembling, . . . and she begins screaming enough for all the women of murdered children, screaming, pleading for help" (74). But why is the cook so frightened? Why do males "tremble" in La Llorona's presence?

As José E. Limón suggests, La Llorona, "the legendary female figure" that dominates the cultures of Greater Mexico, is a "distinct relative of the Medea story and . . . a syncretism of European and indigenous cultural forms" (1986a, 59). While various interpreters of La Llorona have not accorded her a resistive, utopian, and liminal history (viewing her instead as a passive and ahistorical creature), Limón systematically takes us through what he calls the "genesis and formal definition of this legend," arguing that "La Llorona as a symbol . . . speaks to the course of Greater Mexican history and does so for women in particular" (74).

As far back as Fray Bernardino de Sahagún's transcultural chronicle of the New World, *Florentine Codex* (1578), La Llorona, Limón writes, "appeared in the night crying out for her dead children" (68). Let me hasten to add that another Spanish chronicler, the foot soldier

Bernal Díaz del Castillo, likewise collected and recorded indigenous Amerindians' narrations telling her tale of loss: "At night, in the wind, a woman's voice was heard. 'Oh my children, we are now lost!' Sometimes she said, 'Oh my children, where shall I take you?'" (Castillo, quoted in Castañeda-Shular, Ybarra-Frausto, and Sommer 1972, 98). In later colonial versions (as reported by Frances Toor), the legend incorporates other forms: a lower-class woman is betrayed by an upper-class lover who has fathered her children; she then kills the children and walks crying in the night.[11]

In Limón's utopian reading, La Llorona's "insane infanticide" can be said to be a "temporary insanity *produced historically by those who socially dominate*" (86; his emphasis). Seen in this historical light, that Viramontes's wailing washerwoman grieves and searches for her lost child (finding Geraldo in her kidnapping of Macky) is not something that is produced inherently but rather by the history that begins with Cortés's conquest of Mexico. If all children of loss in the Américas (produced by Euroimperialism) are also children of need, then they are also what Limón sees as potentially "grieving, haunting mothers reaching for their children *across fluid boundaries*" (87; my emphasis). We may now be in a better position to understand why the manager of the Cariboo Cafe is so frightened by the washerwoman/La Llorona. In her act of infanticide, La Llorona "symbolically destroys" what Limón argues is "the familial basis for patriarchy" (76).

Nevertheless, Viramontes offers her readers a startling paradox: while her folktale in section three always suggests the symbolic destruction of patriarchy—represented in the washerwoman's fight to the death with the police at the story's end—there also remains the washerwoman's utopian desire to fulfill the last stage of her territorial rite of passage, namely, her dream of incorporation, or better yet, what Castillo calls the washerwoman's "project[ed] . . . dream of re-incorporation, of returning her newborn/reborn infant to her womb" (1992, 91). Viramontes writes, "She wants to conceal him in her body again, return him to her belly so that they will not castrate him and hang his small, blue penis on her door, not crush his face so that he is unrecognizable, not bury him among the heaps of bones, of ears, and teeth, and jaws, because no one, but she, cared to know that he cried. For years he cried and she could hear him day and night" (1985, 74).

Like Rigoberta Menchú, the exiled Quiché Indian who was awarded the Nobel Peace Prize in 1992, the washerwoman (even in her abject solitude) becomes finally an eloquent symbol for indigenous peoples and victims of government repression on both sides of the South-North border. When confronted in the zero zero cafe by the Los Angeles police, "with their guns taut and cold like steel erections" (74), the washerwoman resists them to the bitter end rather than unplug her dream of an incorporated, transnational family: "I will fight you all because you're all farted out of the Devil's ass . . . and then I hear something crunching like broken glass against my forehead and I am blinded by the liquid darkness" (75).

Our subject here has been the intercultural and transnational experiences of migrant border-crossers from the South into the North represented as a complex series of traversing and mixing, syncretizing and hybridizing. As both Chávez and Viramontes emphasize in their narratives, migrant U.S.-Mexico border-crossing cultures are often formed under powerful economic and political constraints. Like the black British diasporic cultures of Stuart Hall and Paul Gilroy, U.S.-Mexico border cultures share what James Clifford has described as a "two-sidedness, expressing a deep dystopic/utopian tension. They are constituted by displacement (under varying degrees of coercion, often extreme)" (1992a, 6). And as Chávez and Viramontes adamantly argue, U.S.-Mexico border-crossing cultures represent alternative interpretive communities in which folkloric and postnational experimental narratives can be enunciated. What is finally remarkable about Viramontes's "The Cariboo Cafe" is that borders "become bonds among peoples, rather than the articulation of national differences and the basis for exclusion by the collaboration of the United States and [Central American] regimes" (Harlow 1991, 152). In other words, in Viramontes's "zero zero place" a worlding of world historical events has erupted—from Cortés's Euroimperialism to the Reagan-Bush wars in Central America—and has come to be embodied in the haunting, resisting figure of La Llorona. This is a story to pass on, to pass through the fluid borders of world literature.

HOLLYWOOD CROSSROADS

No less important than the complex migrant border crossings explored in Viramontes's "The Cariboo Cafe" are the postnational dramatizations of Hollywood (the American Dream) as another multicultural carceral neighborhood, complete with high-tech Los Angeles Police Department mobilizations, INS raids of undocumented workers in downtown sweatshops, drive-by gang shootings, skinhead hate crimes against gays and people of color, and chauvinist "Seal the Border" campaigns. If Mike Davis is right that Los Angeles's culture is conjured as either "sunshine" or "noir,"[12] historically structured either around rich, privileged boosters from the Owens and Chandler families to the Republican mayoral administration of Richard Riordan or around radicalized debunkers from Carey McWilliams to the recent multiracial and transclass participants in the Rodney King uprising, how can we begin to situate critical work about Los Angeles by Chicanos/as such as Viramontes, Rechy, Los Illegals, and (Kid) Frost? Do their cultural critiques add nuances to the revival of southern California noir—a revival Davis notes has been made up of "writers and directors [who] revitalized the anti-myth of [Los Angeles] and elaborated it fictionally into a new comprehensive history" (1990, 44)?

My view is that analyzing Rechy's Hollywood fiction within Davis's megaspatial view of Los Angeles as it actually exists can help us begin to understand how Los Angeles, once "the most *Waspish* of big cities in the 1960s" (104), now contains more multicultural diversity than New York. If demographers are correct that Latinos/as now make up one-quarter of California's population, and the number is expected to almost triple from 5.8 million in 1985 to 15 million in 2020, isn't it crucial for intellectuals to take seriously what Chicano/a writers are saying?

Paradoxically, Rechy's cultural interventions—from the lyrical *City of Night* (1963), *Numbers* (1967), *This Day's Death* (1969), and *The Vampires* (1971) or controversial *Sexual Outlaw* (1977) to his defiant Los Angeles fiction *Bodies and Souls* (1983) and *The Miraculous Day of Amalia Gómez* (1991)—have yet to be interpreted by his mainline or subcultural critics as texts emerging from and responding to his Mexican-American background in El Paso, Texas, or as cultural critiques inspired and contained by his extended southern California borderlands consciousness. As Juan Bruce-Novoa points out, Chicano protonationalist critics have largely ignored Rechy because he is an openly gay Chicano writer;[13] and even as savvy a cultural critic as Jonathan Dollimore, though superb in exploring Rechy's "rages against oppression" and his attributing "extraordinary political potential to transgressive sexuality" (1991, 214), seems largely unaware of Rechy's U.S.-Mexico borderland past. Don't these biographical referents inform Rechy's insistence on seeing himself as an outlaw?

From as early as 1958, in his autoethnographic essay "El Paso del

Norte" (first published in the *Evergreen Review*), Rechy has been representing what many Chicano/a lesbian and gay writers such as Gloria Anzaldúa, Cherríe Moraga, and Arturo Islas call their bridge consciousness, a consciousness that allows them to explore and exploit their double vision as both participant and observer and as displaced subjects across multiple discourses.[14] Not surprisingly, for Rechy, his U.S.-Mexico border consciousness includes both El Paso and Cuidad Juárez, for "the Rio Grande, which in the Southwest is a river only part of the time and usually just a strait of sand along the banks, . . . divides the United States from Mexico [but only] geographically" (quoted in Castañeda Shular, Ybarra-Frausto, and Sommer 1972, 158). Culturally, of course, "the Mexican people of El Paso," he continues, "more than half the population, . . . are all and always completely Mexican. . . . They speak only Spanish to each other and when they say Capital they mean Mexico DF" (158).

Written partly as a U.S.-Mexico borderland hipster's response to a xenophobic and historically misguided 1950s *Time* magazine feature describing Mexican *braceros* as a "line of desperate ants," as "mustached, strawhatted men . . . invading America," Rechy's "El Paso del Norte" can be read as a powerful cultural intervention that questions the dominant Anglocentric view of Mexican migration to the United States. Looming behind his rage is his vivid memory of seeing, as a teenager in El Paso, a dead *bracero* in the Rio Grande, a haunting memory that he returns to years later in *The Miraculous Day of Amalia Gómez*: "I remember a dead *bracero* near the bank of the Rio Grande, face down drowned in the shallow water, the water around him red, red, red. Officially he had drowned and was found, of course, by the Border Patrol. And his wife will go on thinking forever he made it with a beautiful blonde Georgia woman—loaded with toothpaste" (1972, 160).

Satirizing the nativist Anglocentric view—"Well, isn't it natural, those wetbacks wanting to come into America?—Christ, they heard about sweet-tasting toothpaste" (159), Rechy, in a perversely tragicomic narrative, rebuts the magazine's conventional "push-pull" view of Mexican migration. In this view, Mexican workers are pushed from their country by destitution and lured into the United States by the promise of the American Dream, what the mainline magazine article called "sweet-tasting toothpaste." But the reality of Mexican migration, as Rechy suggests and the legal scholar Gerald López argues, is something very different, for the United States "actively promoted migration" through its legal treaty with Mexico (the 1942 Bracero program) that "encouraged Mexican workers to fill lower echelon jobs in the country" (López 1981, 642).

Although Rechy is generally silent on the politics of sexual transgression in "El Paso del Norte," his defiant outlaw sensibility is already apparent, created from both the hypocrisy of the Catholic Church (priests are depicted in "bright drag") and the terms of his racial oppression in white supremacist Texas.

> In Balmorhea, with its giant outdoor swimming pool (where that summer the two blond tigers and I went swimming, climbed over the wall and into the rancid-looking night water) there were signs in the two-bit restaurant, in Balmorhea-town then, that said *We do not serve mexicans, niggers or dogs.* That night we went to the hick movie, and the man taking the tickets said, You boys be sure and sit on the right side, the left is for spiks. So I said I was on the wrong side and walked out. (161; his emphasis)

Later that evening at the home of his friend's aunt, Rechy again encounters nativist white supremacy in Texas head on: "The aunt waited until the Mexican servant walked out and then said, miserably, Ah jaist caint even eat when they are around. And because earlier had made me feel suddenly a Crusader and it was easy now, I walked out of the diningroom and said well I shouldnt be here to louse up your dinner lady" (161).

Rechy's U.S.-Mexico "crusader" radicalism, what Dollimore mistakenly calls a radicalism "trapped in romantic/tragic self-glorification inseparable from naive fantasies of revolutionary omnipotence" (especially in *The Sexual Outlaw*) (1991, 214), must be contextualized and read against the author's earlier battles against bigotry in Texas. Lest I overemphasize Rechy as seeing the culture of the U.S.-Mexico borderland in exclusively binary ethno-racial terms, "El Paso del Norte," like *The Miraculous Day of Amalia Gómez,* mocks the family romance of Mexican-American patriarchal culture, especially in his description of how Mexican-American men "really love Mothers" while most "Americans don't." "I don't," Rechy writes, "have a single American acquaintance whose mother faints everytime he comes home and again when he leaves. Mine does. The Mexican mother-love has nothing to do with sex, either. . . . [C]an you imagine making it with your mother if she wears a Black Shawl, and, even if she doesn't, if she acts all the time like she is wearing one?" (1991, 163).

Some thirty years later, Rechy returns to this U.S.-Mexico border sensibility to tell the engrossing tale of a Mexican-American mother, a maid, who migrates in stages from El Paso, Texas, to southern California and who one day finds herself in the midst of a "decaying" neighborhood off Hollywood Boulevard, gazing out of her barred bungalow window at "a large silver cross in the sky" (3).

While Rechy's postnational fable, *The Miraculous Day of Amalia Gómez,* tells us much about the terror and the hope among the unhomely migrant border-crossers in Los Angeles, and he imaginatively thematizes what Homi K. Bhabha (1992b) sees as the postcontemporary "terrains of world literature"—transnational histories of migrants, the colonized, and so on—mainline reviewers and critics by and large refused to acknowledge (much less attempt to comprehend) the centrality of this emergent U.S.-Mexico borderland fable-making, dismissing it as unremarkable and as invisible as the scores of Amalia Gómezes in our midst. For instance, in the *New York Times Book Review* Karen Brailsford wrote that Rechy's novel was "not so remarkable" after all and that it contained "an unbelievable denouement that's as awkward as the novel's title" (1992, 16). One wonders what this reviewer would say about magic realist fables such as Gabriel García Márquez's "Balthazar's Marvelous Afternoon," or how she would explain former LAPD chief Darryl F. Gates's brutal militarization that led to the thousand fires of rage that consumed Los Angeles in spring 1992. At any rate, the highbrow reviewer completely misses the fundamental irony of Rechy's *fábula*—that the Hollywood of movie fantasy has become the Hollywood of all-too-real violence and racial unrest.

My own view is that Rechy's socially symbolic *fábula* about how Amalia Gómez and her three children live and die in southern California conveys a great deal about who we actually live with in our communities and how our communities either fail to live up to or have fallen short of what used to be called the American Dream. As the novel begins, Amalia Gómez works hard as a housekeeper in Los Angeles, for "she liked being in pretty apartments in California, and she was paid in cash, without deductions, and that was essential to her day-to-day survival" (1991, 42). And she works equally hard as a mother, a cook, a part-time seamstress, and an avid consumer of mass-mediated culture in the extended U.S.-Mexico *frontera,* especially the romantic Pedro Infante mariachi songs on the radio, Hollywood movies such as *The Song of Bernadette,* starring a smashing Jennifer Jones, and the *telenovela* passions on local Spanish TV. Rechy's hypothesis is that the invisible Amalia Gómezes in our communities are essential to the economy, indispensable to middle-class everyday life, and even intimately connected to the American ideological consensus. Paraphrasing Ralph Ellison, Rechy pointedly asks, Who knows but that, on lower frequencies, Amalia Gómez and her children speak for us?[15]

If readers like Brailsford think that Rechy is exaggerating the struggles of Amalia Gómez and her family, then we should take a brief look at Amalia Gómez's life as represented in Rechy's displaced fable. Born in El Paso, Texas, and trained by her mother to believe in the mysteries of the Blessed Holy Mary, Amalia Gómez is raped at fourteen and later forced by her parents to marry the young man, Salvador, who assaulted her. After another unhappy marriage, to a brutal U.S. Latino Vietnam veteran, Gabriel, Amalia Gómez migrates to Hollywood hoping to fashion a better life. Like thousands upon thousands of other *solas* with children, she works her way to southern California by cleaning houses and sewing in downtown garment sweatshops, surviving on the day laborer's jobs that pervade what economists call the secondary labor market. Still unable to make do with these jobs, Amalia "occasionally took in piecework to do at home. Her children would help. Gloria would adjust the expensive labels, Juan would then glue them on the garment, and Amalia would sew them" (56).

Throughout her migrations in California, Amalia flees barrio after barrio in East Los Angeles "to keep [Juan] and Gloria from drugs and killings and gangs that had taken Manny" (8). When she finally settles in a rented stucco bungalow in Hollywood, Amalia finds herself in the midst of "cars left mounted on bricks [and] everywhere . . . iron bars on windows" (6). More by force of habit than anything else, Amalia Gómez, a "legal" Mexican American, keeps afloat by hustling as a housekeeper, but more often than not she feels "some anxiety about her regular workdays because 'new illegals'—Guatemalans, Salvadorans, Nicaraguans without papers—were willing to work for hardly anything at all" (6).

Twice divorced from U.S. Latinos, Amalia is more and more consumed by her desire to find a hardworking and nonabusive husband and father for her three children, a task made all the more problematic by her penchant for U.S. Latino "men with holy names." Though mostly mired in her work as a maid, her everyday experiences often take her beyond the edge: "Worries about Juan!—handsomer each day and each day more secretive, no longer a happy young man, but a moody one. . . . And who wouldn't worry about Gloria? So very pretty, and wearing more and more make-up" (8). Manny, "her beloved firstborn," hangs himself at the Los Angeles County jail.

As if her everyday family life were not remarkable enough, Amalia's best friends, Milagro (Miracle) and Rosario (Rosary), find themselves consumed by southern California borderlands culture: Milagro, who cannot cope with her incorrigible gang-banging son, survives by spinning "accounts of the romantic travails in her serials" (77) to her factory co-workers, and Rosario becomes entangled in the murder of an INS agent who has abused scores of undocumented workers: "Jorge killed a *migra*. . . . [He] paid a *coyote* to bring his youngest son with his wife across the border and they had to take the dangerous route across the hill because the *migra* now . . . flood the border with lights. . . . Hundreds of people from San Diego drive there each night to add their car lights, shout their support, while desperate people are netted rushing the border—and now snipers wait for them. Yesterday a twelve-year-old boy was killed" (176). In scenes such as these, Rechy dramatizes how the government's doctrine of militarized low-intensity conflict spills over into the lives of everyday people.

There are, however some rewarding—albeit fleeting—moments in Rechy's fable. "Amalia liked watching the parades" that took place "every Saturday night on Whittier Boulevard [where] the young men of East Los Angeles would display their 'customized' cars, growling machines worked on constantly, often prized '50s 'Cheveez'; cars silver-sprinkled red, green, blue; purple birds or fiery flames painted on the sides and hoods" (43–44).

If barrio "parades" of lowriders suggest how Chicanos/as, situated between a rock and Gates's Operation Hammer, elaborate a sense of what Tomás Ybarra-Frausto sees as "a communal consciousness of allegiance" (Castañeda Shular, Ybarra-Frausto, and Sommer 1972, 152–153) and the special *cholo/a* calligraphy and their inner-city crossword graffiti are examples of an alternative expressive culture,[16] Rechy reminds us how these cultural counterpractices are routinely smashed by search-and-destroy missions of the Los Angeles Police Department: "Police helicopters hovered over the unofficial parade. Suddenly light poured down in a white pit. Squad cars rushed to block the side exits off the boulevards. Police motorcycles tangled in and out of lanes. Young Mexicans rushed out of cars. Some were pushed to the ground. There were

Page 114 — El Otro Lado / The Other Side

screams. The police pulled out their guns" (1991, 44). Scenes such as these are hardly unbelievable, for as Davis has painstakingly recorded, the Los Angeles Police Department (especially under former Chief Gates) saturated the barrios of South Central and East Los Angeles with Vietnam-inspired offensives such as Operation Hammer, "jacking up thousands of local teenagers at random like so many surprised peasants" (1990, 268).

If Rechy rages against the militarization of southern California through the Reagan-Gates-Bush doctrine of low-intensity conflict, his fable is deeply rooted in actual search-and-destroy missions, such as the astonishing one that took place in August 1988: "Only a short time ago," Rechy writes, "cops had raided and smashed houses randomly in south central Los Angeles, and amid the wreckage they created in search of unfound drugs in the neighborhood suddenly under double siege, they had spray-painted their own *placas,* their own insignia: Los Angeles Police Rule" (1991, 114). Thus, under the "double siege" of the gang crack cocaine blizzard and the out-of-control Los Angeles Police Department, Amalia and her children become prisoners in their own backyard.

These scenes in Rechy's postnational Chicano fable, of course, only begin to tell the lurid story of the "programmed urban hardening" in southern California. Mike Davis must be congratulated for his summary survey in *City of Quartz* of Gates's sustained raids on non-Anglos in Los Angeles, for he documents what all too many Chicanos/as and African Americans have known for years—that the mostly white male police are liars and extreme fabulators. For years Chief Gates and his Gang Related Active Trafficker Suppression (GRATS) program conducted regular sweeps through barrio neighborhoods to curtail intra-community gang fighting—often on the perverse evidence of high-five greetings or the color of clothing. Davis records how on one particular mission Gates's "Blue Machine" "mounted nine sweeps, impounded five hundred cars and [made] nearly fifteen hundred arrests" (272). Moreover, Rechy's brief allusion to the Los Angeles Police Department as gang-bangers (with their own graffiti *placas*) is scandalously elaborated by the *Los Angeles Times:* "Residents . . . said they were punched and kicked by officers during what those arrested called an 'orgy of violence.' Residents reported the officers spraypainted walls with slogans, such as 'LAPD Rules!' . . . Damage to the apartments was so extensive that the Red Cross offered disaster assistance and temporary shelter to displaced residents—a service normally provided in the wake of major fires, floods, earthquakes or other natural disasters" (quoted in Davis 1990, 276). If, for residents of the Dalton Street apartments, Gates's raid, as Davis writes, was "not quite the My Lai of the war against the underclass," it nevertheless signaled "a grim portent of what 'unleashing the police' really means" (275).

If Los Angeles *es una fábula* (is a fable)—as a mural in Rechy's novel puts it—then the author's hyperbolic representation of everyday life becomes more comprehensible, for a fable, as defined by the *Oxford English Dictionary,* is a narrative "relating to supernatural or extraordinary persons or an incident." In Rechy's fable (complete with animal characters—*coyotes* and *pollos*—and a scathing moral) the supernatural high-tech LAPD raids are the stuff of postmodern myth and its "extraordinary" leader's actions are patently unreal. Who would actually believe that then Chief Gates could tacitly approve of his officers forcing the thirty-two prisoners of the Dalton Street raid "to whistle the theme of the 1960s Andy Grifith [*sic*] TV show . . . while they ran a gauntlet of cops beating them with fists and long steel flashlights" (276)?

In any case, when the dust finally settled, the police, Davis notes, "found neither wanted gang members nor weapons, just a small quantity of dope belonging to two non-resident teenagers" (276). What for years Gates and his predecessors, William Parker and Ed Davis, had been able to deny the 1988 Dalton Street raid confirmed: the cops were gang-bangers in their own right, and non-Anglo citizens (such as Rechy's characters, Amalia, Gloria, Juan, and Manny) are often forced to live under de facto apartheid in Los Angeles.[17]

At a time when many middle-class intellectuals of color are tacitly supporting the exterminist rhetoric and practices of the LAPD (more draconian curfews and police raids on their multicultural communities), it is heartening to see that defiant outlaws such as Rechy are refusing to acquiesce. If Hollywood—the terrain of the American Dream—no longer affords the democratic design for freedom and Los Angeles itself has become an armed fortress, what Davis calls a "fragmented, paranoid spatiality" (238), Rechy maintains throughout his text that power is fundamentally a mechanism of state, church, patriarchy, class, and compulsory heterosexual interests whose work is to silence and oppress dominated groups.

While Rechy is justly famous for narrating how gay males confront and transgress the laws of society ("The law tells us we're criminals so we've become defiant outlaws. . . . Religion insists we're sinners and so we've become soulful sensualists"), in *The Miraculous Day of Amalia Gómez* he throws considerable light on how Chicanas/os are "discriminated against more than most people imagine." Not surprisingly, he is "outraged by any kind of injustice, whether against homosexuals, against women, against Chicanos, against Jews, against whomever" (1991, 28). This leads him to be especially critical of patriarchal and homophobic practices within traditional Chicano male culture.

Although Amalia is fascinated by "the murals scattered about the area, . . . paintings as colorful as those on calendars, sprawled on whole walls" (45), she is haunted and confused by one that depicts a "tall, plumed Aztec [holding] a bleeding, dying city boy in his arms" (56). Though Rechy's heroine intuitively grasps in the murals of East Los Angeles what the art historians Shifra Goldman and Tomás Ybarra-Frausto call "a high idealism" emphasizing the "community-oriented" and "public art forms" of the 1960s (1991, 83), she is troubled by the exclusion of women as historical agents.

To understand how this 1960s liberatory Chicano idealism was at best limited, we need only recall that many Chicano murals of the period reflected the male utopian *carnalismo* philosophy contained in manifestos such as "El Plan espiritual de Aztlán" (The Spiritual Plan of Aztlán). Separatist in nature, the manifesto adopted at the 1969 Chicano Youth Conference in Denver advocated the reclaiming of Mexican lands lost to U.S. empire (the Southwest), a privileging of Amerindian (male) consciousness, and an emphasis on Chicano studies and multiculturalism in higher education. Proclaiming that Aztlán "belongs to those that plant the seeds, water the fields, and gather the crops, and not to foreign Europeans" (quoted in Castañeda Shular, Ybarra-Frausto, and Sommer 1972, 84), the "spiritual plan" grounded us not only in the social philosophy of the Chicano movement but also, as Goldman and Ybarra-Frausto emphasize, in "the themes of Chicano art and letters" (1991, 84).

Rechy's cultural critique of murals celebrating Aztlán and Mexican patriarchy (taken together with his raging against gang violence and the "Blue Machine" killings by the LAPD) is therefore illuminating: "A muscular Aztec prince, amber-gold-faced, in lordly feathers, stood with others as proud as he. They gazed toward the distance. Behind them on a hill pale armed men mounted on horses watched them. At the opposite end of the painting brown-faced, muslin-clothed men stared into a bright horizon. They were the ones whom the Aztecs were facing defi-antly." If "Aztlán es una fábula," it is partly so because its Chicano youth philosophy glorifying Aztec warriors while at the same time excluding women is itself a deception. That the mural depicts "the *con-quistadores* [who] are about to subdue the Indians with weapons" and juxtaposes that image with the Mexican "*revolucionarios* who will tri-umph and bring about Aztlán, our promised land of justice," Rechy presents Amalia's respectful but critical response to the work: "There were no women. Where were they? Had they survived?" (1991, 45).

Fundamentally, Rechy's fable focuses on that May day when Amalia apparently sees "a large silver cross in the sky." But is this the mirac-ulous sign that she has been praying for—the miracle that will solve her family's tragic life in Hollywood? Will Guadalupe, the Holy Mother, appear before "a twice-divorced woman with grown, rebel-lious children" (3)?

As Amalia moves into the day—full of flashbacks to her turbulent childhood in El Paso and flash-forwards to police and gangs rampag-ing through her urban galaxy in Hollywood—she is encouraged by two other hopeful signs: she sees that a rosebush with new blossoms "had managed to squeeze through a large crack in the cement" and two hilar-ious "*espiritualistas* / shamans" assure her that "something big" will occur in her tragic life (109). Thus encouraged, Amalia represses all that has been happening around her, for amid what must seem like nirvana to the white youth culture in Los Angeles, Manny, Juan, and Gloria remain trapped in low-wage employment or county jail or suc-cumb to the underground economy, where more than one thousand Latino and African-American gangs license what Davis calls "crack-dealing franchises."[18]

While Amalia stands at the corner of Sunset and Western rereading Manny's last letter from county jail, she decides to walk over to a neigh-borhood health clinic where she can have her "blood pressure checked" (137). Afterward, she walks briskly down Sunset Boulevard and decides to visit Milagro's housing project near MacArthur Park, where she hopes to get Rosario's address.

Once on the mean streets of what Rechy describes as "the other Hol-lywood," Amalia has a series encounters with eccentric characters—some comical, others emotionally challenged. The first is with a priest, to whom Amalia attempts to confess her previous night's peccadillos with a Salvadoran man named Angel who, not surprisingly, is not at all angelic but a *coyote* who sexually humiliates and abuses her. As the scene unravels, Rechy wryly shows how the Roman Catholic priest ends up masturbating to Amalia's sexually explicit confession:

> I cannot grant you absolution unless—Did he touch you?
> . . . Yes, she whispered.
> When he had already removed your intimate clothes?
> Yes. . . .
> How many times did he touch you?
> Twice . . . Three times. . . .
> Between your legs . . . ? With his tongue? (156–157)

With a Foucault-like precision, Rechy examines how the Roman Catholic Church uses the confession ritual for having the subject of sex spoken about. Rechy here is in complete agreement with Foucault's thesis that "the Christian pastoral always presented [sex] as the disquieting enigma: not a thing which stubbornly shows itself, but one which always hides, the insidious presence. . . . It is . . . a fable that is indispensable to the endlessly proliferating economy of the discourses of sex. What is peculiar to modern societies . . . is not that they consigned sex to a shadow existence, but that they dedicated themselves to speaking of it *ad infinitum,* while exploiting it as *the* secret" (1980, 35; his emphasis).

Thus prevented from appeasing her religious guilt, she decides to visit two *espiritualistas* (spiritualists) for what she hopes will be a *limpieza*— a folk ritual cleansing. But here again Amalia is victimized by her own folk, leading readers to see how she (devoutly if not conventionally Catholic) can find salvation only from within the confines of the Church. As Rechy noted in one of his numerous interviews, "For [Amalia] to liberate herself . . . she has to do it through the very instrument that oppresses her" (Fry 1992, 28). As we will see in the novel's ending, after being rejected by the male-centered Roman Catholic Church—with its entrenched machismo and oppressive attitudes toward divorce and abortion—Amalia has very little recourse but to believe that she cannot help her children to survive unless she has the power to hope.

While Amalia "search[es] for signs of resurrection everywhere" (191), she finds only a bench on Sunset Boulevard "with a picture of Marilyn Monroe" (199). She then steps into a bus that takes her to a "huge shopping complex at the edge of Beverly Hills" (199). Amalia's end is as bloodied and nightmarish as the Los Angeles noir of Davis's *City of Quartz* or the washerwoman's end in Viramontes's "The Cariboo Cafe." Amalia ends up in a panopticonlike mall with video cameras and "sturdy middle-aged" men tracking her every step in "stores with names that were impressive, no matter what they meant" (200).

Amid all these extraordinarily well-policed stores, Rechy's heroine is taken hostage by a man "with crazed eyes" (204). As he presses a gun against her temple, the man is surrounded by scores of uniformed men and their cars and motorcycles. When she finally "thrust[s] the man away from her" (205), bullets rip from their chambers at an astonishing rate. Then "Amalia saw a beautiful spatter of blue shards that glinted and gleamed like shooting stars as they fell on splotches of red like huge blossoms, red roses" (205).

In Amalia's wanderings through Hollywood and Beverly Hills, we see events happening simultaneously to a variety of ethno-racial groups in different parts of the same place, thus thematizing the national mappings that theorists of the novel insist is key to the genre. All of Rechy's *Miraculous Day of Amalia Gómez* appears to be narrated as blistering urban realism. But Amalia's circulation around the apparatuses of late capitalist Hollywood has a different signification. Like Joyce's Bloom wandering around the colonial capital of Dublin in *Ulysses,* it maps a different mass-mediated imperialist capital of culture. Wandering Amalia sees all the glossy advertising at the tony mall; she meets not only her working-class peers on the streets but an intense police and INS presence as well. Amalia's *flânerie*, in this light, signals her attempt to escape from the panoptic surveillance of the border-patrolled state.

On another level, Rechy, a brilliant student trained in the critical philosophy of the New School for Social Research, escapes the textuality of engaged "realist" art through his fable's own splendid destruction of the "real." To pursue this negative dialectical reading, we must not only see the fastidious realism of Amalia's beatings, rapes, and humiliations but also understand how Amalia's oppression and humiliation serve as an analogy for the oppressed and misunderstood artist Rechy himself.

Amalia's life struggle and wanderings in Hollywood concretize Rechy's critical philosophical views about the insurrectionary power thematized through the very form of his genre—the novel. When Amalia has a gun pointed at her head by the man with "crazed eyes," or earlier when Rosario informs Amalia that "for all the destitute people [in the U.S.-Mexico borderland], it's like having a loaded gun held to your head" (77), we grasp Rechy's splendid allusion to Adorno's famous response to the Sartrean "engaged literature" thesis: "It is not the office of art to spotlight alternatives, but to resist by its form alone the course of the world, which permanently puts a pistol to men's heads" (1982, 305). Rechy's fable, we might say, does not so much destroy "realism" as attempt to destroy the destroyer's concept of positivism and realism. In so doing, Rechy explodes from within the form of the novel itself and negates Hollywood realism. Rechy emphasizes this philosophical point in a *Diacritics* interview when he says, "In all my novels, I extend 'realism' into metaphor for deeper meaning. . . . In *The Miraculous Day of Amalia Gómez,* I extend the book into surrealism, and then fable" (Castillo 1995, 119).

If intellectuals have dramatized a noir history of Los Angeles's past—which as Davis argues "actually has come to function as a surrogate public history" (1990, 44)—Rechy's grand achievement, *The Miraculous Day of Amalia Gómez,* captures, from the standpoint of a Chicana housekeeper, the image of the city proliferating in endless repressions in social space. While many postcontemporary urban theorists have offered a facile celebration of the postmodern spaces of the new urban "hypercrowd," they have also been what Davis calls "strangely silent about the militarization of city life so grimly visible at street level" (223). Rechy's Hollywood fable, together with Viramontes's "The Cariboo Cafe," thus openly challenge this silence by providing readers with their own Chicana/o noir.

It is hardly surprising, therefore, that Rechy's denouement takes place in a tony mall in Beverly Hills, a mall full of unsubtle signs warning off the Amalia Gómezes of the world.

> Within a huge circular plastic column, an elevator rose. . . . Amalia stared up, at the arched ceiling of the mall. It had translucent brightness like that of an eternally perfect day. Over the railings on upper floors, shoppers peered down onto the spill of shops. For a moment, she felt dizzy, dazed. Then she saw a sturdy middle-aged man looking at her. . . .
> She hurried into a jewelry store. She was admiring a display of wedding rings when she noticed there was a guard there. (1991, 201–202)

In scenes such as these, Rechy does not turn a blind eye—like many postmodernist architectural critics—to the obvious fact that malls such as the one Amalia finds herself in reinforce urban apartheid. Amalia Gómez, like other pariahs, however, reads all too clearly the meaning of such practices: "She stood in the middle of the mall, aware of herself in this glistening palace. So many people. . . . Did they see her? Yes, they saw a woman who looked out of place, tired, perspiring" (202).

Despite being forced to see herself as an "othering machine," despite her imprisonment as a maid in the secondary job market, and despite living in what was once the demiparadise of Hollywood, Amalia survives her hostage-taking—but not before seeing "a dazzling white radiance enclosed in a gleam of blue and within it hovering on a gathering of red roses stood the Blessed Mother with her arms outstretched to her" (206). Rechy, like Adorno before him, remains convinced that autonomous art contains a utopian moment that points toward a future sociocultural transformation.

The language here is familiar to Chicanos/as: folkloric and religious. "The Blessed Mother" who appears to Amalia is Guadalupe—the Mexican people's version of the Virgin Mary who, as Norma Alarcón suggests, "substituted for the Aztec goddess Tonantzin" (1989, 58). To argue over whether Rechy's denouement is "unbelievable" is downright silly, and misses the social message of the author's fable-making, for Guadalupe—as the anthropologist Eric R. Wolf has taught us—always represents in Mexican folktales "mother, food, hope, life; supernatural salvation from oppression" (1958, 38). Additionally, as Jeanette Rodriguez emphasizes, unlike "other Marian apparitions only Our Lady of Guadalupe comes, not to make a request, but to make an offering, and stays. . . . And the people truly believe that she is alive and present for them" (1994, 128). Understandably, then, Roman Catholic oppression and supernatural liberation are, from Rechy's standpoint, not mutually contradictory but mutually reinforcing. Amalia Gómez suffers and is victimized by the Roman Catholic Church and in the process paradoxically becomes liberated through Guadalupe.

Amalia's constructive, if brief, insight into the convergence of ethno-race and oppression and ethno-race and homosexuality occurs as well in the novel's phantasmatic denouement. While Amalia continually rationalizes (given Los Angeles's conscious policy of social disinvestment in its youth) that Juan has more than likely entered the underground crack cocaine economy to survive, at the novel's end she admits to herself that something very different has happened. Juan has, in fact, decided to make do by homosexual hustling with a young Salvadoran boy: "I sent away that boy Juan brought to live in the garage. I saw his sad young eyes. I knew what I was doing was cruel. But I also knew what was really involved between him and my son" (1991, 197).

Given that most U.S. Latinos/as simply repress the complexities that arise at the intersection of ethno-race and sexuality, it is important to emphasize that Amalia is finally prepared to acknowledge a convergence of ethno-racial formation, homosexuality, and maybe even queer theory. All the more remarkable, perhaps, is that Rechy's attempt to show the literal alliance between Juan and his Salvadoran comrade occurs at the historical moment in Los Angeles when the Salvadorans of Mara Salvatrucha (near MacArthur Park) were waging what Davis describes as "a bloody war against the established power of the 18th Street Gang— the largest and fastest growing Chicano gang which threatens to become the Crips of East L.A." (1990, 316). What we therefore learn from John Rechy's displaced fable, among other things, is that a conventionally understood class liberation that ignores gender, sexuality, and ethno-race will be disastrous.

BORDER NOISE: PUNK, HIP-HOP, AND THE POLITICS OF CHICANO/A SOUND

If the culture of the extended U.S.-Mexico borderlands and transnational migrant history are inextricably linked in Viramontes's "The Cariboo Cafe" and Rechy's *Miraculous Day of Amalia Gómez*—grounding overly global formulations of hybridity, syncretism, and the postcolonial condition—there are still other complex sounds of mass media texts critiquing and complicating the dominant culture's linear views of immigration, the American *Bildung,* ethno-race, and the nation.[19] I refer, of course, to the mass media *rolas* (songs) by U.S. Latino (punk) rockers and hip-hoppers such as Los Illegals and (Kid) Frost.

In his justly famous "Cruising Around the Historical Bloc," George Lipsitz argued that from the 1940s to the late 1980s "Chicano rock and roll music from Los Angeles transformed a specific ethnic culture rooted in common experiences into more than just a novelty to be appropriated by uncomprehending outsiders." Drawing on both "residual" and "emergent" elements in their barrios, mass cultural musicians and cultural activists from Richie Valens to Los Lobos won "some measure of participation," Lipsitz noted, "in the creation and dissemination of mass popular culture" (1986, 149).

The underground emergence of Los Illegals as a significant punk rock band, for example, provides us with still another remarkable illustration of the U.S.-Mexico *frontera*'s persistent cultural clash of migra-

tions, deportations, and INS raids. Mixing the shocking multiple realities of undocumented border-crossers with New Wave/punk sensibilities, Los Illegals was one of the first Chicano bands to stand in between
frontera culture and mass culture, performing a frenzied and over-
whelming electric guitar music that seemed on the surface to be a CD
played at quadro speed.[20] Willie Herrón claims that he started his punk
band "to talk about the experience of being a *cholo,* a low rider, of being
in gangs, all of it" (quoted in Lipsitz 1986, 155). In their transnational
anthem "El Lay (L. A., the law)," from their *Internal Exile* (1983) album,
co-written in vernacular Chicano Spanish by Herrón and the po-mo
artist Gronk, Los Illegals represent Los Angeles as it actually is for the
millions of *indocumentados/as* and unhomely.

Parado en la esquina
Sin rumbo sin fin
Estoy in El Lay,
No tengo donde ir
Un hombre se acercó,
Mi nombre preguntó
Al no saber su lengua,
Con el me llevó
¿Esto es el precio
Que pagamos
Cuando llegamos
A este lado?
Jalamos y pagamos impuestos
Migra llega y nos da unos fregasos
El Lay, L. A.
El Lay, L. A.
El Lay, L. A.
El Lay, L. A.
El Lay, L. A.
En un camión,
Sin vuelta me pusieron
Por lavar platos en El Lay me deportaban
Mirar por el cristal,
Sentí pertenecer
Un millión ilegales, no podemos fallar
¿Esto es el precio
Que pagamos
Cuando llegamos
A este lado?
¿Y porque no—podemos quedar
Que Gronk, no borro la frontera?

El Lay, L. A.
Manos fijadas,
Al fin en la frontera
Lo dije que quería,
Mejorar la vida
Familia sin futuro, falta de respeto
¿Adonde fue,
La libertad y justicia?
           (Quoted in Loza 1993, 231–232)

Standing on the corner / Got nowhere to go / I'm here in El Lay, / Got no place to stay / A man came up to me / And he asked me my name / Couldn't speak his language, / So he took me away / Is this the price / You have to pay / When you come / To this side? / We come to work, we pay our taxes / Migra comes and they kick us on our asses / El Lay, L. A. / He threw me on the bus / That headed one way / I was being deported, for washing dishes in El Lay / Looking out the window, / I felt I belonged / A million illegals, we can't all be wrong / Is this the price / You have to pay / When you come / To the USA / I don't know why, we cannot stay / Didn't Gronk erase the border yesterday? / We ended at the border, / Hands above my head / I told him all I wanted, / Was a chance to get ahead / No future for my family, can't even get respect / What happened to / The liberty and the justice that we get?

"The texture of 'El Lay,'" as Steven Loza writes, "is one of unifying forms." "The text," he continues, "conceived through jagged contours of metaphor, satire, and symbolic contradiction, unites itself stylistically with the dissonant harmonic framework and the abrasive, hard-driving rhythmic structure" (232). On a different register, presenting the traditional push-pull view of Mexican migration to the United States that we saw in Rechy's "El Paso del Norte," "El Lay" sums up a complex view of U.S.-Mexico migrant border crossing in moral and historical terms, exhorting the listener to answer the following questions: Hasn't the U.S. government actively promoted Mexican migration since 1942 with the Bracero treaty? Haven't millions of undocumented laborers built up unreasonable expectations that their employment as dishwashers and their presence as taxpayers will continue? Should residency be the only route to legal and cultural citizenship? And what are the moral obligations of the destination country that arise from these dedicated workers' involvement in our communities?

By exposing the moral hypocrisy of Los Angeles, which hyped itself in the late 1980s as "A City for a Future," Los Illegals produced a musical style of crisis emphasizing their outlawed and "illegal" politics, for even the band's name suggests the new face of the U.S. Latino/a youth subculture in southern California. Much as these young *indocumentados/as* themselves, the punk musical style in "El Lay" is angry, sharp, and loud: the lyrics are shouted by Herrón in an exaggerated voice, supported, and, on first listening, blasted away by a barrage of overamplified electric guitars and dizzying Afro-Cuban drumming. "El Lay," as the music critic Iain Chambers wrote in another context, is a "rude blast" directed against "the pretentious domain" of mainline pop music (1986, 172).

Los Illegals' cryptic reference to "Gronk" and his "erasing the border yesterday" needs some elaboration: the self-conscious and irreverent musical quotations and ironic poses (The Clash and Rock Against Racism) offer listeners a presentation of actualities of U.S.-Mexico migrant culture, deconstructing Herrón's and Gronk's earlier utopian attempts, as members of the urban ASCO collective, to "erase the border" in their urban performance art pieces. Herrón and Gronk (together with the video/photo artists Pattsi Valdez, Marisela Norte, and Harry Gamboa, Jr.) were *veteranos/as* of the "blowouts" at Garfield High School in the late 1960s and early 1970s, and through their ASCO "happenings," such as their memorable "Walking Mural" (1972) in which the members gathered on Whittier Boulevard, they were "intent on transforming muralism from a static to a performance medium" (Gamboa 1991, 124). Los Illegals' self-conscious and playful riff goes further; it has a critical edge to it, warning against the postmodern collapsing of history into theoretical wish fulfillment.

In brief, the musical "chaos" that Los Illegals performed in their transnational anthem "El Lay" forces a stark reappraisal of pop music's own politics and cultural sounds. As Chambers said of British punk in general, "El Lay" disrupts the distinction "between mainstream and margin, between avant-garde and popular, and between music and 'noise'" (1986, 172). We might also note that Los Illegals set aside a monocultural and monological sound and replace it with a multiple-layered, bilingual sound of their own.

If 1980s British punk offered Los Illegals and other Chicano bands such as The Brat and Los Cruzados a more democratic and dialogic vernacular form for exploring and transforming the everyday life of the *indocumentado/a* in Los Angeles, 1990s gangster rap, hip-hop, and black

British jungle (often in wild combinations) are the privileged expressive forms appropriated in (Kid) Frost's *East Side Story* (1992). From the very title of his work, (Kid) Frost (Arturo Molina) attempts to talk back to Hollywood's mass cultural constructions in which U.S. Latino/a gang life is used to entertain audiences. The intertextual reference here, of course, is to *West Side Story,* a film depicting gang life in the 1950s. As Martin Sánchez Jankowski says, films such as *West Side Story, Fort Apache/The Bronx,* and *Colors* "depict gangs as composed of poor or working-class males who lack the skills and desire to be upwardly mobile and productive citizens. Essentially, they are not only 'losers' but 'losers' who are also primitive and brutally violent. Their values are painted as both anathema to the values held by the society as a whole and a threat to them (society's values)" (1991, 300).

Moderating his earlier romanticized and misogynist rap persona in his debut *hispanic causing panic* (1990) and deconstructing attempts to essentialize rap as the "authentic" black noise of the U.S. northeastern 'hood, (Kid) Frost responds to Hollywood's typically colonial symbology in hybrid rap songs such as "I Got Pulled Over," "Penitentiary," and "Chaos on the Streets of East Los Angeles," all of which feature sirens, gunshots, and racist LAPD radio conversations among white male cops as "backdrops" to the out-of-control gang-banging and drive-by shootings in East Los Angeles. While occasionally presenting uncritical hymns of Chicano protonationalism in such songs as "Another Firme Rola (Bad Cause I'm Brown)" and offering his listeners lurid fantasies of teenage *cholo* male violence (he recalls how at fourteen he relished his first .32 Barreta handgun), (Kid) Frost resists outright mistranslation and appropriation by the hegemonic mass media in songs such as "Mi Vida Loca," "Home Boyz," and "These Stories Have to be Told." In the latter interlingual hip-hop song, the Chicano rapper begins to rehearse for us a variety of mestizo/a identifications and social relations not yet permissible in the urban U.S.-Mexico *frontera:*

> . . . and this little cholito who got himself in a mess
> his plaqueazo was guero,
> and everywhere daddy went
> the batos quieren pedo.
> So as the tiempo went on,
> the hatred for guero just got more strong.
> So guero started packing the filero
> cuz the guys in the barrio, the block, the ghetoo

were all trying to get him.
He wanted out, to forget his past,
but they won't let him.
So he moved out of state and changed his name. . . .
I know this story's getting kinda old,
but it has to be told. (1992)

Although Mike Davis might justly see (Kid) Frost's interventions as merely another Hollywood attempt "to mine Los Angeles's barrios and ghettoes for every last lurid image of self-destruction and community holocaust" (1990, 87), I prefer Lipsitz's apt observation that when Los Angeles's expressive culture's forms (gangster rap, hip-hop, *caló*, reggae) rub together they are not concessions to the pressures and demands of Anglocentric Hollywood but attempts to use vernacular forms most likely to appeal to masses of hip-hop audiences across the Américas. Likewise, I am persuaded by the historian Robin D. G. Kelley's graceful insight in *Race Rebels* (1994) that West Coast hip-hop in many ways anticipated and prophesied the 1992 transclass upheaval in Los Angeles. Kelley's provocative reading of gangster rap overlaps with Rechy's riffs on Hollywood in *The Miraculous Day of Amalia Gómez,* for both thematize everyday events in the extended *frontera* of southern California as grounded in the "rap sheets" of their male protagonists.

Thus envisaged, West Coast gangster rap, in Kelley's words, opens "a window into, and a critique of, the criminalization" of youths of color (1994, 187). Moreover, (Kid) Frost's hip-hop songs, like Ice T's songs, take on in their form and content "a sort of street ethnography of racist institutions and racial practices" (190). Heard and read collectively, Chicano/a punk, *conjunto,* polka, *technobanda,* and hip-hop songs speak to what social theorists call the "deindustrialization" of North America. Paraphrasing Marx, we might rightly conclude in listening to Los Illegals, Los Tigres del Norte, and (Kid) Frost, among others, that young documented and undocumented men and women make their own history but not under circumstances of their own choosing.

(Kid) Frost's excursions, moreover, into a material hybrid reggae/hip-hop/*caló* sound as in "Home Boyz," or a phat jazz *mestizaje* as in "La Raza," push the logic of his project to its antiessentialist conclusions by fusing local sounds with pop forms rooted in the borders and diasporas of the Américas. Frost's "La Raza," for example, thematizes collective memory in its lyrics and melody (from El Chicano's classic "Viva Tirado") to construct what on the surface appears to be a Chicano protonationalism. Nevertheless, in the act of declaring himself "brown and proud," he consciously echoes James Brown's 1968 song, "I'm Black and I'm Proud," thus grounding an intercultural mass-mediated alliance with the African-American community. Frost then brings the music full circle by using a vocal style innovated by the OG ("official ganster") hip-hopper Ice T, paying tribute to the cut and mixings established within the southern California hip-hop tradition. One last comment is in order here to emphasize the complexities of (Kid) Frost's "La Raza." In sampling El Chicano's wonderful "Viva Tirado," arguably one of the most famous "authentic" Chicano sounds of the Chicano Youth Power social movement, he acknowledges that it was first written and performed by the African-American jazz composer Gerald Wilson. "Music and its rituals," as Paul Gilroy writes in *The Black Atlantic,* "can [therefore] be used to create a model whereby identity can be understood neither as fixed essence nor as a vague and utterly contingent construction." Thus envisaged, (Kid) Frost's southern California *frontera* identification remains the outcome of "practical activity: language, gesture, bodily significations, desires" (102). "These significations," Gilroy continues, "are condensed in musical performance by acting on the body through the specific mechanisms of identification and recognition that are produced in the intimate inter-action of performer and crowd" (1993, 102).

This examination of U.S.-Mexico border culture—from Helena María Viramontes and John Rechy to Los Illegals and (Kid) Frost—shows something of the richness of cultural critique in and around (trans)national identity and demonstrates also the dimensions of an emergent Chicano/a oppositional practice. The cultural forms examined above— the short story, the fable, and punk and hip-hop music—are simultaneously sites of ethno-race, class, gender, sexuality, and transnational identity. Further, I think it bears some repeating that these sites are not interchangeable. As Viramontes, Rechy, Los Illegals, and (Kid) Frost demonstrate again and again in their works, cultural forms can no longer be exclusively located within the border-patrolled boundaries of the nation-state. Chicano/a America therefore defines itself as a central part of an extended *frontera.* Its cultures are revitalized through a "re-Hispanicization" of migratory populations from Mexico and Central America.

Fundamentally, as the texts by these writers and musicians suggest, the cultures and politics, Central and North American, of the extended borderlands have become the very material for hybrid imaginative processes that are redefining what it means to be a Chicano/a and U.S. Latino/a. As Juan Flores and George Yúdice emphasize, "The fact is that [U.S.] Latinos, that very heterogeneous medley of races and nationalities, are different from both the older and the new ethnicities" (1993, 199). Moreover, U.S. Latinos/as constitute a new powerful and demographically rich social movement. Thus envisaged, *la frontera* of the United States and Mexico may very well turn out to be another alternative to what Gilroy described as "the different varieties of absolutism which would confine culture in 'racial,' ethnic, or national essences" (1991b, 155). U.S.-Mexico border culture is always already localized and global, and this is why our monocultural national categories are not the most sensible structures for understanding these emergent expressive cultural practices.

POSTSCRIPT

> A firestorm of rage and destruction is consuming Los Angeles' inner city, but Downtown itself is an eerily quiet ghost town. . . . Thanks to riot television coverage, hundreds of thousands of white Southern Californians are visiting South-central L.A. for the first time in their lives. . . . Because of television's monomaniacal insistence on "black rage," most will also miss the significance of the participation of thousands of poor Latinos in what may be modern America's first multi-ethnic riot.
>
> Mike Davis, "The L.A. Inferno" (1992, 59)

Will the politics of backlash and the Reagan-Bush-Clinton doctrine of low-intensity conflict target new and old U.S. Latino/a ethno-racial populations in California? Will ugly, chauvinistic "Light Up the Border" campaigns and nativist legislation like Proposition 187 continue to go unchecked, like weeds, along the U.S.-Mexico *frontera?* Will California sheriff's deputies (caught on videotape on April 1, 1996) keep clubbing with their erect batons defenseless undocumented border-crossers like Alicia Sotero, Enrique Funes, and José Pedroza? Will our own home-grown *intifada* (intimated in the cultural work of Viramontes, Rechy, Los Illegals, and [Kid] Frost) "be fueled by a generation's collapsing hopes in the future" (59)?

6

Tijuana Calling

Travel Writing, Autoethnography, and Video Art

Tijuana is one of the major laboratories of postmodernity. In 1950 it had no more than sixty thousand inhabitants; today it tops one million, with migrants from every region of Mexico, especially Oaxaca, Puebla, Michoacán, and Mexico City.
    Néstor García Canclini, *Culturas híbridas* (1990)

All the major metropolises have been fully borderized. In fact, there are no longer visible cultural differences between Manhattan, Montreal, Washington D.C., Lost Angeles or Mexico Cida. They all look like downtown Tijuana on a Saturday night.
    Guillermo Gómez-Peña, *The New World (B)order* (1992)

El otro lado es la solución. / Por todas partes se oye el rumor. / Me voy de aquí. (The other side is the solution. / From every direction the rumor is heard. / I will leave from here.)
    Maldita Vecindad, "Mojado" (1991)

James Clifford once broadly described travel writing as a "paraethnographic" genre (1988, 24) and twentieth-century ethnography as "an evolving practice of travel writing" (1992c, 96). Rethinking "culture and its science, anthropology, in terms of travel," Clifford suggests, allows one to question "the organic, naturalizing bias of the term culture—seen as a rooted body that grows, lives, dies" (101). Culture theorized as "sites traversed"—as travel—thus enables one to concentrate on "differently centered worlds" and "interconnected cosmopolitanisms" (103).

In *Imperial Eyes,* Mary Louise Pratt suggests that travel was always part of a profound colonial encounter. European naturalists, sentimental travel writers, and their postcolonial traveling heirs, in other words, are "intertextually" part of the imperial infrastructure. Alexander von

Humboldt, for example, "never once stepped beyond the boundaries of the colonial infrastructure—[he] couldn't, for [he] relied on networks of villages, missions, outposts, haciendas, roadways, and colonial labor systems to sustain [himself] and [his] project for food, shelter, and the labor pool to transport [his] immense equipment" (Pratt 1992, 127). Almost all European male travel writers depended on local native inhabitants, almost all enjoyed semiofficial status, and their very well-being was guaranteed by the military.

Using Clifford's and Pratt's multiple insights about travel writing, autoethnography, and empire, I want to explore how four postcolonial "Alta" and Baja California travel writers and a performance video artist have, in various styles and forms, anatomized the exemplary border site of Tijuana, Mexico. Through a vivid imperializing rhetoric or an experimental counterautoethnographic expression, Beverly Lowry, Luis Alberto Urrea, Rubén Martínez, Richard Rodriguez, and Guillermo Gómez-Peña variously represent Tijuana as a constructed, contradictory, and disputed zone of the postmodern condition of depthlessness, displacement, and material syncretism.[1]

UNDER NORTH AMERICAN EYES

If travel writing as a genre is often about what Pratt calls creating "the domestic subject" of European and U.S. imperialism (4), then I think it might make some sense to begin our "cognitive mapping" of Tijuana by examining a paradigmatic article that appeared in the "Sophisticated Traveler" series in the *New York Times*.[2] Typically, the articles in this series are, as Rob Nixon astutely notes, "effectively literary advertisements, simultaneously dispatched to millions of readers, for solitary spots and uncorrupted 'authentic' cultures" (1992, 61). Thus in the same issue that extols the little island of Malta as a "palimpsest of cultures" (4), we also find Beverly Lowry's essay, "In Tijuana, Tacky Days and Velvet Nights." As we can infer from Lowry's catchy title, she displays an unreflective Californian's patronizing view of Baja California. Lowry's stance is complexly symptomatic: "It's a shock, how fast it happens. Your senses tell you what maybe your mind had not figured on: Tijuana is not San Diego. Baja is not California. You see the vendors and you *know.* You're in a different country. Even the light seems different. Smoky but sharper, more direct" (1992, 22; her emphasis).

From the very start, Lowry asserts her authoritative claims with a highbrow U.S. sensibility—confident that her *New York Times* readers share her assumptions about the "natural" differences between the northern metropole and its periphery to the South. These relations of core and periphery are articulated through Lowry's nuanced metaphors of light and darkness. Tijuana's light, she insists, is "sharper" and "more direct" than, say, the muted, nicer grays and beiges of San Diego, California. An imperial trope, we might say, following Pratt's logic, is immediately present here in Lowry's travel writing: the shocking mastery of the geopolitical border, the aestheticizing adjectives, and the subtle perceptions anchored in the traveler's gaze. The scene is also carefully ordered from the vantage point of a socially constructed white *norteamericana/o*: "you see," "your senses tell you what your mind has not figured on," "you know," and so on. At work throughout Lowry's article is what Pratt aptly has described in a different context as "the relation of *mastery* predicated between the seer and the seen" (1992, 204; her emphasis).

It is precisely the tone of the sophisticated traveler from Alta California that Lowry strains after in the essay. She is so set on seeing Tijuana and its inhabitants as other(s) that it is shocking that the travel writer can be so unaware that there are other postcolonial interpretations of Tijuana. Even her brief history of Tijuana's "golden age" is exclusively cast from the Anglocentric position: "In the 20s and early 30s, Tijuana was chic and full of promise. Movie stars went for the gambling casinos, the drink, the track. Tijuana was exotic; also liquor flowed. Then things changed. . . . Fashions changed. Tijuana became yesterday's great place to go" (22). What is striking in this brief account is that Lowry never attempts to see Tijuana's "underdevelopment" as a result of policies directly undertaken by the colossal to the North. And if Tijuana is "yesterday's great place to go," then, we might ask, why do more North American tourists (over fifty million per year) travel to Baja California's Tijuana than, say, to Alta California's Disneyland?

Attempting to win over an eager audience of U.S. tourists, in the remainder of the article Lowry describes Tijuana's "tackiness," its inauthenticity, its dirtiness, and its premodernity. For it is the rhetorical denunciation of Tijuana's tourist attractions that, ironically, feeds the very industry she denounces. As Nixon has noted about travel writing in general, "One might suggest that the rhetoric of antitourism is one of the surest ploys for enticing tourists" (1992, 61). It is tempting, therefore, to see in Lowry's article the relationship between tourism and antitourism as less a style of Manichaean aesthetics than as a shallow dialectic. While Lowry snubs one of Tijuana's major hotels ("The swimming pool water was tepid and uninviting"), its coffee shops ("the coffee was bad everywhere I tried it in Tijuana"), and its jai alai palace ("I was wild to go in, to see if the interior lived up to my expectations. To my great disappointment, the palace was dark. . . . The computers were down"), she continues her quest for the real, true, and authentic Tijuana sites that scores of tourists both love and hate (1992, 23, 25).

Playing off her "negative" U.S. tourist experiences, Lowry then rhapsodizes on the reified production of Tijuana's frenzied consumerism:

> You can buy a lot of things in Tijuana. Perfume is duty free and almost half-price. So is liquor. As long as they are for personal use and not to sell, many prescription drugs can be bought over-the-counter. . . . Boots are amazingly cheap. Bargain-priced Rolex and Cartier watches are everywhere. (22)

And later:

> I went to an open-air-marketplace called Plaza de Artesanías, where I could find handcrafted goods. The marketplace was a series of small shops and stands. . . . I didn't buy anything. There was just too much of everything and in the end all of it started to look the same. (75)

If Lowry avoids playing into the hands of Tijuana's staged reification —she refuses to buy any of the local artisans' handcrafted goods—she nevertheless is quite adept at verifying its on-sight markers that proliferate around her, thus contributing to the dialectical process of maintaining a tourist gaze of the border cityscape. On the Avenida Revolución, for example, "still the main event" in Tijuana, tourists do "what they wouldn't dream of doing at home; all it takes is wearing a funny hat" (24). She also highlights and juxtaposes Tijuana's other points of interest —the statues of Cuahútemoc, Abraham Lincoln, and the Plaza de Zapatos "where some 200,000 pairs of shoes are for sale" (74).

Lowry's "In Tijuana, Tacky Days and Velvet Nights" is notable, finally, because she consistently shows how unselfconscious she is about her own privileged perspective. While her essay hardly accounts for Tijuana's new demographic explosion of refugees and migrants from the South, her inability to feel anything for the city's forlorn subaltern is astonishing. Although she can give readers the "reality effect" of how "street urchins and beggars on the avenue swell" and "relentless children press crocheted crosses and boxes and chiclets into your arms" (89), all that she can remark about the Tijuanans is that "the people there seemed both cynical and sweet at the same time" (89).

To be sure, Lowry is sympathetic neither to the material hybrid and heteroglossic (sub)cultures of Tijuana nor to Tijuana's explosion of migrants who make up the underbelly of this U.S.-Mexico border metropolis. Suffering from a version of tourist homesickness, Lowry crosses the militarized border (without any problems) and, once safely back in Alta California, immediately notes how "the light softened. Familiar billboards and motel signs appeared, then the suburbs of San Diego. The houses . . . painted in soft gray, blue, or beige" (89). Briefly, operating in Lowry's travel article is what Pratt sees as exemplary of travel writing in general: "a discourse of negation" and "devaluation"— "the official metropolitan code of the third world, its rhetoric of triviality . . . and rejection" (219). Lowry's purpose in Tijuana is to search out, judge, and rhetorically mug the local.[3] Despite the fact that she is on largely unfamiliar turf, the U.S. travel writer claims the authoritativeness of her nuanced instrumentalized gazing. What Lowry sees is innocently all there is. Readers hardly get a sense of the limitations of her universalized panoramic view.[4]

The negative, devaluative, and detached view of Tijuana characteristic of Lowry's travel writing (what we might characterize as "under North American eyes") is by no means the only paradigm that grounds most Alta Californians' view of Baja California, though it is a familiar one. Chicano writers from the (extended) U.S.-Mexico borderlands have drawn quite different cognitive maps of Tijuana and San Diego. As Chicanos, north from Mexico, they do not easily take up the unreflective colonialist gazes of mainstream metropolitan writers. Against Lowry's characteristic impulse to condemn what she sees in Tijuana, I now want to turn to four U.S.-Mexico border writers and travelers who recenter Tijuana from a traditionally peripheral position to a more liminal one, and who experimentally portray themselves by using a mix of local and global symbologies, terms, and genres. Rather than conventional travel writers or ethnographers, the group of U.S.-Mexico border writers discussed here may be described as what Pratt splendidly calls "autoethnographers," who refashion traditions through cross-cultural contact. "Autoethnography" or "autoethnographic expression," in Pratt's definition, "refer to instances in which colonized subjects undertake to represent themselves in ways that engage with the colonizer's own terms"

(1992, 7). This comparative approach opens up a more fully histori-cized and interactive cultural studies project.

TRAVEL, EVANGELIZATION,
AND AUTOETHNOGRAPHY

One of the most riveting and paradoxical border autoethnographies about Tijuana is Luis Alberto Urrea's *Across the Wire* (1993). We might even be inclined to comprehend Urrea himself as a bundle of contra-dictions oscillating between travel writer and Baptist evangelist, Baja Tijuana and Alta San Diego, Mexican father and white North Ameri-can mother. But Urrea gives us little evidence that he feels overly divided by these public and personal contexts. Rather, Urrea's particular slant is that of the "native" autoethnographer, a sensitive, participant observer of the Mexico-U.S. *frontera:* "*Across the Wire* deals with my experi-ences in parts of the Borderlands that no tourist will ever see. It is sub-jective and biased, and I believe that is the way it should be. I have avoided presenting the people who live there as 'noble savages.' Poverty ennobles no one; it brutalizes common people and makes them hungry and old" (2).

Diametrically opposed to the disassociated and largely ethnocentric portrait of Tijuana offered by Beverly Lowry, Urrea casts himself as a positioned geocultural subject—"biased" and "subjective"—who will offer us a hard-nosed representation of the Mexican border megalopolis "that no tourist will see." "Wrung from about fifteen hundred pages of notes gathered with the [Spectrum Incorporated] missionaries from 1978 to 1982," Urrea's narrative tells, in wire-tight fragments, the sweep-ing stories of refugees and migrants who live on the Mexican side of the California borderlands. Part travel writer, part observer participant, and "official translator" of the crew of Baptist relief workers he joins, Urrea documents the heroic struggle of the newly arrived Tijuanans who are largely invisible to the swarms of U.S. tourists who only "do" the Avenida Revolución.

Urrea's *Across the Wire* touches on the themes and divisions of travel writing and ethnography. It describes the Mexican border habitat of the refugees, their lack of nutrition and health care services, and their everyday rituals and desires. The picture is not of a smoothly functioning (sub)culture. The voiceless and powerless refugees—as displaced indi-viduals from El Salvador, Guatemala, Nicaragua, and Mexico's *frontera sur*—are in desperate trouble, and Urrea powerfully documents this fact. "In Tijuana and environs," he wryly notes—overturning colonialist rhetoric about U.S.-Mexico border contamination and pathology—"we met the many ambassadors of poverty: lice, scabies, tapeworm, pinworm, ringworm, fleas, crab lice. We met diphtheria, meningitis, typhoid, polio, *turista* (diarrhea), . . . whooping cough. We met madness and demon possession" (10). The autoethnographer is also particularly vivid in his postmodernist warlike dispatches describing the militarized U.S. *frontera* contact zone: "At night, the Border Patrol helicopters swoop and churn in the air all along the line. You can sit in the Mexican hills and watch them herd humans on the dusty slopes along the valley. They look like science fiction crafts, their hard-focused lights raking the ground as they fly" (11).

From the start Urrea finds himself enmeshed in a complex culture at the Tijuana municipal garbage dump, a border habitus involving local wars over turf, intragroup politics, and creative bilingual borderspeak. He enters the thick of the fray by consciously aestheticizing the view of San Diego from the hilltop Tijuana dump:

> One of the most beautiful views of San Diego is from the summit of a small hill in Tijuana's municipal garbage dump. People live on that hill. . . . They scavenge for bottles, tin, aluminum, cloth. . . . In that stinking blue haze, amid nightmarish sculptures of charred ribs and carbonized tails, the garbage-pickers can watch the buildings of San Diego gleam on the blue coastline. The city looks cool in the summer when heat cracks the ground and flies drill into their noses. (31)

As a travel writer in Tijuana (whose discourse begins with looking), Urrea, like Beverly Lowry before him, is stunned by the views of the U.S.-Mexico border landscape. Attempting to grasp the stark contrasts between Tijuana's "nightmarish" squalor and the "gleam[ing]" city of San Diego "on the blue coastline," he is preoccupied by a geocultural aesthetics of place. His sensitivity to scale, form, and beauty manifests itself ironically, for he cannot not articulate the economic differences between the South and the North.

Using the techniques of the classic ethnographer, who typically attempts to explain unfamiliar cultural systems in the hinterlands to those in the "main" lands, Urrea works hard at making the refugee's habitus on the hill understood: "Each *dompe*," he writes, "has its own culture, as distinct as the people living there. . . . Each of these *dompes* has its own pecking order. Certain people are 'in.' Some families become power brokers due to their relationships to the missionaries who invariably show up. . . . Some *dompes* even have 'mayors'; some have hired goons, paid off by shady syndicates, to keep the trash-pickers in line" (31–32).

A context of unequal exchange, wherein the subaltern Tijuanans must pay what Urrea calls "a ransom" to other border citizens higher on the class scale, is introduced into the mix. The importance of this process for Urrea is twofold. First, he can show the sociological and political forces that the newly arrived migrants constantly struggle against. Second, he then can move on in his jolting dispatches to the harrowing stories of the migrants and refugees to whom he gives aid in the *dompes*. Throughout *Across the Wire*, he desires to respond simultaneously to those North American xenophobes who view the migrants' journey from the South to the North as pathological and to those Mexican bureaucrats in Mexico City who see Tijuana and its inhabitants as inauthentic, culturally contaminated by the North. "A Mexican diplomat once confided to me," Urrea recalls, "'We both know Tijuana is not Mexico. The border is nowhere. It's a no-man's-land'" (20). But it is also, we learn, the place where Urrea himself was born.

Early on, the evangelist-traveler introduces the Amerindian Pacha, a woman with "startling eyes" whose flight from Mexico's *frontera sur* stops at the U.S.-Mexico border dump site. "Pacha's eldest daughter offered to pay me to smuggle her across the border," he writes. "She was pregnant—her husband had gone across the wire and never come back. She watched for him on a neighbor's television. I told her I couldn't do it. . . . On New Year's morning, she had her baby in the free clinic in Tijuana. The nurse took the infant and dunked it in a tub of icy water. It had a heart attack and died. It was a girl" (40). This postmodern realist tale sets in motion a series of extraordinary refugee and migrant stories, including stories of rape, gang *matanza* (massacre), and demon possession.

The autoethnographer wants to shake up his jaded Alta California readers: "There is a sad swirl of humanity in Tijuana. Outsiders eddy there who have simply run out of strength. If North America does not want them, Tijuana wants them even less." He also implores his readers to look hard for this "sad swirl of humanity": "To see them, . . . climb up the little canyons all around the city, where the cardboard shacks and mud and smoke look like a lost triptych by Hieronymous Bosch" (19–20).

If Urrea's *Across the Wire* is a compendium of brutal fragmentary vignettes of the Tijuana *dompe* that "smelled like hell" (44), it is also laced with the evangelist's tenderness for the "outcasts of the outcast" (20). His portrait of Ana María, a young garbage-picker referred to as "Negra," is especially memorable: "Negra was a tiny barefoot girl who had curly black hair and large, startling white teeth. She was so skinny that she was firm as wood; when you picked her up, you could feel her angular pelvis and the chicken-wing bones in her back" (59). Like the majority of refugee children in Tijuana, Ana María—originally from Michoacán—lives in a decayed shack with her mother and sister. Not surprisingly, Ana María's father is nowhere to be seen in the garbage dump. His "obvious destination was clearly visible about three miles to the north, being patrolled by helicopters" (59). Urrea movingly recounts how Ana María, always in her smoky "brown-grey" dress, became an apprentice to his evangelical work. She "help[ed] me give out food to the women, whispering secrets in my ear," and even initiated him in the daily rituals of fastidiously picking trash. "We'd take our poles and wade into the mounds. She wanted tin cans to sell for scrap, and any unbroken bottles were small treasures" (60).

Urrea understandably becomes attached to Ana María, and he painfully recalls his inability to give her the big doll that she begs him for one Christmas: "I had no money at the time. None. When not in Tijuana, I worked as a part-time tutor in a community college for roughly four hundred dollars a month. One of the students at the college overheard me talking about this poor girl with no Christmas, and surprised me a few days later with a thirty-dollar doll with red hair and blinking eyes. When Negra opened the package, she cried" (61).

Fundamentally, *Across the Wire* is a minimalist tale of the autoethnographer's deeply felt struggle to make sense of Pacha's and Ana María's (as well as other refugees') forlorn lives: "For me, the worst part was the lack of a specific enemy. We were fighting a nebulous, all-pervasive *It*. Call it despair. Call it the Devil, the System, Capitalism, the Fruits of Mexican Malaise. It was a seemingly endless circle of disasters. Long after I'd left the wheel kept on grinding" (10–11; his emphasis). Nevertheless, for all his careful insights into the real human hurts of poverty in the U.S.-Mexico borderlands and his powerfully articulated rage at and admiration for the Tijuanans' *lucha* (struggle), we are left with Urrea's silence on his own imperial complicity as missionary and traveling ethnographer.

Across the Wire travels bumpily within the imperial context. Urrea's deeply fraught emotional struggle to understand the refugees' enemy cannot be reduced to what he poetically calls a "nebulous, all-pervasive It." Pacha and Ana María are part of a larger group of powerless, "unhomely" migratory individuals who are in flight. Refugees, as Bertolt Brecht once put it, are "messenger[s] of ill-tiding" (quoted in Nixon 1992, 23). "The wheel that keeps on grinding," to use Urrea's trope, is the tyranny and catastrophe imposed on the refugees by the Reagan-Bush-Clinton military-supported Centroamericano governments to the South.

On another level, Urrea turns a blind eye to the very epistemological issues raised by his compassionate book. Are insider, observer participants able to study the displaced migrants and refugees without asserting power over them? Do missionary and ethnographic texts needlessly contribute to the hegemonic social science process of culture collecting? Lest I be misunderstood, Urrea's *Across the Wire* passionately smuggles across the U.S.-Mexico border line a discrepant cosmopolitan world that never has been acknowledged by either Mexico or the United States. My hesitation is that Urrea's book might have been conceptually stronger if he had reflected more on the evangelist-anthropological processes themselves—what Clifford described as anthropology's "specific dialectics of power, of translation" (1992b, 125).

All the more frustrating is Urrea's inability to acknowledge that the forms of imperial dominion have often been concretized in the personas and functions of the traveler, especially the missionary and the anthropologist. It goes without saying that the Spectrum Baptist missionary and the traveling border autoethnographer dramatically unite in Urrea's work. Clifford's astute meditations on the Christian evangelist and the anthropologist are worth quoting in full:

> The figure of the Christian evangelist is, of course, as old as the Pentecostal gift of languages to the Apostles. The persona of the anthropologist is newer, more narrowly identified with the modern imperial period. However, the two roles are the products of a common cultural heritage: an amalgam of Greek rationality and Christian universalism. If the evangelist goes to the end of the earth to transform the heathen, the ethnographer goes to study them. Both participate in a restless Western desire for encountering and incorporating others, whether by conversion or comprehension. (126)

While Urrea readily (defensively) acknowledges that he "never intended to be a missionary," that he "didn't go to church," and that the Baptist preacher Erhardt George von Trutzchter got him "involved in the hardships and discipline he calls Christian Boot Camp" (1993, 21), his autoethnography remains trapped in the antinomy of the missionary and the ethnographer. Thus envisaged, *Across the Wire* uncovers the predicament Urrea unconsciously sets up for himself: a contemplative and spiritual concern for the refugees and an evangelistic will to convert them. Urrea, following in the high rhetorical colonial discourse tradition, thus can write of the traveling Amerindians Pacha and José, "They were pagans when they came north, of full Indian blood, and not used to the church services or ministers" in the Tijuana garbage dump (38). He can also confess, "God help me—it was fun. It was exciting and nasty. I strode, fearless, through the Tijuana garbage dumps and the Barrio of Shallow Graves. I was doing good deeds, and the goodness thrilled me. But the squalor, too, thrilled me" (27). This druglike sanctimonious intensity is the postmodernist predicament of the autoethnographer-evangelist in the militarized U.S.-Mexico borderlands, for throughout *Across the Wire* Urrea not only maps *la frontera* as a Vietnamlike spatial war zone but also describes what Michael Herr in *Dispatches* called (borrowing from Chicano "grunts" in Vietnam) *la vida loca*—the hallucinogenic excitement, the military structures of eroticism, the intensities and "rushes" that feel like euphoria.[5]

There is an already given vision to Lowry's and Urrea's travel writing about Tijuana. If the traveling *norteamericana* tourist seeks what Paul Fussell has called "the security of cliché," the traveling evangelist (unwittingly) moves toward "appropriating" the other (1980, 39).

WRITING HYBRID CULTURES

Rubén Martínez's autoethnography-*crónica*[6] *The Other Side* (1992)—which translates to "El Otro Lado," the name *centroaméricanos* and *mexicanos* give to California and the United States—supplements the vision of Tijuana provided by Lowry and Urrea. Because of Martínez's personal background, the son of a Mexican father and a Salvadoran mother, displaced by the Latin American diaspora from the South into the North, it is hardly surprising that one of the book's central quests is the discovery of "home." Through experimental *crónicas,* interviews, poems, photographs, and spiritual meditations, Martínez gathers his border-crossing writings from Los Angeles, San Salvador, Mexico City,

Havana, and Tijuana to explore what he announces in the book's original hardback subtitle: fault lines, guerrilla saints, and the true heart of rock 'n' roll. He is particularly adept at querying the presumption that cultural and political identities are tightly secured categories by recording powerful conversations with Salvadoran FMLN guerrilla exiles, East Los Angeles hip-hop graffiti artists, mestizo *rockeros* in the "funky hoyos" of Mexico City, and Tijuana performance artists. As Alejandro Portes puts it, Martinez "drags us mercilessly through the back alleys where [the roots of the U.S. Latino drama] are lived and endured every day" (1993, 40).

But Martínez, unlike Lowry and Urrea, from the start scrambles the geopolitical map of the U.S.-Mexico border:

> I have lived both in the North and the South over my twenty-nine
> years, trying to be South in the South, North in the North, South in
> the North and North in the South. Now I stand at the center—watching
> history whirl around me as my own history fissures: my love shatters,
> North and South, and a rage arises from within as the ideals of exis-
> tential unity crumble. My quest for a true center, for a cultural, politi-
> cal and romantic home, is stripped of direction. (1992b, 1)

His quest moves across an inter-American space where things are not easily in place—North and South—where the traveler can go across the border line and safely return home. Identity, both cultural and geopolitical, for the author, is never a homecoming (neither Los Angeles nor San Salvador), never a moment of arrival, but seemingly a dizzying departure. For example, in his poem "La Distancia," he characteristically asks, "Why are we always leaving / to arrive nowhere?" (75). And when he journeys to San Salvador to report on the devastating earthquake of 1986 for the *L.A. Weekly,* and to check up on his ailing grandparents, he ruefully writes of what he calls "another homecoming. My second home. My first home. My no-home" (30). Such a deconstruction of "home" allows the autoethnographer from Los Angeles to undo the traditional home/abroad oppositions so common in travel writing. Caught between cultures and ethno-racial group formations in the Américas, none of which, he intimates, is sufficient for him, the travel writer uses his interstitial geocultural space to reflect on the "interconnected cosmopolitanisms" of Los Angeles and Tijuana.

In one of the best chapters in *The Other Side,* "Tijuana Burning," Martínez writes, "I have come here thinking that perhaps by studying this city, I will learn something about Los Angeles. After all, isn't L.A. the new Ellis Island, the up-and-coming multicultural capital of the world, the City of the Future? A kind of inverted reflection of L.A.," he theorizes, "exists . . . in Tijuana . . . , the city without which L.A. would not be L.A." (83). In other words, like Tijuana, Los Angeles is involved in cultural contestation, displacement, and reconversion.[7] Provocatively, Martinez's remappings of Los Angeles anticipate George Sánchez's view that "understanding California's role in [late] twentieth-century American culture is crucial," for presently "Los Angeles International Airport welcomes more immigrants than any other port of entry in American history. Public mythology, however, still reveres Ellis Island and the Statue of Liberty and looks toward Europe. Historical writing on immigration in the U.S. surely suffers from this severe regional imbalance" (1993, 13). My own view is that Martinez's *The Other Side* goes a long way in addressing precisely the hegemonic "regional imbalance" of Anglocentric historiography that Sánchez bemoans and contributes to a major remapping of the American *Bildung* at our *fin de siglo*.

At the cultural level, Tijuana's features, Martínez notes, are radically being redrawn "by a group of young local artists whose work reflects the clashing, the melding, the hybridization of culture that is taking place here, virtually invisible to the Northern eye" (1992b, 84). Like García Canclini's critique of the mass culture industry in *Culturas híbridas* (see chapter 1), Martínez's reading of Tijuana as a site of material "cultural hybridity" is particularly lucid and innovative. In *The Other Side,* Tijuana's (mass) culture industry—represented by its official and unofficial sites at the Casa de Cultura and at various underground cafes and discos such as El Nopal Centenario—is analyzed as a matrix that decenters an artistic experience more compatible with the relocations and deterritorializations that are produced by the fragmentariness and migrations of urban life than with traditional conceptions of high and popular culture. New forms of sensibilities, new faces of production and circuits of cultural flows can be found in what Martínez sees as a "genuine alternative cultural movement" launched by Tijuana's performance artists: "The artists who now make up the Nopal community carefully orchestrated a coup d' état by first approaching the conservative administration as innocent volunteers. Soon they were producing events. . . . [P]erformance pieces . . . and a series of children's workshops replaced the abstract works and traditional theater of the previous managers" (88).

Martínez's particular slant on Tijuana as a materially hybridized city facilitates an alternative way of grappling with what is today known as identity politics—not as a rigid essentialism but rather as the project of a vernacular renovation (what one border artist calls *rasquachismo*) with which diverse groups can take charge of the city. For example, at the working-class club La Estrella, near La Revo, he writes how "the *cumbia*, with its two-chord arrangements and horse-trot rhythm, is a campesino tradition from the south of Mexico, but here it is in urbanized Tijuana, part of the cultural baggage of the millions of Southerners who have come north seeking work" (94–95).

To be sure, the demands made on the concept of hybridity by Tijuana (and Mexico City for that matter) are rather large. Hybridity as performance art "ritual" means for Martínez the transformation of concepts such as high art and popular art. At a more empirical level, Martínez sees hybridity as part and parcel of a new border landscape and diaspora community: "The neon burns, the music blasts. The North is here—the disco music. The South is here—the *norteñas* and *cumbias*." Even Tijuana's architecture reeks of the hybrid: "la Revo today," he quotes a professor of philosophy at the University of Baja California, "[is] a mishmash of Deco, Neo-Colonial, and Bauhaus" (90). Likewise, Martínez's journalistic riffs on what he calls the *corazón de rocanrol* (heart of rock and roll) take us inward to the interior spaces of the "funky hoyos" in and around Mexico City. "Where else," Martinez approvingly quotes a local *chilango* (native of Mexico City), "could [*rocanrol*] have exploded into being other than in the biggest city in the world, where soot and sex and social unrest are legendary" (160). It is here in Mexico City where the traveling journalist explores both the bodies and the faces of young rebellious *punkeros* and *los niños bien* (young people of the upper middle class) at Zona Rosa hangouts like Rockstock and El LUCC with the same freedom that he earlier surveyed the Tijuana landscape. We go inside exotic dance clubs where *rocanrol* bands such as Maldita Vecindad y Los Hijos del Quinto Patio (The Damned Neighborhood and the Sons of the Tenement) "float tequila-inspired riffs . . . , steamrolling crazily toward a great abyss, [and] drunk boys dar[e] each other as they look in the darkness" (165).

Not surprisingly, it is in the interior spaces of the "funky hoyos" where Martínez locates the material hybridity of culture that he had earlier celebrated in Tijuana's performance art scenes and architecture. With what the autoethnographer lyrically describes as "precise fury, styles merged, overturned, and burned" (165), "rock en español" bands such as Maldita Vecindad and Cafe Tacuba perform noisy music of intercultural bricolage. Thematizing what George Lipsitz sees as rock music's "facility for cultural fusion" and its potential for resisting "univocal master narratives" (1990, 136, 149), Mexico City *rocanrol* transculturates music from both the South and the North: "Ska gives way to funk, funk to rap, rap to *son veracruzano,* to *danzón,* to *cumbia* and Mambo" (Martínez 1992b, 156). Like Tijuana, Mexico City's "funky hoyos" are also sites of a new, postmodern cultural dominant: "Mexico City intellectuals are only half joking when they say that postmodernism actually originated here five hundred years ago, with the Conquest and its clash of radically different sensibilities" (157).

What is implicit in Martínez's travel writing about Tijuana and Mexico City is that both cities' hip performance artists act as synecdoches for his analysis of the processes of postcolonial hybridizations. But are all urban metropolises in the Americas borderized? Are Tijuana, Mexico City, and Los Angeles spaces of an extended "neoterritoriality"? Can we reduce Tijuana's place in the Americas to theatrical or architectural style or to the dizzying juxtapositionings of its statues of Cuahútemoc and Lincoln?

Last, one of the things that surprises us about Rubén Martínez as a cultural listener is that, as Josh Kun wonderfully points out, "music is never where he expects it" (n.d.). For example, when Martínez travels to Havana, he is startled to hear a musical cosmopolitanism that includes salsa, disco, jazz, and the Latin American *nueva canción* (new song). Similarly, he is confounded when he comes across Chicano/a hip-hop graffiti artists in Los Angeles who listen not only to "lowrider oldies" but also to brown and black hip-hop music—"all together now danc[ing] to Easy E and BDP, crossing every border ever held sacred" (1992b, 136–137).

As it stands, Martínez's *The Other Side* can be described as a quintessential U.S.-Mexico border-crossing autoethnography. As Guillermo Gómez-Peña suggests, Rubén Martínez "is a poet who ventures into journalism, and vice-versa. He is a Latino from el norte who travels in search of the other selves—constantly seeking to reveal the richness and the conflicts emerging from the interstices between countries, languages, and generations." Richard Rodriguez goes even farther in his enthusiastic assessment of Martínez's book: "Here is the voice of the new Los Angeles."[8] Gómez-Peña and Rodriguez are both absolutely right, for Martínez's autoethnography writes into existence an alternative geography by mapping an emergent transnational, U.S. Latino/a identity. Indeed, there is an astonishment provoked by the dizzying conjunction of Salvadoran and Chicano hybridities in Los Angeles.

So considered, Martínez's *The Other Side* undoes the stereotyped and essentialized identities that are usually entrenched in rigid geographic locations in cities such as Los Angeles: Chicano East Los Angeles versus Salvadoran Salvatrucha. It might not be too far-fetched to say that Martínez desires a new geography that makes room for a different geocultural, political, and migratory axis—a map that connects civil war–torn El Salvador to the postmodern "scanscoped" police culture of Los Angeles. Late in his autoethnography, Martínez can therefore ask, "Was that a shotgun? In answer, a series of pops. . . . I crouch by the window, look into the hazy balmy night. . . . Now, from afar, another sound begins, like the whine of a mosquito in the darkness of a stifling room in the tropics. The whine becomes a roar that rattles the windows." But, of course, Martínez is not "crouched" in a tropical room in Central America. Rather, he is in a tropicalized Los Angeles: "this is 1991, not 1979, and San Salvador and Los Angeles gang [and police] strife and civil war all at once" (165).

Martínez's final chapter, "L.A. Journal," takes up the discussion of "home" in terms of its opposite—what he calls "anti-home." During one of the now-commonplace LAPD search-and-destroy missions in predominantly U.S. Latino neighborhoods in Los Angeles, the autoethnographer gathers "objects from the living and the dead" from his various travels: a photograph of his exiled Central American girlfriend; a cassette sleeve photo of a rock group from Mexico City;[9] a black-and-white snapshot of an East Los Angeles homeboy and graffiti artist "cradling his brutally scarred arm, [the] result of an evening when the bullets did find their mark"; a decaying leaf from Palm Sunday mass at La Placita; and a "rather ugly postcard entitled 'La Frontera, Tijuana, BC,' that shows an antiseptic-clean highway on one side and a labyrinth of dusty paths on the other" (166). These mementos, Martínez writes, are "as close as I get to 'home.'" For him, "home" comes to be metonymically associated with the South. It is the conducive site of healing, where the individual is sutured with the collective. But the South is also in the North, "because L.A. is my home and L.A. is anti-home. . . . Taking to the road, I've crossed and recrossed the border heading south and north—trying to put things back in place" (166). Martínez's North, Los

Angeles, is first defined negatively as the opposite of home. But the author's "anti-home" is also the enabling space and concept where utopian remappings can be put "back in place."

To conclude our cognitive mapping of Tijuana and the extended U.S.-Mexico borderlands of Alta and Baja California, I want to examine the widely read and much-commented-on autoethnography *Days of Obligation* (1992) by Richard Rodriguez and the experimental video *Border Brujo* (1990) by Guillermo Gómez-Peña. I end with Rodriguez's lucid travel writing and Gómez-Peña's *frontera* videotext because their work provokes both celebration and disdain.[10] It hardly needs emphasizing (for those who followed the controversy over the author's first book, *Hunger of Memory* [1981]) that Rodriguez's admirers were once predominantly white, male editors and reviewers associated with the mainline publishing world in the northeastern United States. Many of the eleven chapters that make up Rodriguez's *Days of Obligation* first appeared in powerful publications such as the *American Scholar, Harper's* magazine, the *New Republic,* and *Time.*

Rodriguez's prestige as a mainstream writer has assisted him in presenting himself as the most renowned Chicano interpreter of the Pacific Rim, including San Francisco, Los Angeles, and Tijuana. Moreover, by moving beyond his literary *Hunger of Memory,* venturing into travel writing, and solidifying his successful career as a senior editor for the Pacific News Services in San Francisco, a contributing editor for *Harper's,* and an "essayist" for the PBS *Lehrer NewsHour,* Rodriguez has achieved a formidable reputation that has surpassed that of the "ex-centric" literary writer. Like V. S. Naipaul, the travel writer and journalist who is "treated as a mandarin possessing a penetrating, analytic understanding of Third World societies" (Nixon 1992, 4), Rodriguez has brilliantly metamorphosed into an "expert" on things (pan-)Latino. Rodriguez has become such an expert that the British Broadcasting Company hired him to serve as what he calls a "presenter" for a television documentary on the United States and Mexico. All the more remarkable, as Rodriguez himself wryly notes in *Days of Obligation,* is that the presenter was "a man who spent so many years with his back turned to Mexico. Now I am to introduce Mexico to a European audience" (1992, xv–xvi).

Rodriguez's *Days of Obligation* is everything that *Hunger of Memory* was not precisely in its obsession to explore North-South relationships in the Americas. While his first work billed itself as "an American story," it had surprisingly little to say about Alta and Baja California. The U.S.-Mexico borderlands of Tijuana and San Diego were of no real interest to him.

In *Days of Obligation* Rodriguez the traveling journalist journeys to Mexico to explore the country "he [once] turned his back to," the country, he claims, he had never really known—his childhood travels with his family in the late 1950s from Sacramento to Tijuana notwithstanding. "This isn't Mexico . . . my mother kept saying, clucking, smoothing. Tijuana is just a border town; you see the worst here, you'll see" (82). Some forty years later, Rodriguez, now a middle-aged man, responds to his mother's cultural tweaking of Tijuana by grandly boasting that Tijuana has become "his America." "I don't want to say that I'm more Mexican, because that is saying too much. . . . [But] I realized how much of Mexico is in California" (quoted in M. Rodriguez 1992, 13). "Tijuana," he continues, "is even more American than San Diego" (13)—meaning, I suppose, that the optimism and energy that was once the exclusive domain of Alta California has also crossed the border into the South.

One of the most powerful images of Rodriguez as traveler is that of Rodriguez as "Pocho," on his knees "heaving" in his tony Mexico City hotel:[11]

> I am on my knees, my mouth over the mouth of the toilet, waiting to heave. It comes up with a bark. All the badly pronounced Spanish words I have forced myself to sound during the day, bits and pieces of Mexico spew from my mouth, warm, half-understood, nostalgic reds and greens dangle from long strands of saliva.
> I am crying from my mouth in Mexico City.
> Yesterday, the nausea began. (xv)

Rodriguez here seems to feel the need to "out-touricize" U.S. tourists, hence the dramatic opening portrait of the traveler from the North suffering from what is popularly known as Montezuma's revenge—nausea and diarrhea. On a different register, the autoethnographer is accurately presenting Mexicans' stereotypical view of the Chicano/a who is unable or unwilling to master the Spanish language. While Rodriguez often indulges in conjuring overused images of Mexico in his travel writing— suffering mothers, machos, and Chingadalupes[12]—his real purpose is to carefully dissect the idea of national identity that has been socially constructed by bourgeois Mexican male intellectuals such as Samuel Ramos and Octavio Paz. As the anthropologist Roger Bartra taught us, Ramos's *Profile of Man in the History of Mexico* (1930) and Paz's *Labyrinth of Solitude* (1950) discussed the supposed inferiority of Mexicans and Chicanos. Ramos's mythical symbol of the nation, as Bartra notes, was the *pelado,* "a kind of urban peasant . . . half-asphyxiated by the city, who has lost the rural paradise and has not found the promised land" (1992, 33). Fundamentally, Ramos depicted in the *pelado* a person dominated by feelings of inferiority and encaged within the cruel theater of melancholy.

Although Rodriguez's *Days of Obligation* does not explicitly contest Ramos's mythical trope of national identity, several sections take Octavio Paz's nationalist work head on:

> In 1959 [*sic*], Octavio Paz, Mexico's sultan son, her clever one—
> philosopher, poet, statesman—published *The Labyrinth of Solitude,*
> his reflections of Mexico. Within his labyrinth, Paz places as well the
> Mexican American. He writes of the *pachuco,* the teenage gang member, and, by implication, of the Mexican American: "The *pachuco* does
> not want to become a Mexican again; at the same time he does not
> want to blend into the life of North America. His whole being is sheer
> negative impulse, a tangle of contradictions, an enigma." (1992, 58)

If the *pelado,* for Ramos, is the "best exemplar" to study the Mexican "because he constitutes the most elemental and well-portrayed expression of the national character" (Bartra 1992, 53), the pachuco in Los Angeles, for Paz, is the perfect trope for describing Chicanos—the "contemptuous" city-dwelling figure who has lost his cultural identity north from Mexico.

Paz's mythic figure of the pachuco, of course, is insulting to Rodriguez the traveler from the North. Paz was writing about the pachuco from his vantage point as bourgeois intellectual from the South. Having come to Los Angeles at about the time of the infamous zoot suit riots, Paz's views of Chicanos were not only parochial but also remarkably ethnocentric: "the *pachuco* is an impassive and sinister clown whose purpose is to cause terror instead of laughter" (1985, 16). The pachuco, for Paz, was a "sadist," a "masochist," and a "criminal" whose only desire in the North was to provoke Anglocentric Los Angeles into paradoxically "redeem[ing] him and break[ing] his solitude" through brutal "persecution" (17). Rodriguez's wry response to Paz is on target: "This was Mother Mexico talking, her good son; this was Mexico's metropolitan version of Mexican Americans. Mexico had lost language, lost gods, lost ground. Mexico recognized historical confusion in us. We were Mexico's Mexicans" (1992, 58). Let me hasten to add that some fourteen years earlier Américo Paredes had set the Chicano/a response to Paz by writing, "Paz's insensitivity to the problems and the potentialities of the young Los Angeles Mexicans is rooted in other causes. He speaks to us not with the voice of the future but with that of the past."[13]

Throughout *Days of Obligation,* Rodriguez displays even less tolerance for Paz's "reflections on Mexico" by disputing one of the classic text's main theses, the North's economic and cultural hegemony over the South.[14] Like Rubén Martínez before him, Rodriguez suggests that the South is in the North, that América Latina breathes in the United States and vice versa. This idea of the "borderization" of the hemisphere is stated early on in an account of one of his visits to Mexico City, sponsored by an American credit card company: "I take it as an Indian achievement that I am alive, that I am Catholic, that I speak English, that I am an American. My life began, it did not end, in the sixteenth century. . . . Here I am in the capital of death. Life surges about me; wells up from subways, wave upon wave. . . . Everywhere I look. Babies. Traffic. Food. Beggars. Life. Life coming upon me like a sunstroke" (24). Mexico, for Rodriguez, is ready to spill over across the wire into the North and take up the whole enchilada.

How different is this view of the inter-Americas from Rodriguez's largely ahistorical visions in *Hunger of Memory.* Nowadays, Rodriguez insists that he would not write his life history as a "pastoral" master narrative, drawing what he now rightly sees as a naive contrast between the innocence of the country and the corruption of the city. That slant, he suggests, would land him in Ramos's and Paz's camps. How can we begin to account for this sea change in Rodriguez's worldview? What happened to Rodriguez's mandarin views of daily life?

Some Rodriguez commentators suggest that his cultural and sexual politics radically changed when he came out of the closet and wrote an article about his native San Francisco entitled "Late Victorians" for *Harper's* in 1990 and which is reprinted in *Days of Obligation.* It is a sweeping essay about the Castro district, gay and yuppie gentrification of Victorian houses, and the domestication of the city and a moving memorial to his friend César who contracted AIDS in the city's bath houses. Rodriguez's article unmasked both the positive and the negative aspects of what he now refers to as the "queer" scene. Although the writer alluded to his own sexual orientations in *Hunger of Memory* when he wrote about the brown muscular bodies of the *bracero* laborers he saw as a young boy in Sacramento ("Queers," he asserts, "understood what I was saying"), Rodriguez now directly claims that "most gay men and women that I know see life at an angle. It's part of our brilliance. Part of the gay culture's excitement to me has been that eccentricity and that rebellion" (quoted in M. Rodríguez 1992, 14).

The other major event, I believe, was Rodriguez's decision to travel to Mexico, "if only to honor [his parents'] passage to California" and to work for the BBC. If the "youth of [his] life was defined by Puritan optimism," he now claims that in middle age he inclines "more toward the Mexican point of view" (R. Rodriguez 1992, xvii). This "Mexican point of view" is precisely what the autoethnographer brings to his spatial representation of Tijuana. We might even say that Rodriguez sagaciously combines the discrepant views of Tijuana by Lowry, Urrea, and Martínez that have appeared in this chapter—Tijuana as a hybrid and cosmopolitan city in the contact zone where refugees from the South interact with tourists from the North. Tijuana, for Rodriguez as it was for Martínez, is a mirror that helps us to better understand San Diego and the rest of Alta California. "Taken together as one," he writes, "Tijuana and San Diego form the most fascinating new city in the world" (106). With NAFTA now ratified, Rodriguez can confidently claim that "Tijuana is an industrial park on the outskirts of Minneapolis. Tijuana is a colony of Tokyo. Tijuana is a Taiwanese sweatshop," implicitly noting the rise of *maquiladora* culture in the borderlands of the world system.

If Tijuana "is poised at the beginning of an industrial age, a Dickensian city with palm trees," San Diego, the autoethnographer suggests, "is a postindustrial city of high-import plastic and despair diets" (84). Like Martínez before him, Rodriguez is particularly successful in redrawing our cognitive maps of the Americas: "San Diego faces west, looks resolutely out to sea. Tijuana stares north, as toward the future. . . . San Diego is the past, guarding its quality of life" (84).

As one of the fascinating new geocultural chroniclers of North-South interactions, Richard Rodriguez assumes a visionary and, in one sense, a special topospatial importance here. As we have seen, he is obsessed with undoing hegemonic readings of Baja and Alta California. He assails the Euro-American imperialist view of San Francisco as "the metaphor for the end of the line. Land's end." "To speak of San Francisco as land's end," he emphasizes, "is to read the map from one direction only as Europeans would read it or as the East Coast has always read it" (28). This reading of the map, Rodriguez argues, is not only provincial and "parochial" but smacks of the cultures of U.S. imperialism at its very worst. Against this east-west axis of the traditional American *Bildung,* the autoethnographer embraces his Mexican parents' geocultural view: "My parents came here from Mexico. They saw San Francisco as the North. They did not share the Eastern traveler's sense of running before the past—the darkening time zone, the lowering curtain" (29). For Rodriguez, the best view of postmodern California is not from the West's west view, as it were, but from the North—the hills of Tijuana.

One feels jolted to see Rodriguez's writing recover a cognitive mapping of Alta and Baja California not seen since, perhaps, Mike Davis's *City of Quartz.* Rodriguez seems to want to put behind the earlier polemical assaults on affirmative action and bilingual education and his early 1980s support for the English-only movement. Whereas in *Hunger of Memory* Rodriguez argued that only through Americanization—his euphemism for assimilation—could Chicanos expect to be incorporated into the United States, in *Days of Obligation* he dialectically negates and overturns that vision: the future of California is in its Latinoization.

IN / DIFFERENT VIDEO ART

Now I want to complete our exploratory mapping of Tijuana with a final analysis of that "euphoric" border city which in the words of Néstor García Canclini "reinvents itself and offers [us] new spectacles" (1992, 41). Let me reemphasize the enormity of a transition that leaves behind the secure clichés of Lowry's descriptions of Tijuana as tacky, velvety, brown kitsch and replaces them with Urrea's, Martínez's, Rodriguez's, and now Gómez-Peña's view of the U.S.-Mexico border megalopolis as having both decentered local and cosmopolitan characteristics. Like Urrea's view of Baja California, Gómez-Peña's description of Tijuana in *Border Brujo*—a video directed and produced by Isaac Artenstein—is that of an "infected wound," an intercultural site where many realities crash and burn, and where border *brujos* (shamans) are simultaneously postcolonial performance artists (with legal green cards) and "illegal aliens" with "typhoid and malaria" who "haven't been documented yet" (1993b, 78, 87).

Guillermo Gómez-Peña no longer casts himself as a border *brujo* or as an Aztec/high-tech theorist. Rather, he is now "the Warrior for Gringostroika"—which also happens to be the title of his collected work. This new nickname, of course, is a bilingual play on words that speaks to the political resonances of his postmodernist performances. As Gómez-Peña remarked in a 1991 *New York Times* feature story (written by Rubén Martínez), "There's been a whole process of self-criticism and change in the [former] Soviet Union, but we haven't had perestroika in the U.S." He continues by noting that "the Warrior for Gringostroika is a self-proclaimed 'social wrestler,' a champion of tolerance, reform, aperture and diversification regarding culture" (Martínez 1991, A5).

Perhaps as visionary as Chicana feminist Gloria Anzaldúa, Gómez-Peña has brought the term *border art*—a loose trope for multicultural tensions across the hemisphere and for what Claire F. Fox calls "a space of fantasy and sociopolitical allegory" (1994, 61)—into the mainstream, national arts discourse in the United States. Presently, he is at the center of a critical debate over his performance work. Conservative art critics, he claims, have labeled him a "reverse racist many times." But, he responds, "they're criticizing me for the wrong reason. My work is precisely about the space *in between* cultures and ideologies" (Martínez 1991, A5; his emphasis). Let me hasten to add that it is precisely this spatialization of "in-betweenness" in Gómez-Peña's work that has captivated audiences from all the Americas and won over the Canadian jury that awarded him the Prix de la Parole at the International Theatre of the Americas (1989) and the Chicago-based MacArthur committee that gave him a "genius" fellowship in 1991.

On stage or in front of the video camera, Gómez-Peña often rehearses his life history over and over again: a childhood in the sooty world capital of Mexico City, a grandmother reciting poetry, and street vendors barking out their wares. In *Border Brujo,* for example, one of his fifteen video alter egos freely confesses, "I'm a child of border crisis / a product of a cultural cesarean . . . born from . . . a howling wound / a flaming wound / for I am part of a new mankind . . . the migrant kind" (1990, 78). Growing up in Mexico City, Gómez-Péna was initially attracted to the theater of the spoken word on the mean streets and its mixing of popular cultural elements with avant-garde influences from all over the world. "Our studio," he told Rubén Martínez, "was the streets of the city" (Martínez 1991, A5). *Acciones poeticas* (poetic actions) became his obsession. His attempts to disrupt the bourgeois surface normality of La Capital, however, were short-lived. After numerous failed attempts to find what he called *el otro México* (the other Mexico), Gómez-Peña decided to do what many Mexicans had done for decades—go north to *el otro lado*.

Landing in the extended *frontera* of Los Angeles in the late 1970s, Gómez-Peña enrolled at the California Institute for the Arts. As Martínez explains, it was in Los Angeles that Gómez-Peña "experienced the existential isolation of exile, which drove his performance work of the time" (A5). In the "Performance Chronology" section of *The Warrior for Gringostroika*, for example, the performance artist includes the striking photograph of his 1979 solo "ritual" entitled "The Loneliness of the Immigrant," a forty-eight-hour "happening" in which he had fellow Cal Arts students wrap him up in an Indian rug and leave him in a tony Los Angeles high-rise. A text placed on a wall next to the elevator read, "Moving to another country hurts more than moving to another house, another face, another lover. . . . In one way or another we all are or will be immigrants. Surely one day we will be able to crack this shell open, this unbearable loneliness, and develop a transcontinental identity" (1993b, 125). From the very start, Gómez-Peña's interest in postmodernist "identity panic" and "transcontinental" performance *rituales* drove his "portable" U.S.-Mexico border-crossing work.

After a few years at the California Institute for the Arts Gómez-Peña tried unsuccessfully to relocate to Mexico City. But realizing that the North lives and breathes in the South and vice versa, he chose to make the liminal border zones of Tijuana–San Diego into what he called his new "studio space" (Martínez 1991, A5). In 1985 Gómez-Peña (along with Emily Hicks, David Avalos, and Michael Schnorr) founded the Taller de Arte Fronterizo / Border Arts Workshop (TAF/BAW), a performance artist collective that staged highly visible performance interventions on the U.S.-Mexico border line and published the lively journal *La Línea Quebrada*.[15] In an early manifesto published in *La Línea Quebrada*, Gómez-Peña indicated that the site-specific borderlands of Tijuana and San Diego forced him to write a different sort of theoretical account about identity and topography: *"Existen muchas fronteras. Demasiadas"* (There exist many borders. Too many). The manifesto itself heightened the dizzying number of cultural contrasts and shocks on the Tijuana–San Diego border: "Mariachis and surfers, cholos and punks, second-hand buses and helicopters, tropical whorehouses and video discotheques, Catholic saints and monsters from outer space, shanty houses and steel skyscrapers, bullfights and American football, popular anarchism and cybernetic behaviorism, Anglo-Saxon puritanism and Latin hedonism. Will they exist in peaceful coexistence or open warfare?" Fundamentally, what the traveling U.S.-Mexico border theorist called for was a new kind of cultural studies "capable of articulating our incredible circumstances" on *la frontera* (1986, 1).

The extended borderland of Tijuana and San Diego, for Gómez-Peña, is a vast textual machine, a hybrid cyborg that also can map out social and bodily realities. Gómez-Peña's Tijuana/San Diego is, like Haraway's "mestiza cyborg" (1991) and Anzaldúa's "Shadow Beast" (1987), a "cybernetic" organism with real potential for "popular anarchism." It is that which challenges, transforms, and shocks. It was therefore in the border zones of Tijuana and San Diego where Gómez-Peña's ideas about "in-betweenness" and cross-cultural relations in the Americas became the dominant theme of his experimental performance work. As he put it in an interview, "There is a great new fusion taking place between . . . the north and the south. . . . And I think that syncretism is as much a part of U.S. culture as it is in Latin America. The only difference is, the U.S. doesn't have a coherent discourse for it. The real wound in contemporary America is a matter of race and identity" (Martínez 1991, A35).

Seen in this light, as "misunderstanding between cultures" in the Américas, Gómez-Peña's *Border Brujo* takes on special meaning as "another strategy to let YOU know we [U.S. Latinos/as] are here to stay, / and we'd better begin developing a pact of mutual cultural understanding" (1990, 76). Emily Hicks's theorizing of border writing (emerging from her work in the TAF/BAW) can be very helpful here, for border writing writ large, she notes, is better conceptualized "as a mode of operation" than as a definition. By choosing what Hicks calls "a strategy of translation rather than representation," U.S.-Mexico border writers such as Gómez-Peña "undermine the distinction between original and alien culture" (1991, xxiii). How, then, does Gómez-Peña "translate" this new, cyborglike megalopolis of Tijuana? How are we supposed to read the rush of electronic video signals that are hot-wired into *Border Brujo*?

It has proved fruitful to think of video art in terms of what Fredric Jameson (after Sartre) calls our postcontemporary epoch's "objective neurosis." "Every age," he writes in his landmark book on postmodernism, "is dominated by a privileged form, or genre, which seems by its structure, the fittest to express its secret truth" (1991, 67). If, as Jameson suggests, literature with a capital "L" has now lost its exemplary status as our age's most privileged form, this is so because "literature" has been displaced by other mass-mediated forms such as commercial radio and television. Jameson goes on to argue that "for over seventy years now the cleverest prophets have warned us regularly that the dominant art form of the twentieth century was not literature at all—nor even painting, or theater, opera or the symphony—but rather film; the first mediatic art form" (68). In other words, film jolted us out of our "logocentrism" and paved the way for the emergence of the great auteurs of the 1950s—Hitchcock, Fellini, and Kurosawa. But, alas, according to Jameson, film and literature no longer stand as "the cultural dominant" of our postmodern "social and economic conjuncture," for the privileged form, "the richest allegorical vehicle" for describing the "system" we presently live in, is, of course, video—both as "commercial tv" and as "experimental video art" (69).

It is within this context of postmodern experimental video art that Gómez-Peña's *Border Brujo* can best be understood. Questions such as the following, therefore, appear on the video screen of U.S.-Mexico border theory: How are we to situate ourselves into the "total flow" of Gómez-Peña's *Border Brujo?* Is this videotext U.S.-Mexico *frontera* entertainment or advertisement in the NAFTA age? The latter question is perhaps easier to answer, for the screenplay's directions inform us that behind the border *brujo*'s *rasquachi* altar-stage, a digital billboard flashes that the performance is being "sponsored by the Turismo Fronterizo" of Baja California.

Border Brujo is, therefore, a deterritorialized visual-aural provocation, a calculated assault on the Alta Californians' act of gazing through North American eyes. At the same time the performance artist wants to "out" any INS or Border Patrol agents who might have come to deport the video auteur and his audience and continue the U.S. government's doctrine of low-intensity conflict:

> No, I have no green card and
> I was illegally hired by the gallery
> the director might receive employer's
> sanctions
> the INS might raid my audience

one of these nights
one of them
might even shoot me

.   .   .   .   .   .

[if] there is a Border Patrol agent in the audience
can he identify himself? (91)

But still other questions remain unanswered: How are viewers of the
fifty-two-minute videotext to sort the flowing electronic material into
thematic blocks and rhythms? How are we to make sense of the video's
scrambled and decentered climaxes, its transitions, the U.S.-Mexico border shaman's howlings, his speaking in Mayan-like tongues, and even
his unequivocal *coraje* (anger)?

To answer some of these questions, let me enumerate a few of the
experimental and hybrid video materials in *Border Brujo*. First there is
the rush of the videotext's soundtrack itself: the music the U.S.-Mexico
border shaman plays at the beginning of the video is "a collage of Tam-
bora, German punk, bilingual songs from Los Tigres del Norte, and
rap opera" (76). This is followed by the shifting multiple personalities
(15) of the U.S.-Mexico border *brujo* himself and his various *rasquachi*
costumes (altar jacket, Batman pins, dark sunglasses, Cheech and
Chong long-haired wigs, various hats—including a mariachi sombrero,
a panama hat sponsoring Corona beer, his wrestler Gringostroika
mask—and his hilarious banana necklace). At this point, there is a dizzying proliferation of what the border *brujo* calls his "Cyber-Bwana" identities and ethno-racial stereotypes of Latinos/as: an urban mestizo, a
Mexico City street vendor, a Tijuana barker, a *cura* (priest) reading a
psalm in Latin, a *vato loco* (smooth-talking gigolo), a *cholo,* a trans-
vestite, a TV evangelist, a Cantinflas dandy, a redneck southern Californian, an upper-class U.S. Latino from Miami, a radio newscaster, a
nativist sailor from San Diego, a hard-core political activist, and the
"schizo" *chilango*/Chicano shaman.

Sometimes these "identities" seem to be combined in the longer solil-
oquies offered by the U.S.-Mexico border *brujo*. Sometimes, as in the
transitions from a pensive Rossini or Beethoven sonata to the mass-mediated beats of Ry Cooder or the *cumbias* from the South, the principle
of postmodern hybridity and bifocality seems all too heavy-handed.
Sometimes the accelerated flow is meant to assault the Alta California
audience; and the total flow of the videotext is occasionally punctuated
with formal signals—for instance, the bilingual slogan "La identidad

es una ilusión optica" (Identity is an optical illusion), which is presumably designed to warn the viewer of the shifting sounds, howlings, and rumbles that are repeated over and over.

All this postmodern shiftiness comes to a dramatic closure in the final shot where the U.S.-Mexico border *brujo* drinks from a bottle of green Herbal Essence shampoo, thus borrowing freely from the connotative language of transnational TV commercials. It is all, after all, a fifty-two-minute visual border *ficción,* or better still, a biting border *burla* (joke). Were you expecting something more serious from a traveling performance artist who typically describes himself throughout the videotext as someone feeling "no ground under my feet / I'm floating, floating" (85), or as "l'enfant terrible de la frontiere" (88), or even as an undocumented video freak addicted to watching Cheech and Chong's classic "doper" films such as *Up in Smoke*—"I'm going through the Big Smoke! I'm going through the Big Smoke" (91)?

One of the most interesting questions posed by *Border Brujo* is that of interpretation. When all the video dust settles, what does *Border Brujo* really mean? And if Emily Hicks is right that border texts do not attempt to "represent" anything at all, then what does *Border Brujo* "translate"? My own sense is that, like Tijuana itself, Gómez-Peña's experimental videotext is probably "about" cultural reconversion (García Canclini 1990), a polysemic visual-aural collage in which a number of hybrid, low-tech/high-tech signals coexist (*norteño* vs. opera, Gregorian chants vs. the *pelado*'s signifyings made famous by Cantinflas, avant-garde vs. *rasquachi*), all with an unmistakable class message: high versus mass culture. All these connotations are seemingly wired in the videotext simultaneously. All the videotext's materials are, in a word, "borderized." We therefore apprehend a constant dialogism of bilingual signifiers thematizing the total flow of the U.S.-Mexico border *brujo*'s crossings, cruisings, and crass cursings.

The question "what is *Border Brujo* about?" finally encourages a thematic answer that the experimental videotext bluntly dramatizes for us:

alien-ation
alien action
alienated
alguien ate it . . .
Aliens the movie
Aliens the album
Cowboys vs. Aliens

Bikers from Aliens
The Wetback from Mars
The Mexican Transformer & his Radioactive
Torta
The Conquest of Tenochtitlán by Spielberg
. . . .
reinforced by your ignorance dear San Diegan. (91)

The video itself gives us the answer. *Border Brujo* is about the alienation of a whole hemisphere, from the Yukon to Kafkapulco. Gómez-Peña's major preoccupation in *Border Brujo* is with what many theorists of postmodernism call the "signifier rather than the signified" (Harvey 1990, 53). The literary critic Ihab Hassan has called it postmodernism's obsession with "participation," "performance," and "happening" rather than with polished "art object(s)" (1985, 123–124). On another, related level, *Border Brujo* thematizes what Gómez-Peña and his TAF/BAW colleagues sought in their frequent celebratory invocations of Deleuze and Guattari's *Anti-Oedipus*—a relationship between capitalism and schizophrenia that prevails "at the deepest level of one and the same economy, one and the same process," for "our society produces schizos the same way it produces Prell shampoo or Ford cars" (quoted in Harvey 1990, 53).

A major consequence that follows from Gómez-Peña's Deleuzian-Guatterian riffs on postmodern Tijuana is that we can no longer conceptualize the U.S.-Mexico border self as "alienated" in the sense that Marx defined it, because to be alienated in the classic sense presupposes a coherent self rather than a scrambled, "illegally alienated" self. By focusing on the "schizo," "*chilango*/Chicano" U.S.-Mexico border *brujo*, Gómez-Peña's videotext unfortunately prevents us from imagining Tijuana as something other than "the Casa de Cambio / foreign currency exchange / the Temple of Instant Transformation / the place where Tijuana y San Diego se entrepiernan [embrace]" (1990, 80).

7

Remapping American Cultural Studies

> In the United States . . . , the real [José] Martí is almost
> forgotten. . . . It is odd that there is no single book that
> explores Martí's ties with the United States. . . . And it is all
> the more surprising because, except for short intervals, the
> 15 years of his prime (1880–1885) were spent in exile in the
> United States, whose inner life he came to know profoundly.
>
> Roberto Fernández Retamar, "Jose Martí" (1995)

How do U.S.-Mexican border paradigms strive for comparative theoretical reach while remaining grounded in specific histories of what José Martí called "Nuestra América," Our America? What do such projects tell us about the cultures of U.S. imperialism and the cultures of displacement? In addition to these questions, this chapter focuses on two late-nineteenth-century articulations of an uneven and contradictory frontier modernism, one situated along the riverbanks of the Rio Grande in South Texas and the other located in the ranchos of Alta California—*fin de siglo* quests for empire, politics, and subaltern difference.[1]

Culturally, I write these days as a teacher and avid consumer of U.S.-Mexico border texts, musics, and cultural performances. Like many U.S. Latino/a intellectuals, I have lived both in the North and in the South, and in the South in the North, as Rubén Martínez once put it (1992b, 1). While I now find myself in what some one hundred fifty years ago was called the northern frontier of Alta California, I spent the first half of my life at the mouth of the Rio Grande in South Texas. My quest for a new mapping of American cultural studies necessarily entails worries about the politics of location.

When I first came to Yale to study American literature in 1973, I knew hardly anything about America. I was nurtured in the rhetoric of the U.S.-Mexico borderlands, what Américo Paredes has called the liminal spaces of "Greater Mexico" (1993, 84). I was absorbed, moreover, in South Texas's attitudes toward *el norte*—a subalternity deepened by the pressures of economic, military, and cultural displacements. This interpretation of America, however, was not given to me in my provincial public school education in South Texas, where history began and ended with the master periodizing narratives of the Alamo. I learned all the hard facts about regional hegemony and global colonialism's cultures, for culture, my teachers believed, always lived somewhere else—never in our own backyard. So I learned all the hard facts, which were, of course, pejorative. But the symbology of the two Americas Martí mapped out for us in "Nuestra América" remained largely hidden from me.

Nothing in my background prepared me for my encounter with the other America—a secular nation living like a dream on the back of a tiger. With the sound tracks of my adolescence recirculating in me (hybrid *corrido* and *conjunto* sounds), I left South Texas to walk down the mean streets of New Haven to discover the rather different musics of America—from Walt Whitman's "I Hear America Singing" to the Funkadelics' "One Nation under a Groove" and Rubén Blades's *salsa* national anthem, "Buscando América."[2] Quickly, I was immersed in the foundational myths of the Puritan ur-fathers, evident everywhere all around me at the Old Campus, from its neo-Gothic buildings named after dissenters like Jonathan Edwards to the mainline literature classes taught in American and British undergraduate seminars and tutorials. Beyond the walled-in panopticon of the Old Campus was something called the New England Way. To see this New England America as a phantasmatics was to historicize my identifications.[3]

The point of these brief personal remarks is not to demonstrate a Manichaean clash of identities and affiliations but to begin mapping out the phantasmatics of Nuestra América's borders in our own complex time. So what began in New England America as mainline American studies became, years later, at an Alta California private university (founded by a prominent robber baron and member of the Gilded Age's "Big Four") a trail into the intricate symbologies of American cultural studies (Saldívar 1991a). In both New England America and in California I encountered an imperial literary and cultural history: Perry Miller's garden variety errand into the wilderness; R. W. B. Lewis's constructions of the American Adam; Harold Bloom's Western canon based on elite European and Euro-American isolates. In California I encountered Yvor Winters's and Wallace Stegner's constructions of the western American literary frontier passages. The America they discovered (both East and West coasts) seemingly (as Sacvan Bercovitch suggests) appeared out of nowhere, out of some Hegelian telos, respectively labeled

"Nature," the New England Mind, the Jeffersonian Way, and the American Frontier thesis, culminating in the Republican party's all-too-familiar and tired "Contract with America."

American literary and cultural studies had developed, as Amy Kaplan suggests in "Left Alone with America," with a method designed not to explore its subject of empire, for "the study of American culture had traditionally been cut off from the study of foreign relations" (1993, 11). This was a simple lesson for someone like me who was steeped in the U.S.-Mexico contact zone, but it required, as they say, time, comparative study, and observation to absorb. My own view of American studies, fully formed (when I studied with Bercovitch at the School of Criticism and Theory at Dartmouth College in 1987), was that mainline America was an "artifact" made foundational text by academics and soldiers, anthropologists and emergent traveling theorists.

Occasionally, as in the work of a Gilded Age, frontier Americanist-ethnologist like Capt. John Gregory Bourke—commissioned as a first lieutenant at West Point Military Academy in 1869, an Indian and Mexican hunter, and later a friend and colleague of the Smithsonian Institution's Maj. John Wesley Powell and follower of Franz Boas and Hubert Howe Bancroft—all of these force fields were embodied simultaneously.[4] Bourke's American studies in the 1890s, I want to suggest, allows us to begin asking, to what extent did disciplines such as anthropology, ethnography, and travel writing legitimate the imperializing project of the U.S. government? (Parenthetically, was one of José Martí's major contributions as an anti-*letrado* in "Nuestra América" a critique also of imperial governing and the artistic repositioning of what he called the consolidation of *bien gobierno*—governing well?)[5]

Bourke's eminent career as a frontier "Americanist" requires a more precise exploration, which I will elaborate below, but even in modest outline form his project as a soldier-ethnologist is a rich and intricate thematization of the famous frontier field imaginary of the United States. As his biographer Joseph Porter put it, Bourke's "fascination with the land, the history and the peoples of the Southwest" not only "compelled [him] to keep extensive diaries" (1986, 4), but to reproduce in the writing of his cultural poetics the paradoxes of Gilded Age imperialist formation.

After graduating from West Point Bourke was ordered by the War Department to Fort Craig, New Mexico, where he began his military and ethnographic espionage, observation, and destruction of Pueblo

Indian cultures. It was during his "after hours" that he wrote his prodigious diary entries, "studied up" the native American Indians of the region, and mastered the Spanish vernacular language of the Nuevo Mexicanos. According to Porter, a pattern developed in New Mexico: after native American Indian (and later Mexican) hunting, Bourke "stoically worked on his diary, recording incidents and details of that day's march, noting the natural scenery, and making cartographic and geological notes" (16).

Throughout much of the 1870s Bourke waged a war against the American Indian tribes of the southwestern United States and was primarily responsible for what his biographer called "the only successful campaign against the Apaches since the acquisition of the Gadsden Purchase" (20). Now a fully developed "hero of the American frontier," as Porter characteristically phrased it, Bourke traveled from New Mexico to Omaha in 1875, where he was ordered to escort the U.S. Geological Expedition to the Black Hills. The soldier-ethnologist and newly self-made "engineer officer" thus turned his attention to the Lakota and Cheyenne peoples and their native cultures. Typical of his diary entries during this period of ethnographic writing and military conquest is the following: "the sooner the manifest destiny of the race shall be accomplished and the Indian as an Indian cease to exist, the better" (49).

Curiously enough, Bourke's destruction of "the Indian as Indian" occurred at the very same time that he was busy collecting notes, plants, animals, and pictographic artifacts of American Indian and Mexican-American cultures—which he readily preserved by sending them to the Smithsonian Institution in Washington, D.C. In other words, Bourke, together with Major Powell, who in 1879 became the director of the Bureau of Ethnology at the Smithsonian, displayed almost *avant la lettre* what Renato Rosaldo calls "imperialist nostalgia," nostalgia "for the very forms of life they intentionally altered and destroyed" (1989, 69).

In 1881, Lt. Gen. Philip Sheridan readily agreed to Bourke's personal request to be reassigned as an "ethnologist" for the Third United Cavalry, for he concurred with Bourke's assessment that there was institutional value in documenting what we now call the cultural poetics of "the people whom we so often had to fight and always to manage" (quoted in Porter 1986, 280). From Chicago, he embarked on a *fin de siglo* tour that took him to Idaho, Texas, and New Mexico. In Santa

Fe he began his fieldwork at the Pine Ridge Agency, observing and writing an account in his diary of the sacred Oglala Sun Dance. As Porter writes, Bourke was "amazed, moved, and impressed by what he saw" (93). These and other extended military and ethnographic search-and-destroy missions allowed Bourke to write up his first ethnographic studies of American Indian people, *The Dance of the Moquis of Arizona* (1884). Later, after he crossed the present-day U.S.-Mexico border near Guaymas in pursuit of the Chiricahua, he completed *An Apache Campaign in the Sierra Madre* (1886), a book largely chronicling his military travails and travels in the western American frontier.[6] For the remainder of his career as a soldier-ethnologist Bourke traveled to and from Arizona, Texas, and Washington, D.C. Although many of his Washington friends attempted to secure for him various positions in the War Department offices, Bourke eventually was ordered in 1891 to rejoin the cavalry unit in South Texas.

José E. Limón offers us in his cogent and provocative *Dancing with the Devil* the first detailed metacommentary on Bourke's ethnographic writings about the South Texas–Mexico border. For Limón, Bourke's interests and fascination with Mexican border culture and folklore stems from a "not too unconscious projection of [his] own uneasy and ambivalent ethnic identity onto the mexicanos" (1994, 4). Bourke's double career as a "literal warrior turned anthropologist," Limón suggests, is not completely an example of colonialist desire, for as a Catholic Irish American Bourke shared the same ethno-racial contradictions of domination as his objects of study (17).

Some of Bourke's most engaging ethnographic writing about the U.S.-Mexico borderlands, Limón asserts, unconsciously represented the *mexicanos* of South Texas as suffering from the very same hegemonic forces that his own Celtic forebears had earlier experienced under the Saxon and Danish invaders of Ireland. In thus "constructing [the cultural poetics of] mexicanos, Bourke was also coping with his own repudiated and projected self-ambivalences" (33). Be that as it may, my own view of Bourke's writing of U.S.-Mexico border culture, elaborated below, focuses more specifically on the molecular and molar dialectics of the cultures of U.S. imperialism.

If U.S. imperialism was also a cultural process, imagined and energized through recognizable signs, metaphors, tropes, and master narratives, Bourke's project of U.S. empire was expressive and "constitutive" (to use Raymond Williams's term) of imperial relations in themselves.

Through his official military reportage and documents relating to the uneven modernizing process of governing well from Fort Ringold, Rio Grande City, Texas, Bourke situated hemispheric and global colonialism's cultures and narratives in terms of what he embodied—a military captain and agent of U.S. empire, a travel writer, and an ethnographer of South Texas border culture. Here in Bourke's frontier—not *frontera*— cultural work, my coordinates travel, nativist modernity, anthropology, and the cultures of U.S. imperialism can be seen as constitutive of each other.

TRACKING THE U.S.-MEXICO BORDERLANDS
IN THE GILDED AGE

Just three years after José Martí warned us of the profound gap between the two Américas, Bourke collected, gathered, and published his first so-called empirical studies of the U.S.-Mexico borderlands. Part travel writer and part participant observer of the Rio Grande Valley from "Point Isabel to Roma," Texas, Bourke wanted his travel writing/ethnographic work to shed light "upon the character of the Mexican population of our extreme southern border" (1894b, 119). Like a latter-day Perry Miller in the African wilderness, Captain Bourke traveled up and down the Rio Grande into what must have been for him and his readers the American heart of darkness. This river project led Bourke, not to Perry Miller's displaced discovery of American studies as Amy Kaplan (1993) has brilliantly shown, but to the discoveries and trespasses of an imperial American border studies, a project overwhelmingly grounded in a rhetoric of "turbulence," "ignorance," debasement, and negation. Like many ethnographers, Bourke began his project by traveling and looking: "As the Rio Grande is the main line of communication, a trip along its waters will be necessary for anyone who desires to become even fairly well acquainted with the general character of the country and that of the people living in it" (1894a, 594–595).

Bourke's 1894 *Scribner's Magazine* essay, symptomatically entitled "The American Congo," demonstrates how U.S. culture in the Gilded Age was already a global phenomenon, or at least already an extralocal and transregional project. While a good part of Bourke's essay is structured around the "being there" of travel writing and ethnographic thick description, it is also entirely underpinned with the theories of Franz Boas's anthropological project. Anthropology for Boas and his generation, as Nicholas Thomas puts it, was "a modern discourse that ha[d] subsumed humanity to the grand narratives and analogies of natural history" (1994, 89). Not surprisingly, "The American Congo" represents the U.S.-Mexico border zone exclusively in terms of its exoticized landscape, its unceasing mesquite, its noisy *urracas* (magpies), and its fantastic javelinas and armadillos—what Alejo Carpentier (1995) calls *lo barroco americano*. A sympathetic reading of "The American Congo" might therefore stress how Bourke was merely following Boas's famous dictum that "cultures differ like so many species, perhaps genera, of animals" (quoted in Thomas 1994, 89). In other words, in "The American Congo" there is not a simple, smoothed-over colonial discourse but a highly ambiguous and ethnically fraught study of Mexican *pelados* and *peones* who are represented by a Catholic Irish-American gunfighter like newly discovered species, as the bearers of particular characters, physiques, dispositions, political organizations, and juridical practices.

My own reading of Bourke's "The American Congo," however, is less idealistic, though I hope not uncharitable. Bourke is to be congratulated for showing how two imperializing hemispheric events made the Rio Grande borderland and its local population "a sealed book" (1894a, 592). Two "ethnic storms," he writes, had erased for the rest of the United States the Greater Mexican population from the national imaginary. The first was Zachary Taylor's "march from Point Isabel, near the mouth of the Rio Grande, to Camargo" and then to Saltillo; the second was "our own Civil War, when the needs of the Confederacy suggested the transportation of all available cotton . . . across the Rio Grande to the Mexican side, and then down to Matamoros, there to be placed on steamers to Nassau and Liverpool" (592). To his great credit, Bourke shows, in decidedly spatial terms, how U.S. imperial culture is irrevocably local and global, for what makes the U.S.-Mexico borderland and its inhabitants "a sealed book" are the competing mappings of global capital, the multiple roots and routes of the black Atlantic, and the submarine discourses of what Glissant calls Antillean discourses.[7] More locally, Fort Ringold, Fort McIntosh, and Fort Brown in South Texas were part and parcel of Zachary Taylor's military campaigns of U.S. empire that resulted in what Limón calls "the American incorporation of the Southwest" (1994, 22).

If the force field of American border studies in the United States was conceived by John Bourke, a soldier-ethnographer, on the swirling coun-

tercurrents of the Rio Grande in the 1890s, Chicano/a cultural studies—
from Américo Paredes in the 1930s to John Rechy and Helena María
Viramontes in the 1990s—has had to challenge and undo Bourke's
plethora of imperializing crude acts constituted in classic American frontier chronicles like "The American Congo," "Popular Medicine, Customs, and Superstitions of the Rio Grande," and "The Miracle Play of
the Rio Grande." Bourke's title "The American Congo" immediately
allows us to metonymically and synecdochically associate his brand of
"American studies" with immediate acts such as conquest, underdevelopment, intervention, intrusion, and domination of the local mes-
tizo/a inhabitants.

At the beginning of the essay, for example, Bourke recalls how a few
years earlier, from his military post at Fort Ringold, he had written about
the borderlands of Nuestra América to the War Department in Washington, D.C.: "I compared the Rio Grande to the Nile in the facts that,
like its African prototype, the fierce River of the North had its legends
as weird and improbable to be found in the pages of . . . Herodotus"
(1894a, 592). Almost in the very next sentence, however, Bourke cor-
rects his rather baroque comparison of the Rio Grande to the Nile by
writing that the border zone between the United States and Mexico can
be better "compared to the Congo than the Nile the moment that the
degraded, turbulent, ignorant, and superstitious character of its populations comes under examination" (594). One of the first constructions
of the U.S.-Mexico borderlands of Nuestra América is therefore cast in
a literalized episode of rhetorical and anthropological war between the
two shifting Américas, built on what Jacques Derrida called "the violence of the letter" by one culture on the other (1976, 107). Culture in
this light is the nimbus perceived by one group when it comes into contact with and observes another one. It is the objectification of everything alien and weird and exotic about the contact group.

Everything about "The American Congo" from this point on draws
attention to Bourke's nativist, modernist, and politically unconscious representations and to the gross imperial inequities in the dominance of Nuestra América and Africa by the cultures of U.S. and European imperialism.
While Bourke painstakingly surveys the landscape, flora, and fauna, he
remains oblivious to his project of imperial gazing—collecting, organizing,
and aestheticizing the landscape, flora, and fauna. His work as a travel
writer-ethnographer of the U.S.-Mexico borderlands enabled and
informed the imperial cultures of the United States to see the Mexicans

of the borderlands as *pelados,* as "lawless ("The Rio Grande Mexican has never known what law is"), and as culturally inferior "fatalists" who indiscriminately practice what he calls a "weird pharmacy" and therapeutics of *curanderismo* (folk-healing medicine) (606).

"The American Congo" gives us a commonsense understanding of the emergent cultures of U.S. imperialism. His mirroring of the African jungle and the *frontera* of Nuestra América all but effaces the local inhabitants of both continents. The geopolitical border contact zone, moreover, is all too much like the underdeveloped continent of Africa for Bourke. The site-specific borderland of the Rio Grande Valley is at once a "Dark Belt" grounded in "chocolate soils," marked by the unspoken signs of the melancholy, the *agachado mestizo* (stooping mestizo), the white man's burden, and the nativist modernist dialectics of barbarism and savagery. "The American Congo" thus founds and enacts a paradigmatic American studies traveling tale: the construction of the ethno-racial male soldier–culture collector in the wilderness *frontera* surrounded by exotic animals, plants, and human cultural practices. Moreover, we can also see Bourke embodying the desire for what Richard Slotkin (1973) calls "regeneration through violence."[8] The captain of Fort Ringold, after all, is in South Texas to hunt down border-crossing revolutionaries like the journalist Catarino Garza, who, as Limón writes, "attempted to bring down the U.S.-supported autocratic dictatorship of Mexico's Porfirio Díaz in 1891" (1994, 29)—coincidentally the very same year that Martí published his incisive critique of the Díaz regime in "Nuestra América." As Martí put it, "Some of the sleeping republics are still beneath the sleeping octopus." "But others," he angrily criticized, "forgetting that [Benito] Juarez went about in a carriage drawn by mules, hitch their carriages to the wind, their coachmen [to] soap bubbles (1994, 826).

I am fully in agreement with Gayatri Chakravorty Spivak's challenge that "transnational Cultural Studies must put [transactions between the Americas] into an international frame" (1993, 262). Here I am supplementing my provisional 1991 reading of Martí's "Nuestra América" by bringing Bourke, Martí, and María Amparo Ruiz de Burton together in an attempt to begin reconceptualizing American cultural studies. But how can we begin to displace what Donald Pease calls the old "field-Imaginary" of American cultural and literary studies?[9] How are we to begin to remap a field that is clearly no longer mappable by any of the traditional force fields I have touched on above. "If we are to benefit," as Carolyn Porter suggests in her splendid review of the emergent inter-American studies, "in trying to construct a new field imaginary, it seems crucial to pursue the logic" of this comparative model (1994, 507). In the remainder of this chapter I will briefly respond to Spivak's and Porter's enormous challenges by remapping the topospatial and temporal dynamics of the Alta California 1848 by turning to Ruiz de Burton's ethno-racial historical romance, *The Squatter and the Don* (1885).

MARÍA AMPARO RUIZ DE BURTON
AND THE ALTA CALIFORNIA 1848

If Bourke's "The American Congo" initiates an empirical and imperializing project of U.S.-Mexico border studies, María Amparo Ruiz de Burton's *The Squatter and the Don* begins to offer readers a subaltern literature of the U.S.-Mexico borderlands. Like Martí, Ruiz de Burton is fascinated with travel and with the art of governing well in the face of what she calls "the hydra-headed monster" of monopoly capitalism (1992, 298). Born and reared in Baja California, María Amparo del Ruiz was the granddaughter of the commander of the Mexican northern borderlands, José Manuel Ruiz. Very much a child of the inter-American Enlightenment, María would distinguish herself from the majority of her fellow Californios, however, by radically critiquing the Gilded Age monopoly capitalists of the United States, who, she claims, are "the Napoleons of this land" (1992, 365).

When Polk sent U.S. forces to secure Baja California in July 1847, fifteen-year-old Señorita "Amparito," with her friends and relatives, met Henry S. Burton, and in the journalist Winifred Davidson's words, "sneered at the proudly confident lieutenant-colonel of the First Regiment of New York Volunteers as he landed his small force and proceeded upon his errand of taking possession" (Davidson 1932, 5). Like many others, Burton had come west as part of the conquering U.S. forces. With the outbreak of the U.S.-Mexico war, Burton arrived from West Point (where he had been an artillery instructor) to begin his command at Monterey, Alta California. From Monterey Burton was ordered to Santa Barbara and then transferred to La Paz, the capital of Baja California. It was in La Paz that Burton "made the acquaintance of the prettiest young lady on the peninsula" (5).

Davidson's *Los Angeles Times Sunday Magazine* feature article,

"Enemy Lovers," is fascinating not only for its biographical informa-
tion but also for its 1932 marriage of eros and ethno-racial politics.
"They were natural enemies," Davidson writes, "Henry by birth, breed-
ing, tastes, and general appearance typically American" [sic]; "Amparo—
'Amparito' for short—being typically Spanish." The article becomes even
more interesting as Davidson, a member of the San Diego Historical
Society, expands on the inter-ethno-racial romance in La Paz: "[Ampar-
ito] fell naturally and unconsciously into the role as pupil, eager to learn
of a newly found teacher" (5).

When the outgunned Mexican forces in La Paz finally attacked the
U.S. Army post, Burton offered Amparito and her mother, Doña Isabel,
transport on the USS *Lexington*, north to Monterey. After four years
of delays and postponements, Henry and Amparito were married. Like
a real-life sentimental novel, "the Burtons," Davidson writes, "[were]
a successful union. In the very bloom of her young womanhood, Mrs.
Burton went East with her husband; and there, particularly in Chicago,
her beauty and grace won her a distinguished place in the best society"
(5). In terms anticipating Davidson's feature story, Hubert Howe Bancroft had memorialized the marriage as follows: "Captain H. S. Burton fell in love with the charming Californian, María del Amparo Ruiz,
born in Loreto, and aged sixteen. She promised to marry him" (1888,
330–331). Deemed by the conservative Catholic forces as a "heretical"
marriage (Catholic and Protestant), other local commentators referred
to the love affair as the union of "natural enemies" (Californio and
Anglo-American) (Davidson 1932, 5).

After the death of her husband (who had contracted malaria while
fighting in the South during the Civil War), María returned to Alta California. Here in San Diego, as Rosaura Sánchez and Beatrice Pita write
in their introduction, she "wrote and produced a five-act comedy of
Don Quixote. Several years later, in 1872, her first novel *Who Would
Have Thought It?* was published by J. B. Lippincott in Philadelphia"
(Ruiz de Burton 1992, 11).

But it is with the publication of *The Squatter and the Don* that Ruiz
de Burton fully works against the grain of dominant U.S. historiography and represents the cultures of U.S. imperialism not only as territorial and economic fact but also inevitably as a subject-constituting
project. While there is much room for debating Ruiz de Burton's politics of location as a subaltern subject, I want to suggest that in *The Squatter and the Don* her narrator is particularly well suited to begin describing

for us the diversity of the Alta California borderlands as a dispersed space of cultural and political displacement.

Additionally, I want to highlight how Ruiz de Burton engages in the fantasy work of transnational identity. In her own represented history diverse kinds of memories and countermemories, knowledges, and discourses intermingle in the novel. What does it mean for our Alta California romancer to name herself "C. Loyal"—Loyal Citizen in America of 1848? How does she play out the complex regime that transforms her into being intimate with mass-mediated culture and political culture? Does she perform in a ritual of consensus how it feels to be a loyal citizen by constructing Alta California as a domestic land and a place where the "actual" and the "imaginary" meet?

Admittedly, if the narrator is not a subaltern subject in the traditional Gramscian subordinate-class sense, she can be seen as a subaltern supplementary subject. I want to argue for the subversive potential of the narrative subject as representative of what Spivak calls the marginal instance, for "the radical intellectual . . . is . . . caught in a deliberate choice of subalternity, granting to the oppressed either that very expressive subjectivity which s/he criticizes or, instead, a total unrepresentability" (1988, 17).

As a writer who painstakingly traces the juridical, political, and erotic activities of the Californios and Euro-Americans in what Michael Paul Rogin (1983) calls "the American 1848" and beyond, Ruiz de Burton functions as a subaltern mediator who is simultaneously an insurgent critic of monopoly capitalism and a radical critic of Anglocentric historiography. Thus envisaged, *The Squatter and the Don*, written only some forty years after the Treaty of Guadalupe Hidalgo, is Ruiz de Burton's strategy for bringing the hegemonic historiography of the United States to a crisis.

In suggesting that Ruiz de Burton does more than write a "local color" sentimental romance, I have in mind not only her cultural critique of the Alta California 1848 but also her engagement with the manifold cultural anxieties of the Gilded Age moment in California—both Baja and Alta. For present purposes, these cultural criticisms and anxieties may be described through two far-reaching projects and events—one internal, local, and literary historical, the other external, worldly, and transnational, "the American 1848." Both events are thematized in Ruiz de Burton's *The Squatter and the Don*.

Any reading of Ruiz de Burton's narrative must begin by recalling that scores of Alta Californios not only had written and dictated their own versions of the monumental historical past but also, as Rosaura Sánchez emphasizes, "had recognized and been driven by a perceived duty to counter hegemonic versions of the Spanish and Mexican periods of California history" (1993, 279). Moreover, through the splendid recent literary historical scholarship of Sánchez's *Telling Identities* (1995) and Genaro Padilla's *My History, Not Yours* (1993), we are now in a better position to see why Alta Californios such as Mariano Guadalupe Vallejo, Juan Bautista Alvarado, Antonio Franco Coronel, Eulalia Pérez, and María Inocenta Pico de Avila had readily agreed to document their *testimonios* about the Alta California experience through Hubert Howe Bancroft, a book dealer, culture collector, and Gilded Age historian. As Bancroft put it in *Literary Industries,* he and his assistants, Thomas Savage and Enrique Cerruti, collected more than "two hundred volumes of original narratives from memory by as many early Californios, native and pioneer, written by themselves or taken down from their lips, . . . of their experiences" (1890, 282).

María Amparo Ruiz de Burton, I believe, strategically aligns herself with the mediated Alta Californio narratives collected by Bancroft and in the process generates in her own ethno-racial romance what Sánchez notes characterized the Alta Californio narratives themselves: "new discourses of ethnicity, new constructs of identity as a marginalized, disempowered, and dispossessed ethnic minority" (1995, xiii). Ruiz de Burton additionally supplements these testimonials by grounding herself in the rhetoric and structures of feeling of sentimentality and romance. If José Martí had translated Ruiz de Burton's *The Squatter and the Don* into Spanish—as he had translated and written about Helen Hunt Jackson's *Ramona* (1884)—he would surely have written that her Alta Californio romance was, like *Ramona,* "our novel," a model full of "fire and knowledge," and a "tear that speaks."[10]

Throughout *The Squatter and the Don* Ruiz de Burton herself suggests the American 1848 by focusing on Don Mariano Alamar, a character based largely on Mariano Guadalupe Vallejo, who had, in November 1875, given Bancroft his five-volume *testimonio, Recuerdos históricos y personales tocante a la Alta California.* It is important to note that Ruiz de Burton was the only Alta Californian woman Vallejo included in his prologue as participating in the Alta California counterhegemonic project: "erudita y culta dama, celosa de la honra y tradiciones de su patria, valiosa esposa, cariñosa madre y leal amiga" (a learned and erudite lady, concerned with honor and traditions of her land, worthy wife, loving mother, and loyal friend). As Padilla suggests, the very title of Vallejo's *testimonio* "establishes a reading position for the [text]: the narrator serves history by telling the story of Mexican California" (1993, 85). Thus, early in the novel, in a poignant chapter entitled "The Don's Views of the Treaty of Guadalupe Hidalgo," Ruiz de Burton displays her close familiarity with Vallejo's strategic subaltern project by representing—in a language reminiscent of Vallejo and other Alta Californios—Don Mariano Alamar's critical responses on first reading the treaty: "I felt a bitter resentment for the treaty said that our rights would be the same as those enjoyed by all other American citizens. But, you see, Congress takes very good care not to enact retroactive laws for Americans; laws to take away from American citizens the property which they hold now, with a recognized legal title" (1992, 67).

If the Treaty of Guadalupe Hidalgo was not entirely responsible for Don Mariano Alamar's land troubles in Alta California, Ruiz de Burton goes to great pains to show how in fact Sen. William Gwin, the originator of the Land Law of 1851, was also culpable. As the historian Leonard Pitt writes, Gwin "proposed a fine-tooth combing of all the titles without exception, for he believed them to be largely inchoate and fraudulent" (1965, 89). Not surprisingly, much of Ruiz de Burton's cultural critique of the American 1848 is a local attack of the three-man commission (the Board of Land Commissioners) who sat in San Francisco and who adjudicated the proofs of all the titleholders who came before them. Ruiz de Burton's strategy throughout the narrative is therefore to thematize the Don's engagement with the multiple constructions of legal authority: "By those laws any man can come to my land . . . , plant ten acres of grain, without any fence, and catch my cattle which, seeing the green grass without a fence, will go to eat it" (1992, 66).

It may be helpful to distinguish Ruiz de Burton's historiographic strategy from other mainline positions, for the squatters in her romance are not mythologized as noble "settlers" and pioneers struggling quaintly in the frontier wilderness. Eight years before Frederick Jackson Turner, in "The Significance of the Frontier in American History," was to turn western American history into his own chronicle of westward expansion, wherein the struggle with the edges and boundaries of "civilization" turned European immigrants into Americans, Ruiz de Burton quarreled with the folk democracy of the western American frontier by giving full play to the hegemonic land laws, railroads, and institutions of commerce and monopoly capitalism. Succeeding chapters ("Pre-Empting under the Law," "The Sins of Our Legislators!" and "The Fashion of Justice in San Diego") provide extensive explorations of what Patricia Limerick calls "the legacy of conquest" (1987) and take radical stances toward the traditional understanding of what Carl Gutiérrez-Jones calls "consensual" relations (1995b, 4). By reconstructing the relationship between power and consent, Ruiz de Burton, we might say, following Gutiérrez-Jones's arguments about postcontemporary Chicano/a narratives, offers us a "vision of institutional power as a dialectic between coercion and hegemony|—|where outright material limits fail, or where they prove inefficient" (4).

Whereas "other writers defuse political violence," Anne E. Goldman writes, "by relocating it in a domestic space defined in opposition to the social domain, Ruiz de Burton politicizes the familial circle, so that home becomes the locus to articulate a sustained description of conflict in a [inter]national scale" (1994, 130). If the past speaks to us about our present as well as to our future, it is not entirely inappropriate to read Ruiz de Burton's romance as foregrounding what the Chicana poet Lorna Dee Cervantes reterritorializes in "Poema Para Los Californios Muertos" as memories "of silver buckles and dark rebozos . . . / and the pure scent of rage" (1981, 42–43).

Dialectically, love plots and political plots and familial plots overlap in *The Squatter and the Don*. As a historical romance, the narrative, like subaltern writing, is seemingly written in reverse: it points backward to what Northrop Frye calls "medieval quest-romances where victory meant the restored fertility," the union of male and female heroes (1957, 193). A would-be race melodrama, or better still, a future-looking *telenovela, The Squatter and the Don* cooks up libidinal desire (eroticism and heterosexual passion) and patriotism throughout (binational passions for George Washington's tomb and the Mexican national celebrations of Cinco de Mayo and 16 de Septiembre). If Ruiz de Burton's romance does not take us into its lovers' bedroom, it does play on inciting its readers' desire to be there (to paraphrase Sommer [1991, 34]).

In her remarkable *Foundational Fictions*, Doris Sommer redefines romance as "a cross between our contemporary use of the word as a love story," a genre in which readers (particularly women) leave behind their everyday lives and live out their secret desires and passionate phantasmatics, and a "nineteenth-century use that distinguished the genre as more boldly allegorical than the novel" (1991, 5). Nathaniel Hawthorne's self-designation as a "romance writer" in *The Scarlet Letter* captures this generic distinction more spatially, as "a neutral territory, somewhere between the real world and fairyland, where the Actual and the Imaginary meet, and each imbue itself with the nature of the other" (1980, 45).

It is precisely this generic crossing of *The Squatter and the Don* as a popular love story and a liminal narrative located between "the Actual and the Imaginary" that I want to explore below. Like other star-crossed lovers (Romeo and Juliet, Hester and Dimmesdale), the lovers in Ruiz de Burton's narrative undergo various travails and tragedies. But they also represent "an erotics of politics" (Sommer 1991, 6), thematizing specific ethno-racial formations, economic interests, and future idealized states. Put differently, *The Squatter and the Don* does not keep the dialectics of difference (race, ethnicity, class, and gender) pure, but—like other romances—"marr[ies] hero to heroine across former barriers" (Sommer 1991, 123).

By presenting a variety of heterosexual unions between Euro-American Protestants and Californio Roman Catholics, Ruiz de Burton's novel looks to a future of utopian unions in the American 1848. Erotics and politics thus join forces, exhorting idealized Euro-Americans and Californios to be fruitful and create the new national symbolism. Seen in this light, eroticism and nationalism are master tropes for each other in modern and modernizing romance narratives. They function, as Sommer argues, as allegories for each other.

From the very start of *The Squatter and the Don,* when Mercedes Alamar stumbles all over Clarence Darrell at her father's rancho, Ruiz de Burton treats us to "burning blushes" and "eyes emit[ting] rays full of attractive, earnest" intentions (1992, 99). Clarence and Mercedes's "love at first sight" encounter spirals seemingly out of control for most of the novel, but Ruiz de Burton subtly reminds her readers that she is perfectly self-reflexive about her genre: at one point, Elvira tells her sister Mercedes not to despair of the many obstacles the older generation of Darrells and Alamares put in front of them, for it turns out Clarence is not a nefarious squatter and thus their "romance is spoiled" (141). "It would have been so fine—like a dime novel—," Elvira continues telling sad Mercedes, "to have carried you off bodily by order of infuriated, cruel parents, and . . . marry you, at the point of a loaded revolver to a bald-headed millionaire. Your midnight shrieks would have made the blood of passers-by curdle! Then Clarence would have rushed in and stabbed the millionaire, and you, falling across his prostrate body said: 'Tramp or not I am thine'" (141). In this allusion to the mawkish dime novels popular in the United States, Ruiz de Burton shows she understands how (if her romance's political critique is to be widely read) *The Squatter and the Don* has to be aimed rhetorically to an American reading public hungry for gratuitous ethno-racial adventure.

As we follow the lovers' on-and-off wedding engagement, the love story of *The Squatter and the Don* produces a libidinal surplus value, allowing us—as Sommer suggests—to overcome the cultural, political, and ethno-racial roadblocks placed in front of them. Thus, after Mercedes and Clarence agree to marry on September 16 (the date Miguel Hidalgo initiated Mexico's liberation from Spanish imperialism in 1821), the battles between Darrell and Mariano over *honor* and shame create for the young lovers a socially symbolic and transcendent purpose. These obstacles, moreover, heighten the lovers' desire for a new national symbolic, which in Ruiz de Burton's words is "capable of emanicipat[ing] the white slaves of California" (372).

The Squatter and the Don is dense with the emplotments of romance and filled with the cultures of sentiment—but with a Californio difference: vaquero cattle drives and violent confrontations over cattle raising versus farming. For example, when Don Mariano Alamar proposes that the Euro-American squatters raise cattle rather than aspire to being Jeffersonian farmers, a white supremacist squatter proclaims, "I ain't no vaquero to go busquering [*sic*] around" (94), suggesting that Californio vaqueros are ethno-racially inferior to him. Cattle and things vaquero, I want to suggest, are the historical romance's political unconscious. They surround the Euro-American squatters and the Californios, and they are a continual focus of energy (shooting and protecting) and attention through much of the narrative. Ruiz de Burton even gives her readers an extraordinary epic cattle drive led by Don Mariano and his sons across mountains to get the cattle to market. The sacrifice of the cattle, the paralyzing of Victoriano, and the Don's attack of pneumonia in the mountains constitute the text's economic and moral base. The sacrifice of the cattle and the metaphorical crippling of the Don and his sons underwrite almost everything that follows in the romance. Interestingly, within the cultural form of sentimentality (indulgence in excessive structures of feeling), Ruiz de Burton's cattle drive teaches us how men (both squatters and Alta Californios) are enmeshed in accepting pain and, within the context of our emergent gunfighter national imaginary, giving it.

Ruiz de Burton, of course, critically "signifies" on this male vaquero imaginary when, late in the novel, she sets up a modern Hegelian battle on horseback between the supposed master (William Darrell) and his ethno-racialized slave (Don Mariano). Accusing Don Mariano of parading Mercedes "like a pretty young filly" before his son, "to get his money" (248), William, "livid with rage," induces a fight to the death with Don Mariano by beating him with his horsewhip. "Damn you!" Darrell screams out, "can't make you fight. Won't you be insulted, you coward" (248). The more sophisticated and able vaqueros, Victoriano and Everett, "dash their horses" between Darrell and Mariano, "the blow" falling on their backs (248). When Darrell again "lift[s] his whip to strike" Don Mariano, Gabriel lassos the master into submission. Darrell "instantaneously felt as if he had been struck by lightning. . . . His arms fell powerless by his side, and the iron hoop seemed to encircle him . . . [for] the coil of the reata held him in an iron grip, and he could not move" (249). If *The Squatter and the Don* juxtaposes the ritualized Roman Catholic "marriage lasso" that ties the inter-ethno-racial couple Clarence and Mercedes to that of Gabriel's dramatic "iron-hooped" homosocial "lassoing" of Darrell, this scene also alludes (through the images of the *reata* [rope]) to the historical lynching of a Mexican woman, Josefa, who allegedly stabbed to death a man by the name of Cannon in the summer of 1851 in the gold rush town of Downieville.[11]

As a dizzying double-voiced text, the narrative also thematizes cultural conflicts over land, racial status, class positionings, ethnicity as discursive excess—all within the framework of Californio-centered ideas of what the historian Ramón Gutiérrez calls in a related context *honor y vergüenza*.[12] In other words, if naming is at once the setting of a boundary and the repeated inculcation of a norm, Ruiz de Burton's text is excessively overdetermined by shifty and shifting multiple interpellations. Don Mariano, for example, refers to the Alta Californios as "we, the Spaniards" (66) and in more Latin American frames of reference as "Spano-Americans" (67). At other times, however, the Don takes on a more local appellation as in "I am afraid there is no help for us native Californians," or when reading the Treaty of Guadalupe Hidalgo, he casts himself as a dispossessed child of Mexico. The Don's shifting interpellation as a "Spano-American" or as a native Alta Californio is both reiterated and, of course, challenged by various authorities reinforcing or contesting this apparently naturalized naming. Thus, throughout the narrative, white squatters refer to the Don as well as to other Alta Californiosas "inferior" (222), "lazy" (222), "ignorant" (222), and "vaquero" "greasers" (249).

At times, the historical romance veers uncontrollably toward passionate Hispanophilia (perhaps an apology for the Spanish conquest of the Américas), as is clearly the case when Don Mariano sees the colonialist founding of the California missions and their defense as "not a foolish extravagance" (176); most of the time, however, the narrative subaltern subject puts the U.S. government on trial (the novel ends with a stirring chapter entitled "Out with the Invader," a call for the nation's removal of the railroad monopolists Leland Stanford, Collis Huntington, Mark Hopkins, and Charles Crocker, who are "the Napoleons of this land" [365]).

Although *The Squatter and the Don* relies on the mythic time of medieval romance to tell its love story, Ruiz de Burton uses her own authorial time 1846–1884 to ground her readers in the rhetoric of U.S. imperial temporality—Rogin's "American 1848." Rogin's brilliant reperiodizing makes a telling parallel between President Polk's signing of the Treaty of Guadalupe Hidalgo, securing Texas as U.S. territory, and the red revolutions in Europe. "There was a crisis over slavery from the Mexican peace treaty in 1848 through the passage of the 1850 compromise and the enforcement of its fugitive slave provisions in 1851," Rogin writes, and these same dates, 1848–1851, also mark the triumph of the revolution in France and its final defeat by Louis Bonaparte (1983, 103). If the promises of the French Revolution were destroyed by the class war that followed in Paris, the promises of the American Revolution were contradicted and negated by the U.S.-Mexican war. Rogin's American 1848, in other words, creates a startling historical resonance between the United States and France and allows him to construct one of the most significant ideological readings of Melville's *Moby Dick*.

What happens, though, to Rogin's American 1848 if it is "Alta" Californiaized? What might happen if we viewed 1848 not merely as an episode in the violent history of the borderlands of Nuestra América? What if U.S. imperialism were displaced from its location in a national imaginary to its protoempire role in the Américas and the rest of the world? This is precisely what Maria Amparo Ruiz de Burton wishes to map out—spatially and hermeneutically—in *The Squatter and the Don*, for the U.S. war with Mexico not only casts the "shadow of the Civil War" but, more significantly, opens up the Américas to the Big Four and its government's incorporation of the geopolitical arena. The point is not to make Martí's Cuba or Ruiz de Burton's Baja and Alta California the new protagonists but rather to see parataxically one story in relation to another, to note the new politics of location and respatialize the cultures of displacement. *The Squatter and the Don* thus embodies the historical and ethno-racial conflicts of the time, explores its sources, and manufactures through its erotics of politics conciliatory gestures to escape it.

But before the subaltern narrative subject begins to emplot her tale of romance (both as love story and as national allegory of land loss), she tells us in chapter 1 of the multiple roots of the New England Way farmer, William Darrell (Clarence's father), a recent immigrant to Alta California. While William is presumably well off in his "Alameda farm house," the historical romance begins with Darrell sitting up late with his wife, Mary, attempting to persuade her of his grand design "to locate somewhere in a desirable neighborhood" (1992, 55). Relocate he does, building a "casa grande" on the rancho of Don Mariano Alamar, an Alta Californio cattle rancher. We then move from the immediate authorial present of 1884 to the American 1846–1848, when William and his family "had crossed the plains . . . in [a] caravan of four wagons, followed by . . . five horses and choice Durham cows" (56).

Some twenty-four years later William tells his wife that he is still poor in Alameda and that all he has "earned is the name of squatter" (56). Believing that that the Alamar rancho's land grant title has been "rejected," and encouraged by the crude nativists and fellow 1846 immigrant travelers that "San Diego is sure to have a railroad direct to the Eastern States," William Darrell travels south to the Alta California borderlands and takes up 640 acres belonging to Don Mariano Alamar. Unbeknown to him, however, his son, Clarence, on his mother's wise counsel, purchases these lands from the Don, falls hopelessly in love with the Don's sixteen-year-old daughter, Mercedes, and, by investing in the stock market and Arizona mines, earns over a million dollars.

By focusing on Clarence's mining interests, Ruiz de Burton subtly moves her romance out of the myth and symbols of western American historiography that represented life in the American West, as one eminent New West American historian put it, as "labor free" (Limerick 1987, 99). Clarence's engagement in mining thus takes precedence over the Don's cattle and the squatter's farming enterprises. As Limerick emphasizes, "no industry had a greater impact on Western history than mining." As Ruiz de Burton's romance shows, mining not only brings thousands to Alta California but also creates what Limerick calls "settlements of white people where none had been before" (99). As a result of Clarence's investment in mines, he not only becomes incredibly wealthy but also, ironically, helps displace the very Alta Californio family he will eventually marry into.

The remainder of the (trans)national romance becomes a tale of star-crossed lovers, particular regionalisms, economic interests, and competing cultural values—all wonderfully chronicled through the chronotope of what Ruiz de Burton lyrically calls "sentimental twilight" (1992, 169). The soap opera passions of the squatter's son and the Don's daughter spill over to Ruiz's sentimental readership in a move by the author to win what Sommer says about romances in general, "partisan minds and hearts" (1991, 4). All of this makes for a coherent plotting; the narrative moves through dizzying "reconciliations" and "amalgamations," to reimagine the Alta Californio 1848. When Clarence and Mercedes (after years of delays and fantastic tragedies) are eventually reunited and marry, Doña Josefa and her daughters can only weep "all the time," teaching us the mass-mediated lessons of what the most popular Univision *telenovela* of all time announced in its title: "Los ricos también lloran" (The Rich Also Cry).[13]

Put in more cultural materialist terms, Ruiz de Burton's *The Squatter and the Don* ends by dramatically illustrating the proletarianization (notwithstanding Mercedes Darrell) of the majority of the Alta Californios. This is allegorized for us in the scene where Gabriel Alamar falls from a roof in San Francisco—"carrying," the author writes, "his hod full of bricks up a steep ladder." "In that hod of bricks," Ruiz de Burton continues, "not only his sad experience was represented, but *the entire history* of the native Californians . . . was epitomized. The natives . . . having lost all their property, must be hod carriers" (1992, 352; her emphasis). Curiously enough, some one hundred years later, the Chicano novelist Alejandro Morales in his California chronicles *Reto en paraíso* (1983) and *The Brick People* (1988) would explore in magic realist detail how Mexicano and Chicano/a "hod carriers" were largely "instrumental[ized]" in the construction of Anglocentric utopias, paradises which were also monuments of barbarism."[14]

Let us recall the scene I began with, where Don Mariano reflects on reading the Treaty of Guadalupe Hidalgo, especially the treaty's articles promising to deal fairly with the Californio/Mexicano people who became U.S. residents by default:

> I remember, calmly said Don Mariano, that when I first read the
> text of the treaty of Guadalupe Hidalgo, I felt bitter resentment . . .
> against Mexico, the mother country, who abandoned us—her children—
> with so slight a provision of obligatory stipulations for protection. But
> afterwards, upon mature reflection, I saw that Mexico did as much as
> could have been reasonably expected at the time. . . . How could Mex-
> ico have foreseen that when scarcely half a dozen years should have
> eclipsed the conquerors would, "In Congress Assembled," pass laws
> which were to be retroactive upon the defenseless, conquered people,
> in order to despoil them? (1992, 66–67)

It is worth stressing that in Ruiz de Burton's hands, the U.S.-Mexico
border contact zone outlined in the Treaty of Guadalupe Hidalgo is a
signifier not simply of discrepant movements but, more significantly, of
political struggles to define the local as distinctive community, in historical contexts of displacement.

If *The Squatter and the Don* puts the U.S. government on trial, it
also challenges hegemonic U.S. history (cultural and literary) by bringing it to a crisis. Official U.S. history, as we know, did not exist as a
profession until the late nineteenth century, as David J. Weber argues
in *The Spanish Frontier in North America,* for only a few Englishmen
and Anglo-Americans wrote histories about Californios, Tejanos,
Nuevo Mejicanos, and so on. From their English forebears, Weber
explains, Anglo-American historians "had inherited the view that
Spaniards [and later Mexicans and Chicanos] were cruel, avaricious,
treacherous, fanatical, superstitious, cowardly, corrupt, . . . decadent,
indolent and authoritarian, a unique complex of pejoratives" (1992,
336). Thus, as one of the squatters routinely says, "Those greasers aren't
half crushed yet. We have to tame them like they do their mustangs, or
shoot them" (Ruiz de Burton 1992, 73).

Throughout *The Squatter and the Don* Ruiz de Burton counters this
intense Hispano/Californio-phobia by strategically representing the Don
and his clan as subaltern ironists. As Don Mariano puts it, "The set-
tlers want the lands of the lazy, the thriftless Spaniards. Such good-for-
nothing, helpless wretches are not fit to own lordly tracts of land. It
was wicked to tolerate the waste, the extravagance of the Mexican government. The American Government never could have been, or ever
could be, guilty of such things. But, behold! . . . [T]his far-seeing Congress . . . goes to work and gives to railroad companies millions upon
millions of acres of land" (175). If theory, in the words of William V.

Spanos, "has taught us . . . that the institutional production and consumption of literary texts constitutes one of the most important and powerful means of legitimating and reproducing the dominant cultural and sociopolitical formation" (1995, 12), it is hardly surprising that Ruiz de Burton's romance received nary a review or an extended interpretive essay from the local San Francisco media and literary establishment. The emergent national literary canon in the United States and its multiple institutional machinery (English departments, presses, journals, accrediting agencies, etc.) largely succeeded in burying Ruiz de Burton's ethno-racial romance, just as Bancroft censored the *testimonios* of the Alta Californian, thus paving the way for what Spanos calls the U.S. *"Pax Anthropologica"* (12).

In sum, Ruiz de Burton shows how the interracial love between Mercedes Alamar and Clarence Darrell sets the limits of the national imagined community and simultaneously deromanticizes the traditional plot of the western U.S. romance. With unrelenting cultural critique and literary grace the author shows how followers of the New England Way set out to systematically exploit the Californios. Moreover, she moves beyond the binary opposition of white squatters versus Alta Californios by demonstrating how both the Alta Californios and the squatters are pawns ruled by Leland Stanford and the railroad robber barons. Late in the novel, Don Mariano visits Governor Stanford and tries to convince him of the benefits of allowing the Texas Pacific to come into San Diego. The author's portrait of Stanford's ruthlessness is nothing short of devastating: "You don't seem to think of business principles," Stanford tells Mariano Alamar. "You forget that in business every one is for himself. If it is to our interest to prevent the construction of the Texas Pacific, do you suppose we will stop to consider that we might inconvenience the San Diego people?" (1992, 316). Leland Stanford's railroads function in the historical romance as a great symbol of national and capitalist unity. It is a complex industrial phenomenon that transforms California into a state and joins it to the United States and to América Latina by linking commerce and communication among widely dispersed local communities, both North and South. As the New West American historian George Sánchez explains, "Railroad development in Mexico occurred almost entirely during the *Porfirato*—the reign of dictator Porfirio Díaz from 1876 to 1910." Not surprisingly, "the same financial magnates that controlled the Southern Pacific, Santa Fe, and other railroads . . . became the major shareholders in Mexican railroads. Financiers J. Pierpoint Morgan, Jay Gould, Collis P. Huntington, Thomas Nickerson, and Thomas Scott dominated investment in railroads on both sides of [the U.S.-Mexico] border" (1993, 22). Díaz thus underdeveloped Mexico through the development of the monopoly capitalists. It is therefore understandable that the inter-American anti-imperialist José Martí, in his "Prologue to the Niagara Poem," could in a dialectically modernist rhetoric write, "Una tempestad es más bella que una locomotora" (A tempest is more beautiful than a locomotive) (1978, 214).

The Squatter and the Don is an interpreter's guide to the late nineteenth century's emergence into what social theorists call monopoly capitalism.[15] Virtually every scene near the romance's ending is a socially symbolic commentary on Stanford, Hopkins, Huntington, and Crocker, the Big Four who paid for the building of the Central Pacific railroad, thereby consolidating a monopoly that controlled the state and individuals alike. Ruiz de Burton comes down hard on the Big Four for contributing to the demise of the Alta Californios and for the ruination of communities like San Diego, which was once a "fresh and rosy" town (1992, 171). According to the Don's son-in-law , San Diego's fall began when "the managers of the Central Pacific railroad" bribed congressmen and committed "open fraud" (297). The Big Four are represented as wanting to "grab every cent that might be made out of the traffic between the Atlantic and Pacific Oceans," hardly caring if "people are ruined" or if towns "are made desolate" in California (298).

Ruiz de Burton's critique of the monopolists is driven by both a molecular and molar logic, for the demise of the Alta Californios foretells the larger demise of the American nation-state and its citizens. In the conclusion, "Out with the Invader," Ruiz de Burton alludes to the idea that the monopolists were contributing to a new stage of capitalism. The Big Four's momentum knows no borders, for their monopoly is characterized by the development of mechanisms to absorb economic surpluses. Straightforwardly, like Martí's "Nuestra América," the romance warns of the monopolists' power to "take the money earned [through plunder] to go and build railroads in Guatemala and British America" (370).

What is the point in juxtaposing Bourke's imperialist and Martí's and Ruiz de Burton's anti-imperialist chronicles of the borderlands of Nuestra América? In the dispersed archives of "The American Congo," *The*

Squatter and the Don, and "Nuestra América" we can track the almost forgotten histories of the cultures of U.S. imperialism. These narratives shed light on the late-nineteenth-century world of everyday life in advanced capitalism and how *letrado* and anti-*letrado* intellectuals write for and against the uneven development of modernization and modernity. These chronicles help us remember the world systems that catalyzed the rise of what Edward Said (1993) has described as the truncated century of U.S. empire. "The American Congo," "Nuestra América," and *The Squatter and the Don* maintain a clear awareness of the obstacles to "outing the invader," as Ruiz de Burton put it some one hundred years ago. Yet these chronicles also express a great hope for an alternative chronicle of the Gilded Age—what José Martí proposed as a total rejection of the monumentalist European university for the American: "The European university must yield to the American. . . . The history of America, from the Incas to the present, must be taught letter perfect, even if the Argonauts of Greece are never taught" (1994, 823). These alternative archives are indispensable for pursuing crucial political visions—worlds after "The American Congo" and American empire, after contracts with America, after nativist Proposition 187s and so-called illegal aliens.

AFTERWORD

Frontejas to El Vez

> With [Elvis's songs, Lincoln's speeches, and Melville's nov-
> els], there is a presentation, an acting out, a fantasy, a perfor-
> mance, not of what it means to be an American—to be a
> creature of history, the inheritor of certain crimes, wars, ideas,
> landscapes, but rather a presentation, an acting out, a fan-
> tasy of what the deepest and most extreme possibilities and
> dangers of our national identity are.
>
> Greil Marcus, *Dead Elvis* (1991)

It is now time to consider what has been gained by our bumpy voyage
over the landscape of recent thought on U.S.-Mexico border culture
and society. The journey began by acknowledging how U.S.-Mexico
border texts can be seen as nodes in a network of seemingly unrelated
discourses such as novels, poetry, political rhetoric, aesthetics, popular
corrido, conjunto, punk, and hip-hop music, visual art, and travel writing. The situatedness of *Border Matters* within this *frontera*-crossing
scholarship has provided us with close readings of literary narratives
by Américo Paredes, Arturo Islas, Carmen Lomas Garza, Helena María
Viramontes, and John Rechy; poetry by José Montoya, Bernice Zamora,
and Alberto Ríos; and U.S.-Mexico border music by Los Tigres del
Norte, Los Illegals, and (Kid) Frost. Throughout our travels I have placed
my critical gaze within a broad theoretical framework, for example,
when I illuminated the Greater Mexico border sensibilities of intellectuals such as Paredes or when I evaluated the strengths and weaknesses
of the new interpretive ethnography and social histories of Renato
Rosaldo, Néstor García Canclini, George J. Sánchez, and Vicki Ruiz
and the autoethnographies of Beverly Lowry, Luis Alberto Urrea,
Richard Rodriguez, and Guillermo Gómez-Peña.

Border Matters encompasses scholarly fields that are in general iso-
lated even from "interdisciplinary studies." While there are splendid
books that apply textual analyses to anthropological studies, that
apply critical theory to Chicano/a literature, and that use cultural stud-

ies methods to read Chicano/a art and subcultures, or emergent border and diaspora texts that analyze the mobility and transformations of intercultural practices, there are few books that attempt to combine all these practices.[1] *Border Matters,* I believe, addresses each of these areas and engages all of them by discussing them in relation to one another.

By focusing our attention on the heterogeneous and uneven U.S.-Mexico border discourse, certain benefits, I hope, have accrued. First, a welter of overlapping arguments shared by disparate thinkers and writers has become apparent as never before. Virtually all the U.S.-Mexico border intellectuals encountered in this survey were extraordinarily sensitive to ontological issues such as what happens when different worlds confront one another or when border-patrolled boundaries are crossed. To be sure, a certain caution about the uncritical acceptance of U.S.-Mexico border paradigms may seem to be warranted. The writers, activist-intellectuals, musicians, and painters who have contributed to the U.S.-Mexico border discussion might, for example, be dismissed, as some have characterized postmodernism, as elaborating the latest trendy intellectual fashion. But dismissing U.S.-Mexico border discourses as a trendy paradigm of crossing, circulation, and resistance, in my view, fails to do justice to the complexities of the transfrontier issues of our time. As the cultural studies scholar Rosa Linda Fregoso suggests, the U.S.-Mexico border paradigm "has a more politically charged meaning, referring to geopolitical configurations of power and to power relations within a cultural process" (1993, 64).

I want to end by discussing the dangerous crossroads music of two performers who use the geopolitical U.S.-Mexico border as a site to thematize transcultural and local issues: Tish Hinojosa and El Vez, the self-described "Mexican Elvis."

Shortly after dark on a foggy Friday night in San Francisco an excited crowd lines the sidewalk along Geary at Fillmore Street. The multiracial, transcultural crowd (including Joan Baez and Dr. Loco) have come here from all over the city and the East Bay for a performance by Tish Hinojosa, accompanied by the electric accordion Texas-Mexican riffs of Santiago Jimeñez, Jr., and the solitary yodeling of Don Walser. While most performers have their followers, the fervor for Tish Hinojosa (fig. 5) and her U.S.-Mexico border musical be-in seems to be unique. An electric *rasquachi* atmosphere spills over into the mean streets. Right in front of us, Joan Baez practices singing a song in Spanish, the words surrounding us, trapping us, making it hard for us to see her in line sur-

Figure 5. Tish Hinojosa. Photograph by Joe Compton. Courtesy Rounder Records.

rounded by her entourage of *mujeres* (women). Later, she will sing this song with Hinojosa, the grain of their voices rubbing against each other and their audience. There is something about Hinojosa's border tour that is in concert with the extended U.S.-Mexico borderlands at this moment. Hinojosa's tour (to paraphrase Dr. John's song) is the right tour in the right place at the right time.

According to Hinojosa, her music (straight out of San Antonio) deserves a new name all its own—what she lyrically calls *Frontejas* (a combination of the Spanish words *frontera* and *Tejas*). *"Frontejas,"* she writes, is "a sound, a language, a feeling, a place formed by the river of culture and time washing over those who contemplate and investigate. We are pebbles shaping the current that creates tomorrow" (1995). Indeed, Hinojosa plays an eclectic blend of U.S.-Mexican border styles, mixing elements of *corridos, cumbias,* folk, rock, and country and western lyrics and lilting melodies. Her sophisticated undersongs cover an astonishing range of stories and issues, from romantic love ("Pajarillo Barranqueño") to inter-American songs of solidarity with feminist intellectuals such as Elena Ponaitowska ("Las Marías") to a wild, whirling *corrido* dedicated to, in Hinojosa's words, "the scholarly renegade," Américo Paredes. "Con Su Pluma en Su Mano" is a classic *corrido* alluding to the famous 1910 Texas-Mexican border ballad "Con Su Pistola en Su Mano" (With His Pistol in His Hand).

Although some San Francisco music journalists mislabeled Hinojosa as a "woman balladeer," or a Tejana *"corridista,"* the key to her popularity rests with the simple power of her songs to disentangle the segregated musical boundaries that divide the mass-mediated music industry in the Américas into monolingual genres and market segments.

Firmly grounded in some of the most enduring ethno-racial and musical traditions of the U.S.-Mexico border, Tish Hinojosa presents a music in touch with what George Lipsitz, in a related context, describes as "a music in touch with tomorrow—a music that displays the possibilities of the world that is on its way, but not yet here" (1993, 3).

The gender and dissident ethnographic consciousness that makes for exciting music also helps to explain the emphasis in Hinojosa's lyrics on her mother's *domesticana* experiences. "We knew [my mother, Cuquita] could sing," she writes in the compact disk's liner notes. "She confirmed this to us when she'd let loose on Manuel Ponce's 'Estrellita' a cappella. It wasn't until her death in 1985 that we learned of her childhood dreams [to pursue professional musical training] from those who had known her when she was young" (1995). While both men and women attended her border tour in equal numbers, the response she received from women at the Fillmore was jolting.

Part of the power of these U.S.-Mexico border songs lies in lyrics that always tell truths and that depict the problematic of unequal power relationships. In listening to Hinojosa sing at the Fillmore, I am reminded of how segregated we really are in our everyday, mass-mediated lives.

I am reminded, too, of Lipsitz's painful but graceful insights about popular culture and how it "often works to compress the infinitely diverse ways we have of living our lives on a terribly small number of themes and motifs" (1993, 5).

It is Hinojosa's hybrid combinations of U.S.-Mexico border music and lyrics that deserve our attention. The foot-stomping polka rhythms of "Pajarillo Barrenqueño" and its shrieking accordion playing by Jimeñez lure many of us at the Fillmore into doing a hard *tacquachito* on the dance floor. Similarly, the Texas-Mexican orchestra-inflected "Polka Fronterrestrial" duet with Ray Benson turns crisis-divided and propositioned California into a soaring, utopian moment of *transfrontera* solidarity: "Stars across a border sky / A symphony of light / in motion celebrating the night / here between the earth and sky . . . en revolucional brillando / en polka fronterarevolucionidad" (1995).

The Spanish-language lyrics of "Las Marías" issue a call for *vida* (life) and *libertad* (liberty), for all of the anonymous Marías who have left their *ranchitos* and livestock in the South and find themselves entrapped in kitchens in the North. "Las Marías" calls for a world in which subaltern women, together with their homemade "altars salty with tears" can find in the future "justice, peace, and culture" (1995). This sophisticated and complicated gendered stance across borders takes tangible form in the song's structure—its Spanish-language lyrics and Texas-Mexican accordion instrumentation celebrate a world in which women work and struggle together.

Part of the passion, *coraje* (rage), and emotion of Hinojosa's songs comes from her experience as a Chicana growing up in the South Texas *frontera*. Through feminist-inspired lyrics, Mexican and "Tex-Mex" musical forms, and songs like "Las Marías" that reject gender inequality as a result of the global political economy and embrace solidarity and culture, the songwriter positions herself as one of the newest performer-activists in the long revolution of cultural creativity among Chicanas in the U.S.-Mexico borderlands. This long legacy of struggle not only acknowledges feminist intellectuals such as Poniatowska across borders but also memorializes border writers such as Paredes. As Hinojosa writes, "Paredes was sparking the faces of many Mexican-American students, as well as uncovering some buried Texas history" (1995).

On the level of U.S.-Mexico border culture, this "buried history" of the cultures of U.S. imperialism poses great challenges to Chicana/o artists. Its legacy of conquest has not only rendered the dynamic cultural life of the site-specific *frontera* invisible to the rest of the United States but has also obscured the important hybrid cultural forms that workers from both sides of the border have produced.

It is, therefore, entirely fitting that Hinojosa dedicates her song "Con Su Pluma en Su Mano" to the Paredes family. Like all serious *corrido* composers, Hinojosa begins her song by asking her audience's permission to sing "sin tristeza ni maldad" (without sadness or malice) about Paredes's place in the U.S.-Mexico borderlands. Her opening stance lets her audience know that the central issue of her *corrido* is the life history of a U.S.-Mexico border intellectual. With this appropriate beginning, the singer then presents what Paredes himself called "a counterpointing of rhythms," "high register singing," and "rigor" (1958, 209). Contrapuntally combining musical and poetic material, the singer rapidly narrates a changing imagistic song in which her protagonist is born in 1915 and struggles along the bloody border in his childhood, and all the while "his eyes [see] things that have to be recounted" (1995).

Throughout her *corrido*, Hinojosa uses traditional poetic language to compare Paredes's counterdiscourse to the border itself. Certainly Hinojosa, as Limón claims of the *corrido*'s performance, must respond to her "relationship" to her "community," which in turn helps shape her own song (1992, 14). "Paredes," she sings, "won respect for us Chicanas/os" by traveling "the world" and fighting "en la guerra mundial." Years later, after the war, he returns to Texas, where he makes the white supremacist gatekeepers "nervous" by writing "palabras justas bien presentabas" (well-presented words of justice) (1995).

Of particular interest in Hinojosa's *corrido* is the singer's self-reflexiveness. Through her formal opening and closing of the song, the *corrido* flows from the social and back again through its references to her communal audience. Hinojosa's *corrido*, like the classic *corridos* of the U.S.-Mexico border conflict and the Mexican Revolution, functions as a repository of the historical data for a public that has not had access to the emergent counterdiscourses produced by Paredes in the academy. Unlike the classic *corridos*, however, Hinojosa in her *despedida* (farewell) offers her listeners neither the portrait of the male hero nor a character similar to what María Herrera-Sobek calls "the *canción de gesto*," or song of anger (1990, xiii). Instead Hinojosa's border ballad salutes Paredes the U.S.-Mexico border writer, singer, and radio disc jockey who passes down the long *corridos* of struggle contained in folklore: "I'll always treasure," she sings, the *corridos* "he has taught me," and "that's why I'm here to bring you this ballad because I've been an alumna of Paredes" (1995). Hinojosa's songwriting contributes to the ever-transforming genre of transfrontier writing. Her songs in *Frontejas,* on a more general level, thematize the many contradictions subaltern women feel about their everyday lives—especially their desire for peace in the face of the global political economy.

Although he does not use U.S.-Mexico *corridos* to do his cultural border work, the southern California performance artist El Vez (Robert Lopez) displays the same intense negotiations with identity that characterize the artists and writers we have examined in the preceding chapters. His declarations of cultural pride imaginatively use rockabilly riffs, signs, and symbols to testify to the Lipsitzean proposition that popular culture "enables people to rehearse identities, stances, and social situations not yet permissible in politics" (1994, 137). Indeed, El Vez's "borderization" of North America's pop icon Elvis serves as a concrete site where social relations are not only constructed but envisioned as well (fig. 6). El Vez's political songs, we might say after Louis Althusser, do not merely reflect reality in the *frontera,* they help construct it.

Thus envisaged, popular music helps Robert Lopez—a former member of the punk band the Zeros and present-day curator of the folk art gallery La Luz de Jesús in Los Angeles—to thematize and circulate local struggles for undocumented border-crossers visible at the national and transnational level. If "rock en español," as the music critic Josh Kun suggests, "has rapidly become one of the most popular genres in the world of commercial Latin music, proving that there is more to [the Américas] than pop *solistas* and brassy *banda* workouts" (1995, 28), El Vez joins *rockeros en español* such as Mexico's Cafe Tacuba and Maldita Vecindad, Argentina's Los Fabulosos Cadillacs, and Chile's Sexual Democracía in bringing one of the biggest noises yet into hemispheric inter-American musical circulation.

With a mass following in California, El Vez is one of the most recent rockers *en español* to be featured on MTV Latino and Jay Leno's *Tonight Show.* Hard-edged guitar work, tight rockabilly drumming, and slick vocals and inflections à la Elvis highlight his blend of Vegas glitter and Los Angeles frenzy. As Sandy Masuo puts it, El Vez's "music is a sort of an out-of-control *School House Rock* for adults" (1995, 84).

Admittedly, if it is true that El Vez's music (like the original *el rey*'s music) can be all things to all people, his U.S.-Mexico border sounds inevitably cut both ways. El Vez's performance art has been honed within

Figure 6. El Vez. Courtesy Big Pop and the artist.

the postmodern cultural dominant of spectacle and pastiche: "There's been a resurgence of younger Elvises," he notes, "but I like all Elvises" (quoted in Masuo 1995, 84). Thus, on one level, Lopez's music can function as a highly decentered tribute to what Greil Marcus describes as Elvis "the polite rocker, the country boy in Hollywood[,] true folk artist and commodity fetish" (1991, 26). Like Guillermo Gómez-Peña's performance art, El Vez's borderization of Elvis (complete with extravagant attire—mariachi pants, penciled mustache, and gelled pompadour), however, uses the economy of commodity circulation—compact disks—as a vehicle to protest against Proposition 187, the English-only movement, and the like. "Rather than an impersonation of Elvis," Masuo writes, "El Vez is a translation—or, as Lopez's business card proclaims—an incredible stimulation" (1995, 85).

Over the past two years El Vez has recorded five albums: *Fun in Español, Merry MeX-Mas, How Great Thou Art—El Vez's Greatest Hits, Aye Aye Blues,* and his best-known *Graciasland,* a blistering deterritorialization of Memphis geography and U.S.-Mexico border carnival and art. His cover of Elvis's "It's Now or Never," for instance, is a call for gang peace in the barrioscapes of Los Angeles:

> It's now or never, please no more gangs,
> People are dying, don't you understand
> Mañana will be too late, it's now or never it's not too late
> . . . .
> let's stop the hate. (1994)

Likewise, "Go Zapata Go," plugged into Chuck Berry's classic "Johnny Be Good," sings the praises of the Mexican revolutionary Emiliano Zapata, "way down past Louisiana, down in Mexico" fighting for "liberty and land." Implicit in El Vez's representation of Zapata is that, like the other Zapatista, Subcomandante Marcos, Zapata is bigger and more relevant than, say, the Aztec Temple Pilots on Latino MTV.

If Lopez is correct that "Elvis impersonators are almost like the court jesters of our time," then to be El Vez, he reasons, is to be a border trickster to the second power. At his best this is what El Vez accomplishes in songs such as "Immigration Time," which blends Elvis's "Suspicious Minds" with the Rolling Stones' "Sympathy for the Devil." Here he addresses directly the moral hypocrisy of California's and the U.S. government's immigration policy against undocumented Mexican workers:

> I'm caught in a trap, I can't walk out
> Because my foot's caught in the border fence
> Why can't you see, Statue of Liberty
> I am your homeless, tired, and weary.
> We can go on together, it's Immigration Time
> . . . .
> And we can build our dreams, it's Immigration Time.
> Yes I'm trying to go, get out of Mexico
> The promised land waits on the other side.
> Here they come again, they're trying to fence me in
> Wanting to live with the brave and the home of the free. . . . (1994)

Lopez's "Immigration Time" appropriates the major cultural tropes of U.S. immigration writing, a national writing understood in terms of what recent commentators have described as a ritual practice enacting Americanization. Rather than vilify the shared dilemmas of other ethno-racial groups whose icons and narratives have transformed U.S. immigrant writing into national archetypes, El Vez aligns the plight of undocumented Mexican workers with those archetypes and symbologies that scholars such as Werner Sollors and Thomas J. Ferraro have shown to be part and parcel of the national imaginary: WASPs, after all, in Ferraro's words, "fled religious prosecutions," and ethno-racial minorities "were forcibly removed, incorporated, enslaved, and interned" (1993, 7).

"Immigration Time," in my view, thematizes undocumented Mexican border-crossers' desire to move out of the margins (INS border fences notwithstanding) into the larger world where other groups elaborated their representations of America as "the home of the brave" and the "tired" and the "weary." It is, to be sure, a long walk from the border-patrolled fences of the U.S.-Mexico borderlands to New York's Statue of Liberty, but El Vez's song speaks to the profound degree of cultural self-distancing it takes to be in a position to write protest songs in English for undocumented migrant workers.

I am fascinated by how Lopez constructs in *Graciasland* one of the most incisive commentaries on the spectacle cultures of U.S. imperialism and in the process closes the gap between high literature and popular culture. One of the most complicated and enjoyable songs on *Graciasland* is entitled "Aztlán," El Vez's powerful sampling and reworking of Paul Simon's 1986 "Graceland," a controversial tribute to Elvis's home. Here the Chicano border songwriter directly confronts one of the thorniest problems in cultural studies: Can mass-mediated songs advance cross-cultural identifications while simultaneously claiming what Tish Hinojosa calls *libertad* and *justicia*?

At its most basic level, "Aztlán," like "Immigration Time," calmly queries notions of national boundaries that mainline Americans mostly take for granted:

> The river Rio Grande is carving like a national scar
> I am following the river making wetbacks
> Where my parents crossed to be where they are.
> I'm going to Aztlán, where I wanna be. . . .
> Homeboys, Chicanos, Latinas, and we are going to Aztlán
> My traveling companions, La Virgen, Miss Liberty,
> A map and my MEChA books

Well I have reason to believe, we all have been deceived
There still is Aztlán. (1994)

Lopez, the well-read folk art curator, decenters in "Aztlán" Simon's earlier postmodern lyrics of angst by breaking into the long cultural conversation in Chicano/a studies about the significance of Aztlán.

According to legend, Rafael Pérez-Torres writes, "Aztlán names the
Mexican homeland—the land of seven caves (Chicomostoc), the place
of the Twisted Hill (Colhuacán), the place of whiteness (Aztlán)—from
which the Mexica [people] migrated south toward the central plateau
in A.D. 820" (1995, 229). El Vez's song reterritorializes the ideas about
geography, culture, heritage, tradition, and migrations that have driven
Chicano/a discourse since at least 1965. It embodies what Pérez-Torres claims is "the history of dispossession endured by Mexicans, Mex-
ican-Americans, and Chicanos alike" (229).

If Aztlán as a metaphor for identity based on originary claims on
land needs—as John Rechy argued in *The Miraculous Day of Amalia
Gómez*—to be replaced by other paradigms, El Vez desires to hold on
to some of Aztlán's viability as a symbol. For, as Luis Leal has taught
us, Aztlán "conveys the image of the cave (or sometimes a hill)" representative of men and women's origins and, as a myth, "symbolizes
the existence of a paradisiacal region where injustice, evil, sickness, old
age, poverty, and misery do not exist" (1981, 17). El Vez's "Aztlán"
goes a long way toward dramatizing both the geopolitical and cultural
symbolic economies outlined in Leal's definition, marking on a map how
the Rio Grande became a border in the Treaty of Guadalupe Hidalgo
and "carv[ed] a national scar." More significant, Aztlán becomes in the
song a heterotopic space where documented and undocumented subjects can coexist: "Homeboys, Chicanos, Latinas, La Virgen, [and] Miss
Liberty . . . we're all going to Aztlán."

As a signifier for cultural dispossession and imaginary reconstruc-
tion, "Aztlán" suggests a rather different "audiotopia"[2] than we've seen,
for the song does not celebrate protonationalist Chicano movement
wholeness but makes room for a heterogeneous fragmentariness. El Vez's
approach in "Aztlán" is doubly relevant here because he contests the
traditional pathological view of diaspora and border-crossing experiences. In their much-acclaimed introduction to *Aztlán,* Rudolfo A. Anaya
and Francisco Lomelí, for example, argue that "through Aztlán we come
to better understand psychological time (identity), regional make-up
(place), and evolution (historical time). Without any one of these ingre-

dients, we would be contemporary displaced nomads, suffering the diaspora in our homeland" (1989, iv).

What would be the consequences of El Vez's "Aztlán" if it had tried to set the history of Chicanos/as in a provocative relationship with the modern ethno-racial history of diaspora in the Western Hemisphere? Anaya and Lomelí dismiss without consideration the possibility that something useful might be gained from seeing Chicano/a history in relationship to other histories of ethno-racial terror, undocumented border crossings, exile, and diaspora. El Vez's song raises the possibility that there might be something valuable from which we might learn, as Gilroy argues in *The Black Atlantic,* about the way modernity operates and how the ideologies of humanism have been complicit with the dispersal of humans (1993, 207–212).

The spiritual commentary on suffering in El Vez's "Aztlán" and its profane equivalent, feeling pain for undocumented border-crossers, are splendidly interwoven throughout the song:

> Miss Liberty tells me Aztlán gone, as if I didn't know that
> To get in you need a green card
> And she said losing home is like a bullet in your heart
> I am looking for a place, myth of my people
> That won't get blown apart,
> I'm going to Aztlán, Aztlán. . . .

If the song makes less of the wholeness of identity, place, and historical time that Anaya and Lomelí posit as central to the idea of Aztlán, El Vez seems closer to what Pérez-Torres describes "as the heterogeneity evident in the subject position Chicano/a." I agree with Pérez-Torres that "it is impossible to ignore the role that Chicanos and Mexican migrant workers play within a diaspora history. . . . It is illusory to deny the nomadic quality of the Chicano/a community in flux that yet survives and, through survival, affirms its own self" (1995, 61).

On another level, El Vez's "Aztlán" deterritorializes Simon's "Graceland" by reappropriating on a political level what Simon's song largely erased: South African sounds, especially its *mbube* and *mbaqanga* musical styles. His sampling of Simon's "Graceland" recirculates through the commodity form the intercultural and transracial character of the original song and in the process concretizes the historical fact that we cannot know that "in [our] own back yard . . . to get in you need a green card."

I have been trying to approach El Vez's *Graciasland* and some other texts that share their interests in history and social memory in an experimental spirit. Throughout *Border Matters* I have attempted to draw attention to the variety of ways in which some U.S.-Mexico border writers and activist-intellectuals have begun the work of exploring the terrors of border crossing and diaspora amid the debris of what El Vez calls our "national scar" of manifest destiny and the cultures of U.S. imperialism. To repeat and extend the argument I have made in the preceding chapters, these U.S.-Mexico border writers should not be used to build a smoothed-over canon of ethno-racial wholeness because they operate at other levels than those constructed by national borders.

In exploring a variety of texts, songs, political discourses, and visual cultural productions, I have noted how these different genres have responded to the U.S.-Mexico borderlands in different ways. The history of migration, of forced dispersal in the Américas as represented in vernacular border cultures, challenges us to delve into the specific calculus of the U.S.-Mexico border-crossing condition.

Additionally, by highlighting the contributions U.S.-Mexico border writers have made to mainline America, I mean to remind those made anxious by diaspora's borders that millions of new (im)migrants, many of whom are refugees from Central America, Mexico, Vietnam, Korea, India, and Pakistan, have irrevocably settled in the United States "without papers," as Los Tigres del Norte put it in "Jaula de Oro."

In my state of California, where the University of California Regents have begun dismantling Affirmative Action programs, I take solace in the brave (im)migrant students who enter my undergraduate classrooms at Berkeley, eager to earn the pride of their parents and their U.S.-Mexico borderland teacher. I then imagine how those who taught during the 1920s, 1930s, 1940s, and 1950s must have struggled to educate earlier generations of (im)migrant and refugee students. And I recall the historian Lawrence Levine's words: "[W]e who inhabit the United States at this moment are not unique, nor is our situation. Every previous generation of Americans has had its profound difficulties accepting ethnic and racial groups who did not seem to adhere to some earlier model; every previous generation of Americans had spied in the new immigration its own seeds of dissolution and chaos. . . . And every previous generation of Americans has been incorrect in its fears" (1996, 133).

With this, I give you my *despedido*.

Notes

PREFACE

1. From my "new historicist" colleagues Stephen Greenblatt and José E. Limón I have learned much about the dynamics of "cultural poetics" as a series of circulations and border-diaspora crossings. For Greenblatt, cultural poetics is fundamentally "the study of the collective making of distinct cultural practices and inquiry into the relations among those practices" (1988, 5); and for Limón, cultural poetics includes the roots and routes of "folk" practices. See Stephen Greenblatt's *Shakespearean Negotiations* and José E. Limón's *Dancing with the Devil*. In *Border Matters* I situate the "cultural poetics" along the U.S.-Mexico border "dialectically" within what Lisa Lowe calls "the contradictions of the political and economic spheres" (156) and what Timothy J. Dunn describes as a zone of low-intensity militarized conflict. See Lisa Lowe's *Immigrant Acts* and Timothy J. Dunn's *The Militarization of the U.S.-Mexico Border, 1978–1992*.

2. My use of "ethno-race" relies on the Berkeley historian David Hollinger's formulations in *PostEthnic America*. According to Hollinger, "The concept of race . . . serves us reasonably well when we want to be aware of a pattern of behavior: it refers to the lines along which people have been systematically mistreated on the basis of certain physical characteristics. Race does not serve us at all well, however," he writes, "from a postethnic perspective" (35, 34). Thus Hollinger prefers "to subsume" race "under the more general category ethnoracial blocs" (39). See also Michael Omi and Howard Winant's *Racial Formation in the United States*.

3. See "U.S. Boosts Enforcement along Border," *San Francisco Chronicle*, January 12, 1996, 1, A17.

4. To travel in the "Border Patrol State," Silko writes, "take a drive down Interstate 8 or Interstate 10, along the U.S.-Mexico border. Notice the Border Patrol checkpoints all vehicles must pass through. When the border patrol agent asks you where you are coming from and where you are going, don't kid around and answer in Spanish—you could be there all afternoon. Look south into Mexico and enjoy the view while you are still able, before you find yourself behind the twelve-foot steel curtain the U.S. government is building" (114). See Leslie Marmon Silko's "Fences against Freedom" in *Yellow Woman and a Beauty of the Spirit*.

5. See Donald Pease's "New Americanists." "By the term field-Imaginary," Pease writes, "I mean to designate a location for the disciplinary unconscious. . . . Here abides the field's fundamental syntax—its tacit assumptions, convictions, primal words, and the charged relations binding them together" (11–12).

6. See, for example, Alfred Arteaga's edited anthology, *An Other Tongue*, David Román's splendid "Teatro Viva!" and Yvonne Yarbro-Bejarano's remarkable book on the major Chicana public intellectual, Cherríe Moraga, *The Rights to Passion*.

INTRODUCTION: TRACKING BORDERS

1. For recent discussion of the *corrido,* see John H. McDowell's "The Corrido of Greater Mexico as Discourse, Music, and Event"; Maria Herrera-Sobek's *The Mexican Corrido;* and José E. Limón's *Mexican Ballads, Chicano Poems. Technobanda,* a ruralized *norteño* brass band sound with synthesizers and keyboards and a driving polka beat, is revolutionizing mass-mediated radio in California. In January 1993 the number one radio station in Los Angeles was *banda*-heavy KLAX-FM (La Equis), reflecting the dramatic near-majority (not minority) presence of Chicanos and U.S. Latinos in the state. *Technobanda* and *conjunto* sounds, to be sure, also dominate in northern California: San Jose (KAZA-AM and KLOK-AM) and San Francisco (KIQI-AM and KOFY-AM). See Dan Levy's "Spanish Radio Boom Rides 'Banda' Crest" and David Hayes Bautista and Gregory Rodríguez's "Technobanda." *Technobanda,* as George Lipsitz emphasizes, "registers the most visible, demographic, and political change" (6) in the public and private spaces of California, creating "new social worlds and social relations" and "bear[ing] the burden of making sense of the horrifying changes" (17) in the new transnational economy. See George Lipsitz's "'Home Is Where the Hatred Is.'"

2. Lyrics to Los Tigres del Norte's "Jaula de Oro" can be found in Leo R. Chávez's *Shadowed Lives,* 158, 177.

3. See L. A. Chung's and Phuong Le's "2.1 Million Illegals in California." Of relevance here are Alex Saragoza's insights that "California has approximately 50 percent of all undocumented immigrants in the United States, 78 percent of whom are of Mexican origin. Of all Mexican immigrants granted amnesty under IRCA [the Immigration Reform and Control Act passed in 1986], 55 percent are residents of California. These statistics suggest the intense interaction in the past, present, and future between Mexicanos and the Latino population of California." Personal correspondence with the author, July 27, 1995.

4. Under the Fourteenth Amendment to the U.S. Constitution, anyone born in the United States is automatically a citizen.

5. For superb, though uneven, experimental travel autoethnographies of this "third" country, see Tom Miller, *On the Border;* Ted Conover, *Coyotes;* and Luis A. Urrea, *Across the Wire.* Chapter 6, "Tijuana Calling," examines in detail Urrea's hybrid autoethnography.

6. My understanding of people "between" culture is indebted to Renato Rosaldo's "Ideology, Place, and People without Culture."

7. One must note here Raymond Williams's suggestion that British cultural studies began with his experiences of teaching "adult education" classes in village halls around the south of England in the 1950s. See Williams's *Politics and Letters.* Additionally, it is well worth noting that Richard Hoggart outlined the Birmingham CCCS project in his 1963 essay "Schools of English and Contemporary Society" as follows: "The field for possible work in Contemporary Cultural Studies can be divided into three parts: one is, roughly, historical and philosophical; another is, again roughly, sociological; the third—which will be the most important—is the literary critical." See Hoggart's *Speaking to Each*

Other, 255. When Stuart Hall replaced Hoggart as CCCS director in 1968, he immediately decentered its tidy interdisciplinarity (history, philosophy, sociology, and literary criticism) by focusing on ideological and mass signifying practices. For Hall's views on this subject, see "Cultural Studies and the Politics of Internationalization" and "The Formation of the Diasporic Intellectual" in *Stuart Hall: Critical Dialogues in Cultural Studies,* ed. David Morley and Kuan-Hsing Chen. When Richard Johnson succeeded Hall as CCCS director in 1979, he, too, moved the center in new directions, emphasizing work on the historical constructions of subjectivities. Perhaps Stuart Hall puts it best in his interview with Kuan-Hsing Chen when he reminds us that "British cultural studies in the 1990s is very significantly different" from, say, earlier British cultural studies, for "it is now overwhelmingly preoccupied with new questions, such as national cultures, ethnicity, [and] identities" (394).

8. See Paul Gilroy, *The Black Atlantic.*

CHAPTER 1. CULTURAL THEORY IN THE U.S.-MEXICO BORDERLANDS

1. In "Daring to Dream," Mary Louise Pratt writes, "When it comes to culture . . . Europe has continued to possess the American, especially the Euroamerican imagination, to be its point of reference, regardless of the realities that surround us here" (13).

2. My work on José de Escandón has relied on Herbert E. Bolton's *Texas in the Middle Eighteenth Century* and Hubert J. Miller's *José de Escandón.* Additionally, my brief periodizing of the main phases of the borderlands into Spanish, Mexican, and U.S. contexts relies on Patricia Nelson Limerick's *The Legacy of Conquest,* esp. chap. 7, pp. 222–258. Needless to say, my view of the U.S.-Mexico borderlands differs from the sentimentalized "fantasy history" of the Spanish borderlands constructed (between 1911 and 1965) by Bolton and his students at the University of California at Berkeley. See, for example, Bolton's *The Spanish Borderlands* and John Bannon's edited anthology *Bolton and the Spanish Borderlands.*

3. See Patricia Williams's *The Alchemy of Race and Rights* and Richard Griswold del Castillo's *The Treaty of Guadalupe.*

4. See "Border Patrol Accused of Serious Abuse," *San Francisco Chronicle,* June 1, 1992, A6.

5. My discussion of the politics of postmodernism makes use of Andreas Huyssen's *After the Great Divide,* Julian Pefanis's *Heterology and the Postmodern,* and Santiago Colás's *Postmodernity in Latin America.*

6. See Paul Gilroy's *There Ain't No Black in the Union Jack.*

7. Ibid.

8. See Mary Louise Pratt's *Imperial Eyes.* Also relevant is Edward W. Said's *Culture and Imperialism.*

9. For a rich history of Casteñeda, Sánchez, and Campa, intellectual leaders of the "Mexican American Generation," see Mario T. García, *Mexican Americans,* esp. pt. 3, 231–292. For discussions of Jovita González's cultural work,

see Gloria Treviño-Velasquez, "Cultural Ambivalence in Early Chicana Prose Fiction," and José E. Limón, *Dancing with the Devil,* esp. pp. 60–75. See also Jovita González's 1930s historical romance, *Caballero.*

10. See Oscar J. Martínez, *Border Boom Town,* and Mario T. García, *Desert Immigrants.* For a postcolonial reading of Arturo Islas's *The Rain God* and Gloria Anzaldúa's *Borderlands / La Frontera,* see José David Saldívar, *The Dialectics of Our America.*

11. See the following anthologies produced by the Birmingham Centre for Contemporary Cultural Studies: *Women Take Issue* and *The Empire Strikes Back.*

12. See George Lipsitz, "Cruising Around the Historical Bloc," and *Dangerous Crossroads;* Steven Loza, *Barrio Rhythm;* Rosa Linda Fregoso, *The Bronze Screen;* Carl Gutiérrez-Jones, *Rethinking the Borderlands;* Sonia Saldívar-Hull, "Feminism on the Border"; and José E. Limón, *Dancing with the Devil.* Of particular relevance is Saldívar-Hull's analysis of *telenovela* (soap opera) and romance culture in the everyday lived experiences of Chicanas.

13. See Fredric Jameson, "Reification and Utopia in Mass Culture," and George Lipsitz, *Time Passages.*

14. James Clifford's "Traveling Cultures" and his unpublished essay, "Borders and Diasporas," have helped me work through the complex predicaments of local and cosmopolitan cultures.

CHAPTER 2. AMÉRICO PAREDES
AND DECOLONIZATION

1. José David Saldívar, "Chicano Border Narratives as Cultural Critique" and "On Américo Paredes."

2. See Raymond Williams, "Region and Class in the Novel," in *Writing in Society.*

3. For a parallel view of the emergent border intellectual, see Abdul Jan-Mohamed's essay on Edward W. Said, "Worldliness-without-World, Home-lessness-as-Home." See also, for a reading of Welsh-European Raymond Williams as border novelist and critic, Dennis Dworkin and Leslie G. Roman, eds., *Views Beyond the Border Country.*

4. Américo Paredes was born in Brownsville, Texas, on September 3, 1915. His publishing career began in 1934, when one of his poems received first place in a literary contest sponsored by Trinity College in Texas and when he began contributing poetry to *La Prensa,* the major Spanish-language newspaper of San Antonio, Texas. After graduating from high school, from 1936 until 1943, Paredes wrote for both the English- and Spanish-language editions of the *Brownsville Herald,* contributing feature articles on culture and society. Called into the army during World War II, he served as a war correspondent in the Pacific and later as political editor of *Stars and Stripes,* the military newspaper. As political editor Paredes reported on the postwar trials of Japanese generals accused of war crimes. After the war he lived briefly in Japan, working as a

journalist for the American Red Cross, visiting Korea, and witnessing Mao's revolution in China. In 1950 (with two years of junior college credit) Paredes returned to Texas, completed work on his college degree, and received highest honors in English. Six years later he received his Ph.D. in English from the University of Texas at Austin.

5. My study of Américo Paredes makes use of Ramón Saldívar's *Chicano Narrative*, "Bordering on Modernity," and "The Borderlands of Culture." See also Héctor Calderón, "Texas Border Literature"; and José E. Limón, *Mexican Ballads, Chicano Poems*, 45–80, and *Dancing with the Devil*, 76–96.

6. In 1951 Paredes, while a student at the University of Texas at Austin, completed an extraordinary collection of short stories and sections from *George Washington Gómez* entitled "Border Country." The unpublished collection won first place in a literary contest sponsored by the *Dallas Times-Herald*. In this chapter I do not focus on "Cold Night," "Over the Waves Is Out," and "Gringo," stories from "Border Country" emphasizing the geopolitics of cultural identity along the Texas-Mexico border. Set against the historical backdrop of the Plan de San Diego uprising in 1915, "Over the Waves Is Out" takes its title from Juventino Rosas's famous Mexican waltz "Sobre las Olas." The story is Paredes's allegorical comment on the relation of music and his developing aesthetic desires: "And finally [the music] came, faintly at first, then more distinctly, though never loud, splashing and whirling about, twisting in intricate eddies of chords and bright waterfalls of melody, or falling in separate notes into night, like drops of quicksilver, rolling, glimmering" (1994, 14). "The Gringo" chronicles Ygnacio's everyday life chances at the beginning of President Polk's military invasion of South Texas and Mexico in 1846. Polk had ordered Zachary Taylor to move his U.S. Army to the mouth of the Rio Grande, and Taylor had done so, arriving in South Texas on March 28, 1846. When Mexican troops crossed the Rio Grande in April and then later attacked the U.S. Army at Palo Alto on May 8 and at Resaca de las Palmas on May 9, Taylor counterattacked and won. Paredes's protagonist Ygnacio experiences these struggles firsthand. His father and brother are killed by Texan gringos near Nueces, but Ygnacio's life is spared when the gringos mistake him as one of their own. Nursed back to health by Prudence, one of the gringo's daughters, Ygnacio begins an interracial romance with her. It is quickly ended by the father when he realizes that Ygnacio is just another "greaser." The story ends with Ygnacio, machete and pistol in hand, charging against the U.S. Army "and the guns of Palo Alto [going] off inside his head" (1994, 56).

7. For a groundbreaking reading of Paredes's *"With His Pistol in His Hand"* as a "strong sociological poem," see José E. Limón's *Mexican Ballads, Chicano Poems*, esp. chap. 3, 61–77.

8. For a full analysis of racial segregation in South Texas, see David Montejano, *Anglos and Mexicans in the Making of Texas, 1836–1986*.

9. While the American studies movement was a necessary response to the formalist practices of New Criticism in the United States, it was not and has not been an oppositional movement.

10. For a superb discussion of *corrido* subjectivity, see Ramón Saldívar,

Chicano Narrative, esp. chap. 2, "The Folk Base of Chicano Narrative," 26–46. See also José David Saldívar, "Chicano Border Narratives as Cultural Critique."

11. For an excellent study of John Steinbeck's *The Grapes of Wrath,* see Louis Owens, *John Steinbeck's Re-Vision of America.* Also relevant here is Barbara Foley's *Radical Representations.*

12. For an absorbing study of the Plan de San Diego, see James A. Sandos, *Rebellion in the Borderlands.*

13. My reading of music and political identity draws from Paul Gilroy's "Sounds Authentic." See also Manuel Peña's *The Texas-Mexican Conjunto.*

14. For comparative readings of U.S. and Latin American poetry, see Vera Kutzinski's *Against the American Grain.* Luisa Espinel, as Paredes acknowledges in a long footnote in the volume, popularized the *son* in the Southwest borderlands when she toured "the U.S. with a program of Southwest Mexican songs in the mid-1930s, which she called "Songs My Mother Taught Me" (140).

15. For detailed close readings of these writers, see chapters 4 and 5, below.

16. While Paredes's thematization of Chicano/a everyday life in South Texas as a "colonized" experience under military occupation may strike some as bizarre, more recent historians of Texas agree with Paredes's modernist representations. In *Lone Star* T. R. Fehrenback juxtaposes the position of Chicanos/as in early twentieth-century Texas to that of subalterns in Israel's West Bank. See also Mahmud Darwish's *Victims of a Map.*

17. "Transculturation" was coined in the 1940s by the Cuban sociologist Fernándo Ortíz in a pioneering study of Afro-Cuban culture, *Contrapunteo cubano del tobaco y azucar* (1940). Ortíz proposed the term to replace the paired concepts of acculturation and deculturation that described the transference of culture in reductive fashion from within the interests of the metropolis. Of relevance here is Mary Louise Pratt's *Imperial Eyes.* According to Pratt, "Ethnographers have used [the term *transculturation*] to describe how subordinated or marginal groups select and invent from materials transmitted to them by a dominant or metropolitan culture" (6). See also Gustavo Pérez Firmat's *The Cuban Condition* and Silvia Spitta's *Between Two Waters.* For Pérez Firmat and Spitta, Ortíz's theory of transculturation displaces for U.S. Latino studies the old U.S. "melting pot" metaphor of cultural contact.

CHAPTER 3. CHANGING
BORDERLAND SUBJECTIVITIES

1. See Marta E. Sánchez, *Contemporary Chicana Poetry;* Ramón Saldívar, *Chicano Narrative;* José E. Limón, *Mexican Ballads, Chicano Poems;* Carl Gutiérrez-Jones, *Rethinking the Borderlands;* and Rafael Pérez-Torres, *Movements in Chicano Poetry.*

2. The best introductory essays on Montoya's poetry are Orlando Trujillo's "Linguistic Structures in José Montoya's 'El Louie'" and Olivia Castellanos's "José Montoya." For postmodernist and cultural studies readings of Montoya's

work, see Renato Rosaldo's *Culture and Truth*, 215–217; and José E. Limón's *Mexican Ballads, Chicano Poems*, 95–112.

3. Although Paredes claims that the *corrido* proper entered a "decadent" phase after the 1930s, Montoya's customizing of the *corrido* in the 1960s suggests that the border form can be recuperated and still maintain its cutting edge. See Paredes's *"With His Pistol in His Hand."*

4. For an extensive examination, see Mauricio Mazón's *The Zoot Suit Riots*.

5. See Montoya's "Thoughts on La Cultura, the Media, Con Safos, and Survival."

6. For a detailed examination of early nineteenth-century *corridos*, see Ramón Saldívar's *Chicano Narrative*, esp. chap. 2, "The Folk Base of Chicano Narrative," 26–46.

7. Of relevance to my reading of *corridos* and Chicano/a poetry is Teresa McKenna's splendid "On Chicano Poetry and the Political Age."

8. See Norma Alarcón's "Chicana Feminism," Cordelia Candelaria's *Chicano Poetry*, Chela Sandoval's "U.S. Third World Feminism," Alvina Quintana's *Home Girls*, and Sonia Saldívar-Hull's *Feminism on the Border*.

9. According to Deleuze and Guattari, schizoanalysis must be applied to literary discourse. As an old-fashioned semiotic practice, schizoanalysis reveals the hybrid and fragmented discourse of "deterritorialization." See their *Anti-Oedipus*.

10. My position here is indebted to Gayatri Chakravorty Spivak's "Finding Feminist Readings" in her *In Other Worlds*.

CHAPTER 4. THE PRODUCTION OF SPACE
BY ARTURO ISLAS AND CARMEN LOMAS GARZA

1. The most provocative attempts to understand the impact of Puritan rhetoric on American culture and literature are Sacvan Bercovitch's *The Puritan Origins of the American Self* and *The American Jeremiad*. Bercovitch's project is essentially a study of American ideologies. In *Migrant Souls* Islas challenges the Puritan typological "Flight Out of Egypt" by creating a counterdiaspora in his text.

2. In his posthumous novel, *La Mollie and the King of Tears*, Islas continued to weave genealogies and fates of his border characters. In this novel Louie, a Chicano from Texas, first introduced in *Migrant Souls*, is earning a living in the San Francisco Bay Area.

3. In *Telling Identities* Rosaura Sánchez brilliantly theorizes the topospatiality of nineteenth-century Alta Californio *testimonios* that I am advocating for postcontemporary Chicano/a literature. In Sánchez's formulation, Alta Californio identity is "a representation generated reflexively and collectively within concrete historical, social, and spatial conditions" (37). Alta Californio identity, for her, thus "requires a framework that will allow us to explore not only shifts in positionality in relation to structural location [but also] to different social spaces—the territory, the mission, the *rancho*, the *ranchería*, the territorial administration and the region" (37). Also relevant are the following inci-

sive and erudite Ph.D. dissertations on space in Chicano/a literary and cultural studies: Raúl Villa, "Tales of the Second City"; Margarita Barceló, "Geography of Struggle"; and Mary Patricia Brady, "Extinct Lands, Scarred Bodies."

4. Suffice it to say that in this chapter I want to move away from an exclusively phenomenological poetics and focus our attention on the spatiality of social life, the actually lived and socially produced space of geography and the relations between them.

5. On the ideology of immigration, see Virginia Yans-McLaughlin, ed., *Immigration Reconsidered.*

6. In contradistinction to the male-centered *rasquachismo* (jive aesthetics), Amalia Mesa-Bains offers the spatial poetics of *la domesticana,* "defying the restrictive gender identity imposed by Chicano culture" (1991b, 132). See also Mesa-Bain's excellent "Chicana Chronicle and Cosomology: The Works of Carmen Lomas Garza" in Carmen Lomas Garza's *A Piece of My Heart / Pedacitos de mi corazón.* Mesa-Bains is absolutely right when she theorizes that "as we enter the world of Carmen Lomas Garza's paintings we are struck by her keen observations. We see, witness, watch, peer, scan and behold her gaze. . . . Hers is an instructive gaze" (21). From a more recent perspective, Lomas Garza's *Códice* can be read as a meditation on what Walter Mignolo has called "colonial semiosis" (1995, 8).

7. See Renato Rosaldo's graceful reading of the politics of culture in the short fiction of Denise Chávez, Sandra Cisneros, and Alberto Ríos: "Fables of the Fallen Guy."

CHAPTER 5. ON THE BAD EDGE OF *LA FRONTERA*

1. For more on Guillermo Gómez-Peña's career and performance border art, see Claire F. Fox's excellent essay "The Portable Border."

2. In *Border Writing,* Emily Hicks supplements Gómez-Peña's use of Deleuze and Guattari's desiring machine to explore postmodernism.

3. Nancy Fraser's term, "juridical-administrative-state apparatus," of course, echoes Louis Althusser's phrase, "ideological state apparatus," in "Ideology and Ideological State Apparatuses: Notes towards an Investigation" (in Althusser 1971). In general Fraser's JAT can be understood as a subclass of an Althusserian institutional state apparatus (ISA), and this is how I am using it in this chapter.

4. For more on this cultural and legal redefinition of citizenship, see Renato Rosaldo's "Cultural Citizenship." Rosaldo uses cultural citizenship "both in the legal sense (one either does or does not have a document) and also in the familiar sense of the spectrum from full citizenship to second-class citizenship" (7); he uses the term *cultural* "to emphasize the local people's own descriptions of what goes into being fully enfranchised" (7). Also relevant here is Gerald P. López's "The Work We Know So Little About."

5. Even at the mass-mediated level, the national press rarely mentions Latinos/as when discussing ethno-race relations and urban problems. As Gerald P. López writes, "When people visualize the goings-on in this country they most

often don't even seem to see the 25 million or so Latinos who live here." Thus, it is hardly surprising, López notes, that "we Latinos haven't made it onto some list of nationally prominent folks—in this case, it's 'The Newsweek 100' of cultural elite. . . . Having no Latinos on the Newsweek list might not get under our skin were it not so utterly familiar." See López's "My Turn."

6. For cogent discussions of Mexico's *frontera sur*, see Andrés Fábregas Puig, "Mexico frente a la frontera sur," and Andrés Medina, "En frontera sur y los procesos étnicos."

7. According to Debra Castillo, "What tends to drop out of sight . . . is . . . the *Carib*, the indigenous element that waits, another hidden layer of writing on the scratched surface of the palimpsest, the unrecognized other half of the backdrop against which the transients shuffle, and suffer, and die. What remains undefined is the nameless act of violence that has suppressed the *Carib*, as well as the outline of the form the history of its repression might take" (81). See Castillo's splendid *Talking Back*.

8. In 1942 the U.S. government negotiated a treaty with Mexico popularly known as the *bracero* program, which provided the destination country with the use of Mexicans as temporary workers. When the treaty expired in 1964 generations of Mexicans had "legally" migrated to the United States.

9. As Leo Chávez suggests in *Shadowed Lives*, "While migrants may not sever family ties, those ties are stretched across time, space, and national boundaries" (119).

10. According to Gerald López, "Data strongly suggest that only one to four percent of undocumented Mexicans take advantage of public services such as welfare, unemployment benefits, food stamps, AFDC benefits and the like; that eight to ten percent pay Social Security and income taxes; that the majority do not file for income tax refunds; that all contribute to sales taxes; and that at least some contribute to property taxes" (636). See López's superb monograph "Undocumented Mexican Migration."

11. Frances Toor, *A Treasury of Mexican Folkways*, 532.

12. According to Mike Davis, noir as a genre refers to the southern California writers and film directors—from James Cain to the rap group NWA—who "repainted the image of Los Angeles as a deracinated urban hell" (37). See Davis's *City of Quartz*.

13. See Juan Bruce-Novoa's "The Space of Chicano Literature Update: 1978," in *Retrospace*. See also B. Satterfield's "John Rechy's Tormented World" and Didier Jaén's "John Rechy."

14. For more on the U.S.-Mexico borderlands "bridge" consciousness, see Cherríe Moraga and Gloria Anzaldúa, eds., *This Bridge Called My Back*. According to Norma Alarcón, "The writer in *Bridge* was aware of the displacement of her subjectivity across a multiplicity of discourses: feminist/lesbian, nationalist, racial, and socioeconomic. The peculiarity of her displacement implied a multiplicity of positions from which she was driven to grasp or understand herself and her relations with the real" (28). See Alarcón's incisive "The Theoretical Subject(s) of *This Bridge Called My Back* and Anglo-American Feminism."

15. See Ralph Ellison's *Invisible Man*, 439. Early in the novel, John Rechy writes, "They just don't see us, Amalia knew" (67).

16. See Brenda Bright's "The Meaning of Roles and the Role of Showing."

17. For more on Darryl F. Gates's use and abuse of the Los Angeles Police Department, see Mike Rothmiller and Ivan Goldman's *L.A. Secret Police*. "Unbeknownst to both friends and enemies of the LAPD," the authors write, "[Gates's secret unit, OCID,] maintained secret, Stalinesque dossiers" (1992, 9) on the shakers and movers of southern California. This unit's attitude toward non-Anglos, of course, was not a positive one, for "racism was expected, part of the group's persona. Shrink from it and you were an odd duck, perhaps a pink one" (30).

18. Needless to say, Manny's "entrepreneurial spirit" as a "defiant individualist" in East Los Angeles / Hollywood has to be understood within Martín Sánchez Jankowski's reading of gang business in general: "Gang members' entrepreneurial spirit," he argues, "is both stimulated and reinforced by the desire to resist what they perceive to be their parents' resignation to poverty and failure" (108). See Martín Sánchez Jankowski's excellent *Islands in the Streets*.

19. I have profited from Ella Shohat's sharp critique of the rather loose and ahistorical use of the terms *postcolonial, hybridity,* and *syncretism* in her "Notes on the Post-Colonial." Also relevant here is James Clifford's call in "Borders and Diasporas" for "close attention to discrepant hybridities, with attention to the power relations producing various syncretic forms" (4).

20. Other Chicano New Wave and punk bands in Los Angeles include The Brat and The Plugz. As Steven Loza writes, "[The Brat's and The Plugz's] style has relied on the punk and new wave formations, although certain musical nuances and literary styles still relate to aspects of the historically unique Chicano/Mexican musical tradition" (110). See Steven Loza's exhaustive *Barrio Rhythm*.

CHAPTER 6. TIJUANA CALLING

1. It goes without saying that postmodern theory, a product long associated with East-West discursive spaces (Paris, Frankfurt, London, and New York), is dissected by South-North centers and horizons (San Salvador, Mexico City, Tijuana, and Los Angeles). This chapter maps the South-North experiences of migration and hybridity—working oppositionally against dominant postmodern horizons. See Néstor García Canclini, *Culturas híbridas*.

2. According to Fredric Jameson, "Cognitive mapping in the broadest sense comes to require the coordination of existential data (the empirical position of the subject) with unlived, abstract conceptions of the geographic totality" (52). See Fredric Jameson, *Postmodernism, or, The Cultural Logic of Late Capitalism*. Also relevant is Fredric Jameson, "Cognitive Mapping."

3. "Tourism," Rob Nixon writes, "is symptomatic and constitutive of the inexhaustible quest for ["true," "real," and "authentic" objects and experiences], a quest that is also a form of conquest" (61). See Rob Nixon, *London Calling*.

4. See David Spurr's excellent *The Rhetoric of Empire*. My reading of colonial discourse in U.S.-Mexico border travel writing is much indebted to this book.

5. Indeed, this intertextual debt to Michael Herr's *Dispatches* is highlighted by Luis Alberto Urrea's epigraph at the beginning of *Across the Wire* taken from Herr's book. For a lucid analysis of *Dispatches* and postmodernist war, see Fredric Jameson's *Postmodernism,* 44–45. Also relevant is Chela Sandoval's remarkable and diplomatic critique of Jameson's theorizing of postmodernism in "Oppositional Consciousness in the Postmodern World."

6. According to the Mexican cultural critic Carlos Monsiváis, "En la crónica, el juego literario usa a discreción de primera persona o narra libremente los acontecimientos como vistos y vivido desde la interioridad ajena" (In the chronicle, the playful writer uses to his or her discretion the first person or liberally narrates events as seen and lived from another interiority) (1980, 13). See Carlos Monsiváis, *A ustedes les consta.* I thank Sergio de la Mora for pointing this out to me.

7. "Cultural reconversions," García Canclini writes, "are hybrid transformations generated by the horizontal co-existence of a number of symbolic systems. . . . [Cultural] reconversion . . . challenges the assumption that cultural identity is based on a patrimony, and that this patrimony is constituted by the occupation of a territory and by collections of works and monuments" (32). See Néstor García Canclini, "Cultural Reconversion."

8. Gómez-Peña and Rodriguez are quoted on the back cover of *The Other Side.*

9. The cassette tape Rubén Martínez alludes to probably is that of Maldita Vecindad; their 1989 hit song "Mojado" (Wetback) interestingly contains the haunting refrain alluding to "El Otro Lado" (The Other Side).

10. The U.S. Latino/a critical response to Richard Rodriguez's *Days of Obligation* largely follows this pattern. For instance, the Chicano poet Gary Soto harshly criticizes Rodriguez's "seemingly random opinions" based on what he calls "a grab bag of research." On a more schoolmarmish level, Soto dismisses "Rodriguez's penchant for writing in incomplete sentences, as if a greater mystery is instilled in the reader when documentary evidence is elliptical. He overuses parentheses, dashes, italicized passages and other cosmetic devices that only interrupt the reader's thoughts" (10). See Gary Soto, "Rodriguez Meditates on His Mixed Roots." Similarly, the Guatemalan-American writer Victor Perera writes that "Rodriguez's gnomic prose erects a prickly hedge that keeps the reader at a distance, suspended between sympathy for his dilemma and repugnance at his callous self-absorption" (64). Briefly, for Perera, Rodriguez the traveler comes across as "the detached prig . . . who visits Mexico City on an American Express bus tour for writers, refusing to taste the liquor or engage the natives in meaningful discourse, . . . a self-parodying Hispanic Prufrock (Do I dare eat a taco?)" (64). See Victor Perera, "The Labyrinth of Solitude." More positively, Rubén Martínez confesses, "I write about Richard Rodriguez with trepidation. He is a Berkeley-educated essayist. I dropped out of college. . . . He has been identified—unfairly, I think—as a right-winger because of his views on bilingual education and affirmative action. I identify with the political left. . . . Five years ago, had I been assigned to write about Rodriguez, I would have self-righteously placed him on the other side of the cultural and political bor-

der. Today, I realize that we've always lived on the same side of the border" (18). See Rubén Martínez, "My Argument with Richard Rodriguez." For favorable reviews of Gómez-Peña's live performances of *Border Brujo*, see the following: Cindi Carr in *Artforum* (January 1989): 119; Miriam Horn, "The Art of Ethnic Tensions," *U.S. News & World* Report (December 30, 1991): 79; Kent Neely in *Theatre Journal* (December 1990): 497. George Yúdice takes on Gómez-Peña's global border-crossing pretensions in "We Are Not the World," *Social Text* (1992): 202. Finally, Claire F. Fox astutely notes that Gómez-Pena's concept of the U.S.-Mexico border in *Border Brujo*, like that of his Border Art Workshop colleagues' paradigm, is fundamentally not a social category but "a phenomenological category, . . . something that people carried within themselves" (63). See Claire F. Fox, "The Portable Border."

11. For an excellent discussion of Richard Rodriguez as a paradigmatic "Pocho," see Tomás Rivera, "Richard Rodriguez's *Hunger of Memory* as Humanistic Antithesis."

12. The "archetype of the Mexican woman," Roger Bartra writes, "is the Malintzin-Guadalupe duality—the Chingadalupe [a compound of *chingada* (whore) and Guadalupe], an ideal image that the Mexican male must form of his companion, who must fornicate with unbridled enjoyment and at the same time be virginal and comforting" (160). See Roger Barta, *The Cage of Melancholy.*

13. See Américo Paredes's 1978 essay reprinted in 1993 as "The Problem of Identity in a Changing Culture."

14. Perera writes in his astute review of *Days of Obligation* that Rodriguez here "has a point": "Mother Mexico, with her abundance of oil reserves, her resurgent optimism and can-do president, has kicked up her traces and is poised to overtake her tired, fast-declining neighbor to the North" (63). See Victor Perera, "Labyrinth of Solitude."

15. For a sense of the range of the Taller de Arte Fronterizo group, see David Avalos's *Café Mestizo*, Art Exhibit, 1989; Emily Hicks's *Border Writing;* and Guillermo Gómez-Pena and Jeff Kelly, eds., *The Border Art Workshop.*

CHAPTER 7. REMAPPING
AMERICAN CULTURAL STUDIES

1. My use of the term *frontier modernism* is meant to suggest in part the distinctive nature of modernism along the extended U.S.-Mexico border from, say, the 1840s to the 1940s. I am also using it to describe a set of issues as both a chronological and a qualitative concept.

2. In contrast to my dialogical views of the musics of America, see Ronald Reagan's Inaugural Address, which he delivered on January 21, 1985. Using Frederick Jackson Turner's frontier rhetoric, Reagan declared that "a settler pushes west and sings a song, and the song echoes out forever and fulfills the unknowing air. It is the American sound. It is hopeful, big-hearted, idealistic,

daring, decent and fair. That's our heritage, that's our song. We still sing it." See *Public Papers of the Presidents*, 58.

3. For more on phantasmatic identification, see Judith Butler's *Bodies That Matter*, esp. pp. 93–120.

4. My discussion here makes use of Joseph C. Porter's *Paper Medicine Man* and José E. Limón's *Dancing with the Devil*.

5. See José Martí's "Our America." My present view of Martí as an "anti-*letrado*" (literally, anti-lettered Old World elite) intellectual is much indebted to Julio Ramos's superb *Desencuntros de la Modernidad en América Latina*.

6. Between 1886 and 1891 Bourke wrote the following books: *On the Border with Crook* (New York: Charles Scribner's Sons, 1891); *Scatologic Rites of All Nations: A Dissertation upon the Employment of Excretious Remedial Agents in Religion, Therapeutics, Divination, Witchcraft, Love Philters, etc., in All Parts of the Globe* (Washington, D.C.: W. H. Lowermilk, 1891); and *The Medicine Men of the Apache: Ninth Annual Report of the Bureau of Ethnology, 1887–1888* (Washington, D.C.: Government Printing Office, 1892).

7. See Paul Gilroy's *The Black Atlantic* and Edouard Glissant's *Caribbean Discourses*.

8. In *Regeneration through Violence* Slotkin explores how warfare on the colonial frontier was transformed into a body of narrative lore, which was in turn codified in myth and symbol by mainline U.S. writers.

9. See Donald Pease's "New Americanists." "By the term field-Imaginary," Pease claims, "I mean to designate a location for the disciplinary unconscious. . . . Here abides the field's fundamental syntax—its tacit assumptions, convictions, primal words, and the charged relations binding them together" (1990, 11–12).

10. See José Martí's introduction to *Ramona*.

11. In an unpublished essay, "I Ain't No Vacquero," David Luis Brown splendidly reads the ritualized marriage lasso in the romance against Gabriel's lassoing of William Darrell. Ruiz de Burton, he argues, "counterposes the reata of violent conflict with the feminizing alternative, the double loop of marital unions" (6). For an analysis of the history of the lynching of Josefa, the only woman ever lynched in California, see William B. Secrest's *Juanita*. I thank my student Alexandro Gradilla for bringing this citation to my attention.

12. Ramón Gutiérrez, *When Jesus Came, the Corn Mothers Went Away*. According to Gutiérrez, "*honor* was strictly a male attribute while shame (*vergüenza*) was intrinsic to females. Infractions of behavioral norms by males were dishonoring, in females they were a sign of shamelessness" (209). Ruiz de Burton's romance thematizes the Don's *honor* and his daughter Mercedes's *vergüenza* almost ad nauseum.

13. "Los ricos También Lloran" originally aired on Univision in 1989; it is now televised in reruns all over the world, from Brazil to Russia.

14. For an incisive reading of Morales's fiction, see Gutiérrez-Jones's *Rethinking the Borderlands*, 80–102.

15. See Keith Cowling's *Monopoly Capitalism* and Paul Baran and Paul Sweezy's *Monopoly Capitalism*.

AFTERWORD: *FRONTEJAS* TO EL VEZ

1. See James Clifford's *The Predicament of Culture*, Ramón Saldívar's *Chicano Narrative*, Renato Rosaldo's *Culture and Truth*, Néstor García Canclini's *Culturas híbridas*, and Gustavo Pérez Firmat's *The Cuban Condition*.

2. As Josh Kun suggests, "audiotopias" are "sonic spaces of utopian longings where several sites normally deemed incompatible are brought together not only in the space of a particular piece of music itself, but in the production of social space and geographical space that music makes possible as well." See Kun's wonderful "Against Easy Listening."

References

Adorno, Theodor.

1973. *Negative Dialectics.* Trans. E. B. Ashton. New York: Seabury Press.

1982 "Commitment." In *The Essential Frankfurt School Reader,* ed. Andrew Arato and Eike Gebhardt, 300–318. New York: Continuum.

1984. *Aesthetic Theory.* Trans. Christian Lenhardt. London: Routledge, Kegan and Paul.

Alarcón, Norma.

1989. "Traddutora, Traditora: A Paradigmatic Figure of Chicana Feminism." *Cultural Critique* 13 (Fall): 57–87.

1990. "Chicana Feminism: In the Tracks of 'the' Native Woman." *Cultural Studies* 4/3 (October): 248–256.

1991. "The Theoretical Subject(s) of *This Bridge Called My Back* and Anglo-American Feminism." In *Criticism in the Borderlands: Studies in Chicano Literature, Culture, and Ideology,* ed. Héctor Calderón and José David Saldívar, 28–39. Durham, N.C.: Duke University Press.

1994. "Conjugating Subjects: The Heteroglossia of Essence and Resistance." In *An Other Tongue: Nation and Ethnicity in the Linguistic Borderlands,* ed. Alfred Arteaga, 125–139. Durham, N.C.: Duke University Press.

Almaguer, Tomás.

1994. *Racial Fault Lines: The Historical Origins of White Supremacy in California.* Berkeley: University of California Press.

Althusser, Louis.

1971. *Lenin and Philosophy and Other Essays.* Trans. Ben Brewster. London: New Left Books.

Anaya, Rudolfo A., and Francisco Lomelí, eds.

1989. *Aztlán: Essays on the Chicano Homeland.* Albuquerque: Academia / El Norte Publications.

Anderson, Benedict.

1983. *Imagined Communities: Reflections on the Origins and Spread of Nationalism.* London: Verso.

Anzaldúa, Gloria.

1987. *Borderlands / La Frontera: The New Mestiza.* San Francisco: Spinsters / Aunt Lute.

Appiah, Kwame Anthony.

1991. "Is the Post- in Postmodernism the Post- in Postcolonial?" *Critical Inquiry* 17/2 (Winter): 336–355.

Arana, Ana.
    1992.   "The Wasteland." *San Francisco Examiner Image,* August 30,
        18–26.
Arnold, Matthew.
    1869.   *Culture and Anarchy: An Essay in Political and Social Criticism.*
        London: Smith, Elder.
Arteaga, Alfred.
    1994.   *An Other Tongue: Nation and Ethnicity in the Linguistic Border-
        lands.* Durham, N.C.: Duke University Press.
Baker, Houston A.
    1993.   *Black Studies, Rap, and the Academy.* Chicago: University of
        Chicago Press.
Bancroft, Hubert Howe.
    1888.   *California Pastoral.* San Francisco: The History Company.
    1890.   *Literary Industries.* San Francisco: The History Company.
Bannon, John, ed.
    1964.   *Bolton and the Spanish Borderlands.* Norman: University of Okla-
        homa Press.
Baran, Paul, and Paul Sweezy.
    1966.   *Monopoly Capitalism.* New York: Monthly Review Press.
Barceló, Margarita.
    1995.   "Geography of Struggle: Ideological Representation of Social
        Space in Four Chicana Writers." Ph.D. diss., University of Cali-
        fornia, San Diego.
Barrera, Mario.
    1979.   *Race and Class in the Southwest: A Theory of Racial Inequality.*
        Notre Dame, Ind.: University of Notre Dame Press.
Bartra, Roger.
    1992.   *The Cage of Melancholy: Identity and Metamorphosis in the Mex-
        ican Character.* Trans. Christopher J. Hall. New Brunswick, N.J.:
        Rutgers University Press.
Batalla, Guillermo Bonfil.
    1996.   *México Profundo: Reclaiming a Civilization.* Trans. Philip A.
        Dennis. Austin: University of Texas Press.
Bautista, David Hays, and Gregory Rodríguez.
    1994.   "Technobanda." *New Republic,* April 11, 10–11.
Behar, Ruth.
    1993.   *Translated Woman: Crossing the Border with Esperanza's Story.*
        Boston: Beacon Press.
Benítez-Rojo, Antonio.
    1992.   *The Repeating Island: The Caribbean and the Postmodern Perspec-
        tive.* Trans. James E. Maraniss. Durham, N.C.: Duke University Press.
Benjamin, Walter.
    1968.   "Theses on the Philosophy of History." In *Illuminations: Essays
        and Reflections,* ed. Hannah Arendt, trans. Harry Zohn, 255–266.
        New York: Harcourt, Brace and World.

Bercovitch, Sacvan.
  1975.   *The Puritan Origins of the American Self.* New Haven: Yale University Press.
  1978.   *The American Jeremiad.* Madison: University of Wisconsin Press.
  1991.   *The Office of the Scarlet Letter.* Baltimore: Johns Hopkins University Press.
  1993.   *The Rites of Assent: Transformations in the Symbolic Construction of America.* New York: Routledge.
Beverly, John, and José Oviedo.
  1993.   "Postmodernism and Latin America." *boundary 2* 20/3: 1–17.
Bhabha, Homi K.
  1992a. "Postcolonial Authority and Postmodern Guilt." In *Cultural Studies,* ed. Lawrence Grossberg, Cary Nelson, and Paula Treichler, 56–68. New York: Routledge.
  1992b. "The World and the Home." *Social Text* 31/32: 141–153.
Blades, Rubén, and Willie Colón.
  1995.   *Tras La Tormenta.* Sony Tropical. CDT-81498.
Bolton, Herbert E.
  1921.   *The Spanish Borderlands: A Chronicle of Old Florida and the Southwest.* New Haven: Yale University Press.
  1970.   *Texas in the Middle Eighteenth Century.* Austin: University of Texas Press.
Boon, James A.
  1990.   *Affinities and Extremes.* Chicago: University of Chicago Press.
Bourdieu, Pierre.
  1977.   *Outline of a Theory of Practice.* Cambridge: Cambridge University Press.
Bourke, John Gregory.
  1891.   *On the Border with Crook.* New York: Charles Scribner's Sons.
  1893.   "The Miracle Play of the Rio Grande." *Journal of American Folk-Lore* 6: 89–95.
  1894a. "The American Congo." *Scribners' Magazine* 15 (May): 590–610.
  1894b. "Popular Medicine, Customs, and Superstitions of the Rio Grande." *Journal of American Folk-Lore* (April–June): 119–146.
Brady, Mary Patricia.
  1996.   "Extinct Lands, Scarred Bodies: Chicana Literature and the Reinvention of Space." Ph.D. diss., University of California, Los Angeles.
Brailsford, Karen.
  1992.   Review of John Rechy's *The Miraculous Day of Amalia Gómez. New York Times Book Review,* May 10, 16.
Breton, André.
  1972.   *Surrealism and Painting.* Trans. Simon Watson Taylor. London: Faber and Faber.
Bright, Brenda.
  1984.   "The Meaning of Roles and the Role of Showing: Houston's Low Riders." Unpublished manuscript.

Bruce-Novoa, Juan.

1977.   Review essay on Bernice Zamora's *Restless Serpents*. *Latin American Literary Review* 5/10 (Spring–Summer): 153–154.

1990.   *Retrospace: Collected Essays on Chicano Literature*. Houston: Arte Público Press.

Butler, Judith.

1990.   "The Force of Fantasy: Feminism, Mapplethorpe, and Discursive Excess." *Differences: A Journal of Feminist Cultural Studies* 2/2: 105–125.

1993.   *Bodies That Matter: On the Discursive Limits of "Sex."* New York: Routledge.

Cafe Tacuba.

1994.   *Re*. Warner Music Mexico, S.A. 96784.

Calderón, Héctor.

1991.   "Texas Border Literature: Cultural Transformation in the Works of Américo Paredes, Rolando Hinojoa, and Gloria Anzaldúa. *Dispositio* 26/41: 13–28.

Calderón, Héctor, and José David Saldívar, eds.

1991.   *Criticism in the Borderlands: Studies in Chicano Literature, Culture, and Ideology*. Durham, N.C.: Duke University Press.

Candelaria, Cordelia.

1986.   *Chicano Poetry: A Critical View*. Westport, Conn.: Greenwood Press.

Cantú, Roberto.

1992.   "On Arturo Islas." In *Dictionary of Literary Biography*. Vol. 122: *Chicano Writers,* 2d ser., ed. Francisco Lomelí and Carl Shirley, 146–153. Detroit: Bruccoli Clark Layman Book.

Carby, Hazel.

1987.   *Reconstructing Womanhood: The Emergence of the Afro-American Woman Novelist*. Oxford: Oxford University Press.

Carpentier, Alejo.

1995.   "The [American] Baroque and the Marvelous Real." In *Magical Realism: Theory, History, Community,* ed. Wendy Faris and Lois P. Zamora, 89–108. Durham, N.C.: Duke University Press.

Castañeda Shular, Antonia, Tomás Ybarra-Frausto, and Joseph Sommer, eds.

1972.   *Literatura Chicana: Texto y contexto*. Englewood Cliffs, N.J.: Prentice-Hall.

Castellanos, Olivia.

1978.   "José Montoya: Vision of Madness on the Open Road to the Temple of the Sun." *De Colores*: 82–91.

Castillo, Debra.

1992.   *Talking Back: Towards a Latin American Feminist Literary Criticism*. Ithaca, N.Y.: Cornell University Press.

1995.   "An Interview with John Rechy." *Diacritics* 25/1 (Spring): 113–125.

CCCS (Centre for Contemporary Cultural Studies).

1978.   *Women Take Issue: Aspects of Women's Subordination*. London: Hutchinson.

1982.   *The Empire Strikes Back: Race and Racism in 70s Britain*. London: Hutchinson.

Cervantes, Lorna Dee.

1981.   "Poema Para Los Californios Muertos." In *Emplumada*, 42–43. Pittsburgh: University of Pittsburgh Press.

Chambers, Iain.

1986.   *Popular Culture: The Metropolitan Experience*. London: Methuen.

Chávez, Leo R.

1992.   *Shadowed Lives: Undocumented Immigrants in American Society*. New York: Harcourt Brace Jovanovich.

Chung, L. A., and Phuong Le.

1993.   "2.1 Million Illegals in California." *San Francisco Chronicle*, August 7, 1, A15.

Clifford, James.

1988.   *The Predicament of Culture: Twentieth-Century Ethnography, Literature, and Art*. Cambridge, Mass.: Harvard University Press.

1991.   "The Transit Lounge of Culture." *Times Literary Supplement*, May 5, 1–3.

1992a.   "Borders and Diasporas." Unpublished manuscript.

1992b.   *Person and Myth: Maurice Leenhardt in the Melanesian World*. Durham, N.C.: Duke University Press.

1992c.   "Traveling Culture." In *Cultural Studies*, ed. Lawrence Grossberg, Cary Nelson, and Paula Treichler, 96–116. New York: Routledge.

Colás, Santiago.

1994.   *Postmodernity in Latin America: The Argentine Paradigm*. Durham, N.C.: Duke University Press.

Conover, Ted.

1987.   *Coyotes: A Journey Through the Secret World of America's Illegal Aliens*. New York: Vintage.

Cowling, Keith.

1982.   *Monopoly Capitalism*. London: Macmillan.

Darwish, Mahmud.

1984.   *Victims of a Map*. Trans. A. al-Udarhi. London: Al Saqi Books.

Davidson, Winifred.

1932.   "Enemy Lovers." *Los Angeles Times Sunday Magazine*, October 16, 5.

Davis, Mike.

1990.   *City of Quartz: Excavating the Future in Los Angeles*. London: Verso.

1992.   "The L.A. Inferno." *Socialist Review* 1/2: 57–80.

Deleuze, Gilles, and Félix Guattari.

1977.   *Anti-Oedipus: Capitalism and Schizophrenia*. Trans. Robert Hurley, Mark Seem, and Helen R. Lane. New York: Viking Press.

Derrida, Jacques.

1976.   *Of Grammatology*. Trans. Gaytri Chakravorty Spivak. Baltimore: Johns Hopkins University Press.

Diana, Goffredo, and John Beverley.
   1995.   "These Are the Times We Have to Live In: An Interview with Roberto
            Fernández Retamar." *Critical Inquiry* 21 (Winter): 411–433.
Dobie, J. Frank.
   1935.   *Tongues of the Monte*. Austin: University of Texas Press.
Dollimore, Jonathan.
   1991.   *Sexual Dissidence: Agustine to Wilde, Freud to Foucault*. Oxford:
            Clarendon Press.
Dunn, Timothy J.
   1996.   *The Militarization of the U.S.–Mexico Border, 1978–1992: Low-
            Intensity Conflict Doctrine Comes Home*. Austin: Center for Mex-
            ican American Studies.
Dworkin, Dennis, and Leslie G. Roman.
   1993.   *Views Beyond the Border Country: Raymond Williams and Cul-
            tural Politics*. New York: Routledge.
Ellison, Ralph.
   1982.   *Invisible Man*. New York: Random House.
El Vez.
   1994.   *Graciasland*. Sympathy for the Record Industry. 302.
   n.d.   *How Great Thou Art*. Sympathy for the Record Industry. 199.
Escobar, Arturo, and Sonia Alvarez.
   1992.   *The Making of Social Movements in Latin America: Identity, Strat-
            egy, and Democracy*. Boulder, Colo.: Westview Press.
Ethington, Philip J.
   1996.   "Toward a 'Borderlands School' for American Urban Ethnic Stud-
            ies." *American Quarterly* 48/2 (June): 344–353.
Fehrenback, T. R.
   1968.   *Lone Star: A History of Texas and Texans*. New York: Macmillan.
Fernández Retamar, Roberto.
   1995.   "Jose Martí: A Cuban for All Seasons." *Washington Post Book
            World*, May 14, 8–9.
Ferraro, Thomas J.
   1993.   *Ethnic Passages: Literary Immigrants in Twentieth-Century Amer-
            ica*. Chicago: University of Chicago Press.
Flores, Juan (with George Yúdice).
   1993.   "Living Borders/Buscando America: Languages of Latino Self-
            Formation." In *Divided Borders: Essays on Puerto Rican Identity*,
            ed. Juan Flores, 199–252. Houston: Arte Público Press.
Foley, Barbara.
   1993.   *Radical Representations: Politics and Form in U.S. Proletarian Fic-
            tion*. Durham, N.C.: Duke University Press.
Foucault, Michel.
   1980.   *The History of Sexuality*. Vol. 1: *An Introduction*. Trans. Robert
            Hurley. New York: Vintage Books.
   1987.   "Of Other Spaces." *Diacritics* 16: 22–27.

Fox, Claire F.
  1994.   "The Portable Border: Site-Specificity, Art, and the U.S.–Mexico Frontier." *Social Text* 41 (Winter): 61–82.
Franco, Jean.
  1992.   "Border Patrol." *Travesia: Journal of Latin American Studies* 1/2: 134–142.
Fraser, Nancy.
  1989.   *Unruly Practices: Power, Discourse, and Gender in Contemporary Social Theory.* Minneapolis: University of Minnesota Press.
Fregoso, Rosa Linda.
  1993.   *The Bronze Screen: Chicana and Chicano Film Culture.* Minneapolis: University of Minnesota Press.
Frost, Kid.
  1990.   *hispanic causing panic.* Virgin Records. 2-91377.
  1992.   *East Side Story.* Virgin Records. 92097-4.
Fry, Joan.
  1992.   "An Interview with John Rechy." *Poets & Writers Magazine* 20/3 (May/June): 25–37.
Frye, Northrop.
  1957.   *The Anatomy of Criticism: Four Essays.* Princeton, N.J.: Princeton University Press.
Fuentes, Carlos.
  1992.   *The Buried Mirror: Reflections on Spain and the New World.* New York: Houghton Mifflin.
Fussell, Paul.
  1980.   *Abroad: Literary Traveling Between the Wars.* New York: Oxford University Press.
Gamboa, Harry.
  1991.   "In the City of Angels, Chameleons, and Phantoms: Asco, a Case Study of Chicano Art in Urban Tones (or Asco Was a Four-Member Word)." In *Chicano Art, Resistance and Affirmation: An Interpretive Exhibition of the Chicano Art Movement, 1965–1985,* ed. Richard Griswold del Castillo, Teresa McKenna, and Yvonne Yarbro-Bejarano, 121–130. Los Angeles: Wright Art Gallery, UCLA.
  1989.   *Mexican Americans: Leadership, Ideology, and Identity, 1930–1960.* New Haven: Yale University Press.
García, Mario T.
  1981.   *Desert Immigrants: The Mexicans of El Paso, 1880–1920.* New Haven: Yale University Press.
  1989.   *Mexican Americans: Leadership, Ideology, and Identity, 1930–1960.* New Haven: Yale University Press.
García Canclini, Néstor.
  1990.   *Culturas híbridas: Estrategias para entrar y salir de la modernidad.* Mexico City: Grijalbo.

1992.   "Cultural Reconversion." In *On Edge: The Crisis of Contemporary Latin American Culture,* ed. George Yúdice, Jean Franco, and Juan Flores, 29–43. Minneapolis: University of Minnesota Press.

Gates, Henry Louis.

1992.   "Hybridity Happens: Black Brit Bricolage Brings the Noise." *Village Voice Literary Supplement* 109 (October): 26–27.

Gilroy, Paul.

1991a.   "Sounds Authentic: Black Music, Ethnicity, and the Challenge of a Changing Same." *Black Music Research Journal* 2/2 (Fall): 111–136.

1991b.   *There Ain't No Black in the Union Jack: The Cultural Politics of Race and Nation.* Chicago: University of Chicago Press.

1992.   "Cultural Studies and Ethnic Absolutism." In *Cultural Studies,* ed. Lawrence Grossberg, Cary Nelson, and Paula Treichler, 187–198. New York: Routledge.

1993.   *The Black Atlantic: Modernity and Double Consciousness.* Cambridge, Mass.: Harvard University Press.

Glissant, Edouard.

1992.   *Caribbean Discourses: Selected Essays.* Trans. with an intro. by J. Michael Dash. Charlottesville: University of Virginia Press.

Goldman, Anne E.

1994.   Review of Ruiz de Burton's *The Squatter and the Don. MELUS* 9/3 (Fall): 130–134.

Goldman, Shifra, and Tomás Ybarra-Frausto.

1991.   "The Political and Social Contexts of Chicano Art." *Chicano Art, Resistance and Affirmation: An Interpretive Exhibition of the Chicano Art Movement, 1965–1985,* ed. Richard Griswold del Castillo, Teresa McKenna, and Yvonne Yarbro-Bejarano, 83–96. Los Angeles: Wright Art Gallery, UCLA.

Gómez-Peña, Guillermo.

1986.   "Border Culture: A Process of Negotiation toward Utopia." *La Línea Quebrada* 1: 1–6.

1987.   "Border Culture and Deterritorialization." *La Línea Quebrada* 2/2 (March): 1–10.

1991.   "Border Brujo: A Performance Poem." *Drama Review* 35/3 (Fall): 49–66.

1993a.   *The New World (B)order.* University of California, Santa Cruz, Performing Arts Theater, April 13.

1993b.   *Warrior for Gringostroika.* Intro. Roger Barta. Minneapolis: Graywolf Press.

Gómez-Peña, Guillermo, and Jeff Kelly, eds.

1989.   *The Border Art Workshop: Documentation of Five Years of Interdisciplinary Art Projects Dealing with U.S.-Mexico Border Issues, 1984–1989.* New York and La Jolla, Calif.: Artists Space and Museum of Contemporary Art.

González, Jovita.

1996.   *Caballero.* College Station: Texas A&M University Press.

Gooding-Williams, Robert, ed.
  1993.   *Reading Rodney King: Reading Urban Uprising.* New York: Routledge.
Greenblatt, Stephen.
  1988.   *Shakespearean Negotiations: The Circulation of Social Energy in Renaissance England.* Berkeley: University of California Press.
Griswold del Castillo, Richard.
  1990.   *The Treaty of Guadalupe Hidalgo: A Legacy of Conflict.* Norman: University of Oklahoma Press.
Grossman, James R., ed.
  1994.   *The Frontier in American Culture: Essays by Richard White and Patricia Nelson Limerick.* Berkeley: University of California Press.
Guillén, Nicolás.
  1974.   *Obras poética 1920–1972.* 2 vols. Ed. Angel Augier. Havana: Editorial de Arte y Literatura.
Gutiérrez, Ramón.
  1991.   *When Jesus Came, the Corn Mothers Went Away: Marriage, Sexuality, and Power in New Mexico, 1500–1846.* Stanford: Stanford University Press.
Gutiérrez, Ramón, and Genaro Padilla, eds.
  1993.   *Recovering the U.S. Hispanic Literary Heritage.* Houston: Arte Público Press.
Gutiérrez-Jones, Carl.
  1995a.   "Desiring (B)orders." *Diacritics* 25/1 (Spring): 99–112.
  1995b.   *Rethinking the Borderlands: Between Chicano Culture and Legal Discourse.* Berkeley: University of California Press.
Habermas, Jurgen.
  1983.   "Modernity—An Incomplete Project." Trans. Seyla Ben-Habib. In *The Anti-Aesthetic: Essays in Postmodern Culture,* ed. Hal Foster, 3–15. Port Townsend, Wash.: Bay Press.
Hall, Stuart.
  1980.   Cultural Studies and the Centre: Some Problematics and Problems." In *Culture, Media, Language,* ed. Dorothy Hobson et al., 15–47. London: Hutchinson.
  1990.   "Cultural Identity and Diaspora." In *Identity: Community, Cultural, Difference,* ed. Jonathan Rutherford, 222–237. London: Lawrence and Wishart.
  1992.   "Cultural Studies and Its Theoretical Legacies." In *Cultural Studies,* ed. Larry Grossberg, Cary Nelson, and Paula Treichler, 277–294. New York: Routledge.
Haraway, Donna.
  1991.   *Simians, Cyborgs and Women: The Reinvention of Nature.* New York: Routledge.
Harlow, Barbara.
  1991.   "Sites of Struggle: Immigration, Deportation, and Prison." In *Criticism in the Borderlands: Studies in Chicano Literature, Culture,*

   and Ideology, ed. Héctor Calderón and José David Saldívar, 149–163. Durham, N.C.: Duke University Press.

Harvey, David A.

   1990.   *The Condition of Postmodernity: An Enquiry into the Origins of Cultural Change.* Oxford: Blackwell.

Hassan, Ihab.

   1985.   "The Culture of Postmodernism." *Theory, Culture, and Society* 2/3: 119–132.

Hawthorne, Nathaniel.

   1980.   *The Scarlet Letter.* New York: New American Library.

Herrera-Sobek, María.

   1990.   *The Mexican Corrido: A Feminist Analysis.* Bloomington: Indiana University Press.

Herzog, Lawrence A.

   1990.   *Where North Meets South: Cities, Space, and Politics on the U.S.-Mexico Border.* Austin: CMAS and University of Texas Press.

Hicks, Emily.

   1991.   *Border Writing: The Multidimensional Text.* Minneapolis: University of Minnesota Press.

Hinojosa, Tish.

   1995.   *Frontejas.* Rounder Records Corporation. CD 3132.

Hoggart, Richard.

   1970.   *Speaking to Each Other.* 2 vols. London: Chatto and Windus.

Hollinger, David.

   1995.   *PostEthnic America: Beyond Multiculturalism.* New York: Basic Books.

Hughes, Langston.

   1968.   "The Negro Speaks of Rivers." In *The New Negro,* ed. Alain Locke, 141. New York: Atheneum.

Hutcheon, Linda.

   1988.   *A Poetics of Postmodernism.* New York: Routledge.

Huyssen, Andreas.

   1986.   *After the Great Divide: Modernism, Mass Culture, Postmodernism.* Bloomington: Indiana University Press.

Inglis, Fred.

   1993.   *Cultural Studies.* Oxford: Blackwell.

Islas, Arturo.

   1975.   "Writing from a Dual Perspective." *Miquiztli* 3/1: 3–7.

   1984.   *The Rain God: A Desert Tale.* Palo Alto, Calif.: Alexandrian Press.

   1990a.   "At the Bridge, on the Border, Migrants and Immigrants." Fifth Annual Ernesto Galarza Lecture, Stanford Center for Chicano Research.

   1990b.   *Migrant Souls.* New York: William Morrow.

   1996.   *La Mollie and the King of Tears.* Albuquerque: University of New Mexico Press.

Jaén, Didier.

   1992.   "John Rechy." In *Dictionary of Literary Biography.* Vol. 122: *Chi-*

cano Writers, 2d ser., ed. Francisco Lomelí and Carl Shirley, 212–219. Detroit: Gale Research.

Jameson, Fredric.

1979.   "Reification and Utopia in Mass Culture." Social Text 1: 130–148.

1981.   The Political Unconscious: Narrative as a Socially Symbolic Act. Ithaca, N.Y.: Cornell University Press.

1988.   "Cognitive Mapping." In Marxism and the Interpretation of Culture, ed. Cary Nelson and Lawrence Grossberg, 347–357. Urbana: University of Illinois Press.

1990.   Late Marxism: Adorno, or, The Persistence of the Dialectic. London: Verso.

1991.   Postmodernism, or, The Logic of Late Capitalism. Durham, N.C.: Duke University Press.

1993.   "On Cultural Studies." Social Text 34: 17–52.

JanMohamed, Abdul.

1992.   "Worldliness-without-World, Homelessness-as-Home: Toward a Definition of the Specular Border Intellectual." In Edward Said: A Critical Reader, ed. Michael Sprinker, 96–120. Oxford: Blackwell.

Jay, Martin.

1993.   Downcast Eyes: The Denigration of Vision in Twentieth-Century French Thought. Berkeley: University of California Press.

Johnson, Richard.

1987.   "What Is Cultural Studies Anyway?" Social Text 6/1: 38–90.

Kaplan, Amy.

1990.   "Romancing the Empire: The Embodiment of American Masculinity in the Popular Historical Novel of the 1890s." American Literary History 2/4 (Winter): 659–690.

1993.   "Left Alone with America: The Absence of Empire in the Study of American Culture." In Cultures of U.S. Imperialism, ed. Donald E. Pease and Amy Kaplan, 3–21. Durham, N.C.: Duke University Press.

Kelley, Robin D. G.

1994.   Race Rebels: Culture, Politics, and the Black Working Class. New York: Free Press.

Kershner, Vlae.

1993.   "Wilson's Plan to Curb Illegal Immigration." San Francisco Chronicle, August 10, 1, A13.

Klor de Alva, Jorge.

1986.   "California Chicano Literature and Pre-Columbian Motifs: Foils and Fetish." Confluencia 1 (Spring): 18–26.

Kun, Josh.

1995.   "Rock en español." San Francisco Bay Guardian, August 9–15, 27–31.

n.d.   "Against Easy Listening: Audiotopic Readings and Transnational Soundings in the Américas." In Everynight Life: Dance, Music, and Culture, ed. José Muñoz and Celeste Fraser Delgado. Durham, N.C.: Duke University Press, forthcoming.

Kutzinski, Vera M.
    1987.   *Against the American Grain: Myth and History in William Carlos Williams, Jay Wright, and Nicolás Guillén.* Baltimore: Johns Hopkins University Press.
Laplanche, Jean, and J. B. Pontalis.
    1985.   *Fantasme Originaire.* Paris: Hachette.
Leal, Luis.
    1981.   "In Search of Aztlán." Trans. Galdys Leal. *Denver Quarterly* 16 (Fall): 16–22.
    1985.   *Aztlán y México: Perfiles literarios e históricos.* Binghamton, N.Y.: Bilingual Press/Editorial Bilingue.
Lefebvre, Henri.
    1991.   *The Production of Space.* Trans. Donald Nicholson-Smith. Oxford: Blackwell.
Levine, Lawrence W.
    1996.   *The Opening of the American Mind: Canons, Culture, and History.* Boston: Beacon Press.
Levy, Dan.
    1993.   "Spanish Radio Boom Rides 'Banda' Crest." *San Francisco Chronicle,* March 17, D1, D2.
Limerick, Patricia Nelson.
    1987.   *The Legacy of Conquest: The Unbroken Past of the American West.* New York: W. W. Norton.
Limón, José E.
    1986a.   "La Llorona, the Third Legend of Greater Mexico: Cultural Symbols, Women and the Political Unconscious." In *Renato Rosaldo Lecture Series Monograph* 2, ed. Ignacio M. García, 59–93. Tucson: University of Arizona, Department of Chicano Studies.
    1986b.   "Mexican Ballads, Chicano Epic: History, Social Dramas and Poetic Persuasions." SCCR Working Paper 14, Stanford University.
    1986c.   "The Return of the Mexican Ballad: Américo Paredes and His Anthropological Text as Persuasive Political Performance." SCCR Working Paper 16, Stanford University.
    1992.   *Mexican Ballads, Chicano Poems: History and Influence in Mexican-American Social Poetry.* Berkeley: University of California Press.
    1994.   *Dancing with the Devil: Society and Cultural Poetics in Mexican-American South Texas.* Madison: University of Wisconsin Press.
Lipsitz, George.
    1986.   "Cruising Around the Historical Bloc: Postmodernism and Popular Music in East Los Angeles." *Cultural Critique* 5: 157–177.
    1990.   *Time Passages: Collective Memory and American Popular Culture.* Minneapolis: University of Minnesota Press.
    1994.   *Dangerous Crossroads: Popular Music, Postmodernism, and the Poetics of Place.* New York: Verso.

n.d.   "Home Is Where the Hatred Is: Work, Music, and the Transnational Economy." Unpublished manuscript.

n.d.   "Musical Aesthetics and Multiculturalism in Los Angeles." *UCLA Selected Papers in Ethnomusicology,* forthcoming.

Lloyd, David.

1994.   "Adulteration and the Nation." In *An Other Tongue: Nation and Ethnicity in the Linguistic Borderlands,* ed. Alfred Arteaga, 53–92. Durham, N.C.: Duke University Press.

Lomas Garza, Carmen.

1990.   *Cuadros de familia / Family Pictures.* San Francisco: Talman.

1991.   *A Piece of My Heart / Pedacito de mi corazón.* New York: Free Press.

López, Gerald P.

1981.   "Undocumented Mexican Immigration: In Search of a Just Law and Policy." *UCLA Law Review* 28/4 (April): 616–714.

1989.   "The Work We Know So Little About." *Stanford Law Review* 42/1: 1–13.

1992.   "My Turn." *Newsweek,* November 2, 12.

Los Illegals.

1983.   *Internal Exile.* A & M Records. 7502-14925-1.

Los Tigres del Norte.

1985.   "Jaula de Oro." Profono Internacional.

Lowe, Lisa.

1996.   *Immigrant Acts: On Asian American Cultural Politics.* Durham, N.C.: Duke University Press.

Lowry, Beverly.

1992.   "In Tijuana, Tacky Days and Velvet Nights." *New York Times Magazine,* March 1, 22–25, 74, 89.

Loza, Steven.

1993.   *Barrio Rhythm: Mexican American Music in Los Angeles.* Urbana: University of Illinois Press.

Lummis, Charles F.

1893.   *Land of Poco Tiempo.* New York: Charles Scribner's Sons.

Lyotard, Jean François.

1984.   *The Postmodern Condition: A Report on Knowledge.* Trans. Geoff Bennington and Brian Massuni. Minneapolis: University of Minnesota Press.

McDowell, John H.

1981.   "The Corrido of Greater Mexico as Discourse, Music, and Event." In *"And Other Neighborly Names": Social Process and Cultural Image in Texas Folklore,* ed. Richard Bauman and Roger D. Abraham, 44–75. Austin: University of Texas Press.

McKenna, Teresa.

1991.   "On Chicano Poetry and the Political Age: Corridos as Social Dramas." In *Criticism in the Borderlands: Studies in Chicano Litera-*

ture, Culture, and Ideology, ed. Héctor Calderón and José David Saldívar, 181–202. Durham, N.C.: Duke University Press.

Maldita Vecindad y Los Hijos del Quinto Patio.

    1991.   "Mojado." *Rock de Los 90's.* RCA. 3292-2-RL.

Marcus, George E., and Michael M. J. Fischer.

    1986.   *Anthropology as Cultural Critique: An Experimental Moment in the Human Sciences.* Chicago: University of Chicago Press.

Marcus, Greil.

    1991.   *Dead Elvis: A Chronicle of a Cultural Obsession.* New York: Doubleday.

Marcuse, Herbert.

    1969.   *An Essay on Liberation.* New York: Beacon Press.

Márquez, Antonio C.

    1994.   "The Historical Imagination in Arturo Islas's *The Rain God* and *Migrant Souls.*" *MELUS* 19/2 (Summer): 3–16.

Martí, José.

    1965.   *Ramona: Novela americana.* Vol. 24 of *Obras completas.* Havana: Editorial Nacional de Cuba.

    1978.   "Prólogo al Poema del Niágara." In *Obra literaria.* Caracas: Biblioteca Ayacucho.

    1994.   "Our America." In *The Heath Anthology of American Literature,* 2d. ed., ed. Paul Lauter, 821–829. Lexington, Mass.: D. C. Heath.

Martínez, Jesús.

    1993a.   "Tigers in a Gold Cage: Songs of Mexican Immigrants in Silicon Valley." Unpublished manuscript.

    1993b.   "Los Tigres del Norte en Silicon Valley." *Nexos* (November): 77–83.

Martínez, Oscar J.

    1975.   *Border Boom Town: Ciudad Juárez since 1848.* Austin: University of Texas Press.

Martínez, Rubén.

    1991.   "On the North-South Border Patrol, in Art and Life." *New York Times,* October 13, A5, 35.

    1992a.   "My Argument with Richard Rodriguez: Or, a Defense of the Mexican-American Chicanos Love to Hate." *L.A. Weekly* (October 2–8): 18–21.

    1992b.   *The Other Side: Fault Lines, Guerrilla Saints, and the True Heart of Rock 'n' Roll.* New York: Verso.

    1994.   "The Shock of the New: Anti-Immigration Fervor Is at a Fever Pitch, but the Real Issue Is This: When Will the Old (Anglo) L.A. Join the New (Latino) L.A., and Learn to Dance the Quebradita?" *Los Angeles Times Magazine,* January 30.

Mascia-Lees, Frances, and Patricia Sharpe.

    1992.   "Culture, Power, and Text: Anthropology and Literature Confront Each Other." *American Literary History* 4/4 (Winter): 678–696.

Masuo, Sandy.

    1995.   "El Rey Esta Muerto: Viva El Vez! *Option* 62 (May–June): 82–85.

Mazón, Mauricio.
   1984.   *The Zoot Suit Riots.* Austin: University of Texas Press.
Medina, Andrés.
   1987.   "En frontera sur y los procesos étnicos." *México Indígena* 14/3 (January/February): 24–28.
Mercer, Kobena.
   1994.   *Welcome to the Jungle: New Positions in Black Cultural Studies.* New York: Routledge.
Mesa-Bains, Amalia.
   1991a.   "Chicana Chronicle and Cosmology: The Works of Carmen Lomas Garza." In *A Piece of My Heart / Pedacitos de mi corazón,* by Carmen Lomas Garza. New York: Free Press.
   1991b.   "El mundo femenino: Chicana Artists of the Movement—A Commentary on Development and Production." In *Chicano Art, Resistance and Affirmation—An Interpretive Exhibition of the Chicano Art Movement, 1965–1985,* ed. Richard Griswold del Castillo, Teresa McKenna, and Yvonne Yarbro-Bejarano, 131–140. Los Angeles: Wright Art Gallery, UCLA.
Michaels, Walter Benn.
   1995.   *Our America: Nativism, Modernism, and Pluralism.* Durham, N.C.: Duke University Press.
Mignolo, Walter.
   1995.   *The Darker Side of the Renaissance: Literacy, Territoriality, and Colonization.* Ann Arbor: University of Michigan Press.
   n.d.   "Are Subaltern Studies Postmodern or Postcolonial? The Politics and Sensibilities of Geo-Cultural Locations."
Miller, Hubert J.
   1980.   *José de Escandón: Colonizer of Nuevo Santander.* Edinburg: Nuevo Santander Press.
Miller, Tom.
   1985.   *On the Border: Portraits of America's Southwestern Frontier.* Tucson: University of Arizona Press.
Monsiváis, Carlos.
   1980.   *A ustedes les consta: Antología de la crónica en México.* Mexico City: Era.
Montejano, David.
   1987.   *Anglos and Mexicans in the Making of Texas, 1836–1986.* Austin: University of Texas Press.
Montoya, José.
   1969.   "Los Vatos." In *El Espejo / The Mirror,* ed. Herminio Ríos and Octavio I. Romano, 186–187. Berkeley, Calif.: Quinto Sol Press.
   1980.   "Thoughts on La Cultura, the Media, Con Safos, and Survival." *Metamorfosis* 3/1 (Spring–Summer): 28–34.
   1992.   *In Formation: 20 Years of Joda.* San Jose, Calif.: Chusma House.
Moraga, Cherríe, and Gloria Anzaldúa, eds.
   1983.   *This Bridge Called My Back: Writings by Radical Women of Color.* New York: Kitchen Table Press.

Morales, Alejandro.

1983.   *Reto en el paraíso.* Ypsilanti, Mich.: Bilingual Press/Editorial Bilingue.

1988.   *The Brick People.* Houston: Arte Público Press.

Morley, David, and Kuan Hsing-Chen, eds.

1996.   *Stuart Hall: Critical Dialogues in Cultural Studies.* London: Routledge.

Muñoz, Carlos.

1989.   *Youth, Identity, and Power: The Chicano Movement.* New York: Verso.

Nelson, Cary, Paula Treichler, and Lawrence Grossberg, eds.

1992.   *Cultural Studies.* New York: Routledge.

Nixon, Rob.

1992.   *London Calling: V. S. Naipaul, Postcolonial Mandarin.* New York: Oxford University Press.

Omi, Michael, and Howard Winant.

1994.   *Racial Formation in the United States: From the 1960s to the 1990s.* 2d ed. New York: Routledge.

Ortíz, Fernándo.

1978.   *Contrapunteo cubano del tobaco y azucar.* Caracas: Biblioteca Ayacucho.

Owens, Louis.

1985.   *John Steinbeck's Re-Vision of America.* Athens: University of Georgia Press.

Padilla, Genaro.

1993.   *"My History Not Yours": The Formation of Mexican American Autobiography.* Madison: University of Wisconsin Press.

Paredes, Américo.

1958.   *"With His Pistol in His Hand": A Border Ballad and Its Hero.* Austin: University of Texas Press.

1970.   *Folktales of Mexico.* Chicago: University of Chicago Press.

1976.   *A Texas-Mexican "Cancionero": Folksongs of the Lower Border.* Urbana: University of Illinois Press.

1979.   "The Folk Base of Chicano Literature." In *Modern Chicano Writers: A Collection of Critical Essays,* ed. Joseph Sommers and Tomás Ybarra-Frausto, 4–17. Englewood Cliffs, N.J.: Prentice Hall.

1990.   *George Washington Gómez: A Mexicotexan Novel.* Houston: Arte Público Press.

1991.   *Between Two Worlds.* Houston: Arte Público Press.

1992.   *Uncle Remus con Chile.* Houston: Arte Público Press.

1993.   "The Problem of Identity in a Changing Culture: Popular Expressions of Culture Conflict along the Lower Rio Grande Border." In *Folklore and Culture on the Texas-Mexican Border,* ed. and intro. Richard Bauman, 46. Austin: Center for Mexican American Studies and University of Texas Press.

1994.   *The Hammon and the Beans and Other Stories.* Intro. Ramón Saldívar. Houston: Arte Público Press.

Paz, Octavio.
  1985.   *The Labyrinth of Solitude*. Trans. Lysander Kemp. New York: Grove Press.
Pease, Donald P.
  1990.   "New Americanists: Revisionist Interventions into the Canon." *boundary* 2/17 (Spring): 1–37.
Pefanis, Julian.
  1991.   *Heterology and the Postmodern: Bataille, Baudrillard, and Lyotard*. Durham, N.C.: Duke University Press.
Peña, Manuel.
  1985.   *The Texas-Mexican Conjunto: History of a Working-Class Music*. Austin: University of Texas Press.
Perera, Victor.
  1993.   "The Labyrinth of Solitude." *The Nation* (January 18): 63–65.
Pérez Firmat, Gustavo.
  1986.   *Literature and Liminality: Festive Readings in the Hispanic Tradition*. Durham N.C.: Duke University Press.
  1987.   "Nicolás Guillén between the Son and the Sonnet." *Callaloo* 10/2: 318–328.
  1989.   *The Cuban Condition: Translation and Identity in Modern Cuban Literature*. Cambridge: Cambridge University Press.
Pérez-Torres, Rafael.
  1995.   *Movements in Chicano Poetry: Against Margins, Against Myths*. New York: Cambridge University Press.
Pitt, Leonard.
  1965.   *The Decline of the Californios: A Social History of the Spanish-speaking Californians, 1846–1890*. Berkeley: University of California Press.
Porter, Carolyn.
  1994.   "What We Know that We Don't Know." *American Literary History* 6: 467–526.
Porter, Joseph C.
  1986.   *Paper Medicine Man: John Gregory Bourke and His American West*. Norman: University of Oklahoma Press.
Portes, Alejandro.
  1993.   "The Longest Migration." *New Republic* 208/17 (March 26): 38–42.
Pratt, Mary Louise.
  1981.   "The Short Story: The Long and Short of It." *Poetics* 10: 175–194.
  1992.   *Imperial Eyes: Travel Writing and Transculturation*. London: Routledge.
  n.d.   "Daring to Dream: New Visions of Culture and Citizenship, 1992." Unpublished manuscript.
Puig, Andrés Fábregas.
  1987.   "Mexico frente a la frontera sur." *Mexico indígena* 14/3 (January/February): 8–11.

Quintana, Alvina.
    1996.   *Home Girls: Chicana Literary Voices.* Philadelphia: Temple University Press.
Ramos, Julio.
    1989.   *Desencuentros de la modernidad en América Latina: Literatura y Política en el siglo XIX.* Mexico City: Fondo de Cultural Económica.
Reagan, Ronald.
    1982–   "Inaugural Address," January 21, 1985. In *Public Papers of*
    1991.   *the President: Ronald Reagan, 1985,* 1: 55–59. Washington, D.C.: Government Printing Office.
Rechy, John.
    1963.   *City of Night.* New York: Grove Press.
    1967.   *Numbers.* New York: Grove Press.
    1969.   *This Day's Death.* New York: Grove Press.
    1971.   *The Vampires.* New York: Grove Press.
    1972.   "El Paso del Norte." In *Literatura Chicana: texto y contexto,* ed. Antonia Castañeda Shular, Tomás Ybarra-Frausto, and Joseph Sommer, 158–164. Englewood Cliffs, N.J.: Prentice Hall.
    1974.   *The Fourth Angel.* New York: Viking Press.
    1977.   *The Sexual Outlaw: A Documentary.* New York: Grove Press.
    1983.   *Bodies and Souls.* New York: Carroll and Graf.
    1991.   *The Miraculous Day of Amalia Gómez.* New York: Arcade/Little, Brown.
Rich, Adrienne.
    1986.   "Notes toward a Politics of Location." In *Blood, Bread, and Poetry: Selected Prose, 1979–1985,* 210–231. New York: W. W. Norton.
Ríos, Alberto.
    1982.   *Whispering to Fool the Wind.* New York: Sheep Meadow Press.
    1984.   *The Iguana Killer: Twelve Stories of the Heart.* Tucson: A Blue Moon and Confluence Press.
    1985.   *Five Indiscretions.* New York: Sheep Meadow Press.
Rivera, Tomás.
    1988.   "Richard Rodriguez's *Hunger of Memory* as Humanistic Antithesis." In *Tomás Rivera, 1935–1984: The Man and His Work,* ed. Vernon Lattin, Rolando Hinojosa, and Gary Keller, 28–33. Tempe, Ariz.: Bilingual Press.
Robbins, Bruce.
    1992.   "Comparative Cosmopolitanism." *Social Text* 31/32: 169–186.
Rodríguez, Marcelo.
    1992.   "Hunger of Reality." *SF Weekly,* September 30, 13–14.
Rodriguez, Richard.
    1992.   *Days of Obligation: An Argument with My Mexican Father.* New York: Viking Press.
Rodriguez, Jeanette.
    1994.   *Our Lady of Guadalupe: Faith and Empowerment among Mexican-American Women.* Austin: University of Texas Press.

Rogin, Michael Paul.
　1983.　*Subversive Genealogy: The Politics and Art of Herman Melville.*
　　　　　New York: Knopf.
Román, David.
　1995.　"Teatro Viva! Latino Performance and the Politics of AIDS in Los
　　　　　Angeles." *¿Entiendes? Queer Readings, Hispanic Writings,* ed.
　　　　　Emile L. Bergmann and Paul Smith, 346–369. Durham, N.C.: Duke
　　　　　University Press.
Rosaldo, Renato.
　1988.　"Ideology, Place, and People without Culture." *Cultural Anthro-
　　　　　pology* 3: 77–87.
　1989.　*Culture and Truth: The Remaking of Social Analysis.* Boston: Bea-
　　　　　con Press.
　1991.　"Fables of the Fallen Guy." In *Criticism in the Borderlands: Stud-
　　　　　ies in Chicano Literature, Culture, and Ideology,* ed. Héctor
　　　　　Calderón and José David Saldívar, 84–93. Durham, N.C.: Duke
　　　　　University Press.
　1992a.　"Cultural Citizenship: Attempting to Enfranchise Latinos." *La Nueva
　　　　　Visión* (Stanford Center for Chicano Research) 1/2 (Summer):7.
　1992b.　"Race and Other Inequalities: Decent People and Indians in Arturo
　　　　　Islas's *Migrant Souls.*" Unpublished manuscript.
Ross, Andrew, ed.
　1988.　*Universal Abandon? The Politics of Postmodernism.* Minneapolis:
　　　　　University of Minnesota Press.
Ross, Kristin.
　1988.　*The Emergence of Social Space: Rimbaud and the Paris Commune.*
　　　　　Minneapolis: University of Minnesota Press.
Rothmiller, Mike, and Ivan Goldman.
　1992.　*L.A. Secret Police: Inside the LAPD Elite Spy Network.* New York:
　　　　　Pocket Books.
Ruiz de Burton, María Amparo.
　1992.　*The Squatter and the Don.* Ed. and intro. Beatrice Pita and Rosaura
　　　　　Sánchez. Houston: Arte Público Press.
　1995.　*Who Would Have Thought It?* Ed. and intro. Beatrice Pita and
　　　　　Rosaura Sánchez. Houston: Arte Público Press.
Ruiz, Vicki.
　1987.　"Oral History and La Mujer: The Rosa Guerrero Story." In
　　　　　Women on the U.S.-Mexico Border: Responses to Change, ed. Vicki
　　　　　Ruiz and Susan Tiano, 219–231. Boston: Allen and Unwin.
Ruiz, Vicki, and Susan Tiano, eds.
　1987.　*Women on the U.S.-Mexico Border: Responses to Change.* Boston:
　　　　　Allen and Unwin.
Sahagún, Bernardino de
　1578.　*Florentine Codex.* Trans. and ed. Charles E. Diddle, Arthur Ander-
　　　　　son, and J. O. Anderson. Bilingual edition, 13 vols. Salt Lake City
　　　　　and Santa Fe: University of Utah Press and School of American
　　　　　Research, 1956–69.

Said, Edward W.
  1990.   "Yeats and Decolonization." In *Nationalism, Colonialism, and Literature*, 69–95. Intro. Seanus Deane. Minneapolis: University of Minnesota Press.
  1993.   *Culture and Imperialism*. New York: Alfred A. Knopf.
Saldívar, José David.
  1991a.   "Chicano Border Narratives as Cultural Critique." In *Criticism in the Borderlands: Studies in Chicano Literature, Culture, and Ideology*, ed. Héctor Calderón and José David Saldívar, 167–180. Durham, N.C.: Duke University Press.
  1991b.   *The Dialectics of Our America: Genealogy, Cultural Critique, and Literary History*. Durham, N.C.: Duke University Press.
  1991c.   "Postmodern Realism." In *The Columbia History of the American Novel*, ed. Emory Elliott, 521–541. New York: Columbia University Press.
  1993a.   "Américo Paredes and Decolonization." In *Cultures of U.S. Imperialism*, ed. Amy Kaplan and Donald Pease, 292–310. Durham, N.C.: Duke University Press.
  1993b.   "Arturo Islas—Migrant Soul." *Stanford Magazine* (September): 57.
  1993–   "*Frontera* Crossings: Sites of Cultural Contestation." *Mester* 22/23
  1994.   (Fall/Spring): 81–92.
  1994.   "The Hybridity of Culture in Arturo Islas's *The Rain God*." In *Cohesion and Dissent in America*, ed. Carol Colatrella and Joseph Alkana, 159–173. Albany: State University Press of New York.
  1995.   "The Limits of Cultural Studies." In *The American Literary History Reader*, ed. Gordon Hutner, 188–203. New York: Oxford University Press.
  1996.   "Las Fronteras de Nuestra América: para volver a trazar el mapa de los Estudios Culturales Norteamericanos." *Casa de las Américas* 37/204: 3–19.
Saldívar, Ramón. 1979. "The Dialectics of Difference: Toward a Theory of the Chicano Novel." *MELUS* 6/3: 73–92.
  1990.   *Chicano Narrative: The Dialectics of Difference*. Madison: University of Wisconsin Press.
  1993.   "Bordering on Modernity: Américo Paredes's *Between Two Worlds* and the Imagining of Utopian Social Space." *Stanford Humanities Review* 3/1 (Winter): 54–66.
  1995.   "The Borderlands of Culture: *George Washington Gómez* and Chicano Literature at the End of the Twentieth Century." In *The American Literary History Reader*, ed. Gordon Hutner, 318–339. New York: Oxford University Press.
Saldívar-Hull, Sonia.
  1990.   "Feminism on the Border: From Gender Politics to Geopolitics." Ph.D. diss, University of Texas.
San Francisco Chronicle.
  1992.   "Border Patrol Accused of Serious Abuse." June 1, A6.
  1996.   "U.S. Boosts Enforcement along Border." January 12, 1, A17.

Sánchez, George J.
  1993.   *Becoming Mexican American: Ethnicity, Culture, and Identity in Chicano Los Angeles, 1900–1945.* New York: Oxford University Press.
Sánchez, Marta E.
  1980.   "Inter-sexual and Intertextual Codes in the Poetry of Bernice Zamora." *MELUS* 7/3: 55–68.
  1985.   *Contemporary Chicana Poetry: A Critical Approach to an Emerging Practice.* Berkeley: University of California Press.
Sánchez, Rosaura.
  1987.   "Postmodernism and Chicano Literature." *Aztlán* 18/2: 1–14.
  1991.   "Ideological Discourses in Arturo Islas's *The Rain God.*" In *Criticism in the Borderlands: Studies in Chicano Literature, Culture, and Ideology,* ed. Héctor Calderón and José David Saldívar, 114–126. Durham, N.C.: Duke University Press.
  1993.   "Nineteenth-Century Californio Narratives: The Hubert H. Bancroft Collection." In *Recovering the U.S. Hispanic Literary Heritage,* ed. Genaro Padilla and Ramón Gutiérrez, 279–292. Houston: Arte Público Press.
  1995.   *Telling Identities: The Californio Testimonio.* Minneapolis: University of Minnesota Press.
Sánchez Jankowski, Martín.
  1991.   *Islands in the Street: Gangs and American Urban Society.* Berkeley: University of California Press.
Sandos, James A.
  1992.   *Rebellion in the Borderlands: Anarchism and the Plan of San Diego, 1904–1923.* Norman: University of Oklahoma Press.
Sandoval, Chela.
  1991.   "U.S. Third World Feminism: The Theory and Method of Oppositional Consciousness in the Postmodern World." *Genders* 10 (Spring): 1–24.
  1993.   "Oppositional Consciousness in the Postmodern World: U.S. Third World Feminism, Semiotics, and the Methodology of the Oppressed." Ph.D. diss., University of California, Santa Cruz.
Satterfield, B.
  1982.   "John Rechy's Tormented World." *Southwest Review* 67 (Winter): 78–85.
Secrest, William.
  1967.   *Juanita.* Fresno, Calif.: Saga-West.
Sedgwick, Eve Kosofsky.
  1990.   *Epistemology of the Closet.* Berkeley: University of California Press.
Shohat, Ella.
  1992.   "Notes on the Post-Colonial." *Social Text* 31/32: 99–113.
Silko, Leslie Marmon.
  1996.   *Yellow Woman and a Beauty of the Spirit: Essays on Native American Life Today.* New York: Simon and Schuster.

Slotkin, Richard.

1973.   *Regeneration through Violence: The Mythology of the American Frontier, 1600–1860.* Middletown, Conn.: Wesleyan University Press.

Soja, Edward.

1989.   *Postmodern Geographies: The Reassertion of Space in Critical Social Theory.* London: Verso.

Sollors, Werner.

1986.   *Beyond Ethnicity: Consent and Descent in American Culture.* New York: Oxford University Press.

Sommer, Doris.

1991.   *Foundational Fictions: The National Romance of Latin America.* Berkeley: University of California Press.

Soto, Gary

1992.   "Rodriguez Meditates on His Mixed Roots." *San Francisco Chronicle Review,* November 1, 1, 10.

Spanos, William V.

1995.   *The Errant Art of Moby-Dick: The Canon, the Cold War, and the Struggle for American Studies.* Durham, N.C.: Duke University Press.

Spitta, Silvia.

1995.   *Between Two Waters: Narratives of Transculturation in Latin America.* Houston: Rice University Press.

Spivak, Gayatri Chakravorty.

1988a.   *In Other Worlds: Essays in Cultural Politics.* New York: Routledge.

1988b.   "Subaltern Studies: Deconstructing Historiography." In *Selected Subaltern Studies,* ed. Ranajit Guha and Gayatri Chakravorty Spivak, 3–34. New York: Oxford University Press.

1993.   *Outside in the Teaching Machine.* New York: Routledge.

1995.   "Teaching for the Times." In *Decolonization of the Imagination: Culture, Knowledge, and Power,* ed. Jan Nederveen Pieterse and Bhikhu Parekh, 177–202. London: Zed Books.

Spurr, David.

1993.   *The Rhetoric of Empire: Colonial Discourse in Journalism, Travel Writing, and Imperial Administration.* Durham, N.C.: Duke University Press.

Steinbeck, John.

1939.   *The Grapes of Wrath.* New York: Viking Press.

Suleri, Sara.

1989.   *Meatless Days.* Chicago: University of Chicago Press.

Sweezy, Paul.

1966.   *Monopoly Capitalism.* New York: Monthly Review Press.

Takaki, Ronald.

1993.   *A Different Mirror: A History of Multicultural America.* Boston: Little, Brown.

Thomas, Nicholas.

1994.   *Colonialism's Culture: Anthropology, Travel, and Government.* Princeton, N.J.: Princeton University Press.

Toor, Frances.
    1985.   *A Treasury of Mexican Folkways*. New York: Bonanza Books.
Tranquilino-Sánchez, Marcos.
    1992.   Foreword. In *The Chicano Codices: Encountering the Art of the Americas*. San Francisco: Mexican Museum.
Treviño-Velasquez, Gloria.
    1985.   "Cultural Ambivalence in Early Chicana Prose Fiction." Ph.D. diss., Stanford University.
Trujillo, Orlando.
    1979.   "Linguistic Structures in José Montoya's 'El Louie.'" In *Modern Chicano Writers: A Collection of Critical Essays*, ed. Joseph Sommers and Tomás Ybarra-Frausto, 150–160. Englewood Cliffs, N.J.: Prentice Hall.
Turner, Frederick Jackson.
    1893.   "The Significance of the Frontier in American History." In *Annual Report of the American Historical Association for the Year 1893*, 197–227. Washington D.C.: Government Printing Office, 1894.
Turner, Victor.
    1969.   *The Ritual Process: Structure and Anti-Structure*. Chicago: Aldine.
Urrea, Luis A.
    1993.   *Across the Wire: Life and Hard Times on the Mexican Border*. New York: Anchor/Doubleday.
Valenzuela, José Manuel.
    1988.   *A la brava ese! Cholos, Punks, Chavos Banda*. Tijuana: Colegio de la frontera Norte.
Van Gennep, Arnold.
    [1909]   *Rites of Passage*. Trans. Monika B. Vizedom and Gabrielle L. Caffee.
    1960.   Chicago: University of Chicago Press.
Villa, Raúl.
    1993.   "Tales of the Second City: Social Geographic Imagination in Contemporary California Chicano/a Literature and Art." Ph.D. diss., University of California, Santa Cruz.
Viramontes, Helena María.
    1985.   *The Moths and Other Stories*. Houston: Arte Público Press.
    1995.   *Under the Feet of Jesus*. New York: Dutton.
Webb, Walter Prescott.
    [1935]   *The Texas Rangers: A Century of Frontier Defense*. Boston:
    1965.   Houghton. Reprint, Austin: University of Texas Press.
Weber, David J.
    1992.   *The Spanish Frontier in North America*. New Haven: Yale University Press.
West, Cornel.
    1991.   "Postmodern Culture." In *The Columbia History of the American Novel*, ed. Emory Elliott, 515–520. New York: Columbia University Press.

Williams, Patricia J.
 1991. *The Alchemy of Race and Rights.* Cambridge, Mass.: Harvard University Press.
Williams, Raymond.
 1958. *Culture and Society, 1780–1950.* London: Chatto and Windus.
 1960. *Border Country.* London: Chatto and Windus.
 1964. *Second Generation.* London: Chatto and Windus.
 1973a. *The Country and the City.* New York: Oxford University Press.
 1973b. *The English Novel: From Dickens to Lawrence.* New York: Oxford University Press.
 1976. *Keywords: A Vocabulary of Culture and Society.* New York: Oxford University Press. Rev. ed. 1983, 1986.
 1977. *Marxism and Literature.* New York: Oxford University Press.
 1979a. *The Fight for Manod.* London: Chatto and Windus.
 1979b. *Politics and Letters: Interviews with New Left Review.* London: New Left Books.
 1983. *Writing in Society.* London: Verso.
 1989. *The Politics of Modernism: Against the New Conformists.* Ed. and intro. Tony Pinkey. London: Verso.
 1989– *People of the Black Mountain.* London: Chatto and Windus.
 1990.
 1990. *What I Came to Say.* London: Hutchinson/Radius.
Wolf, Eric R.
 1958. "The Virgén de Guadalupe: A Mexican National Symbol." *Journal of American Folklore* 71: 34–39.
Wong, Shelley Sunn.
 1994. "Unnaming the Same: Thersa Hak Kyung Cha's *Dictée.*" In *Writing Self, Writing Nation,* ed. Norma Alarcón and Elaine Kim, 103–140. Berkeley, Calif.: Third Woman Press.
Wrobel, David.
 1993. *The End of American Exceptionalism: Frontier Anxiety from the Old West to the New Deal.* Lawrence: University of Kansas Press.
Yans-McLaughlin, Virginia, ed.
 1990. *Immigration Reconsidered: History, Sociology, and Politics.* New York: Oxford University Press.
Yarbro-Bejarano, Yvonne.
 1994. "Gloria Anzaldúa's *Borderlands/La Frontera:* Cultural Studies, 'Difference,' and the Non-Unitary Subject." *Cultural Critique* 28 (Fall): 5–28.
 n.d. *The Right to Passion.* Austin: University of Texas Press, forthcoming.
Ybarra-Frausto, Tomás.
 1991. "Rasquachismo: A Chicano Sensibility." In *Chicano Art, Resistance and Affirmation: An Interpretive Exhibition of the Chicano Art Movement, 1965–1985,* ed. Richard Griswold del Castillo, Teresa

McKenna, and Yvonne Yarbo-Bejarano, 155–162. Los Angeles: Wright Art Gallery, UCLA.

Yúdice, George.
  1991.   "El conflicto de posmodernidades." *Nuevo Texto Crítico* 7: 19–33.

Zamora, Bernice.
  1976.   *Restless Serpents*. Menlo Park, Calif.: Diseño Literarios.

Zavella, Patricia.
  1987.   *Women's Work and Chicano Families: Cannery Workers of the Santa Clara Valley*. Ithaca, N.Y.: Cornell University Press.

Zizek, Slavoj.
  1989.   *The Sublime Object of Ideology*. London: Verso.
  1993.   *Tarrying with the Negative: Kant, Hegel, and the Critique of Ideology*. Durham, N.C.: Duke University Press.

Index

acculturation/deculturation, 204n.17
"A César Augusto Sandino" (Paredes), 54
Across the Wire (Urrea), 12–13, 135–40
Adorno, Theodor, 102–3, 119–20, 121
"Africa" (Paredes), 54
"Aguafuerte estival" (Paredes), 54–55
Alarcón, Norma, 12, 121, 207n.14
alienation, 158
allegiance, communal consciousness of, 113
Althusser, Louis, 206n.3
Alvarado, Juan Bautista, 171
American baroque, 66–71, 165
"American Congo, The" (Bourke), 13, 164–65, 166–67, 182–83
American Dream, 109, 111–12
American 1848, 170–72, 174, 177
American Frontier thesis, 161
Americanization programs, 28. *See also* assimilation
"American Lives" course (Islas), 74–75
American Revolution, 177
American studies. *See under* cultural studies
Americas Watch, 19
Amerindians, 81–82, 90, 100, 106–7, 162, 163
amnesty for undocumented immigrants, 96, 200n.3
Ana María (refugee in Tijuana), 138
Anaya, Rudolfo A., 195–96
Anderson, Benedict, 19
anencephalic births, 19
"Another Firme Rola (Bad Cause I'm Brown)" (Frost), 126
Anzaldúa, Gloria, 8, 109
Apache, 162
Apache Campaign in the Sierra Madre, An (Bourke), 163
apartheid, and shopping malls, 120–21
Arana, Ana, 19
Arnold, Matthew: *Culture and Anarchy*, 21–22
art: Adorno on, 103; border, 152; performance, 125, 142–43, 152–53, 154; praxis, 103. *See also* painting
Artenstein, Isaac, 151

ASCO collective, 125
assimilation: and cultural in-betweenness, 28–29; paradigm of, 80–81, 151; resistance to, 59, 79; transculturation, 55–56, 80, 204n.17
audiotopias, 195, 212n.2
autoethnography, 134–51, 209n.6; evangelism in, 138–40; "home" concept in, 139–41, 145–46; hybridity in, 140–51; imperialist context of, 138–39; refugee life captured in, 135–40
Avalos, David, 153
"Aztlán" (El Vez), 194–97
Aztlán legend, 116–17, 195–96

Baez, Joan, 186
Bancroft, Hubert Howe, 169, 171, 181
barrios, 68, 113; phantasmatic aspect of, 87, 88; violence in, 59–60, 62, 126–27
Bartra, Roger, 148, 210n.12
Bauman, Richard, 38, 46
Becoming Mexican American (G. Sánchez), 27–29
Behar, Ruth, x
Benítez-Rojo, Antonio, 97
Benson, Ray, 189
Bercovitch, Sacvan, 49, 73, 160–61, 205n.1
Bernardino de Sahagún, Fray, 105
Between Two Worlds (Paredes), 39, 52–56
Bhabha, Homi K., 95, 111
Big Four (railroad barons), 177, 181, 182
Birmingham Centre for Contemporary Cultural Studies. *See* CCCS
"Birthday of Mrs. Piñeda, The" (A. Ríos), 68
birth defects, 19
Black Atlantic, The (Gilroy), 12, 196
black British jungle, 125–26
black diaspora, 12, 19, 35
Blades, Rubén, x
Bloom, Harold, 160
Board of Land Commissioners (San Francisco), 172
Boas, Franz, 164–65

Wong, Shelley Sunn, 7, 29
workers, undocumented, 193–94; citizenship status of, 7, 124; numbers/types of, 6, 95–96, 200n.3; space and movements repressed, 6–7. *See also* immigrants, Mexican; immigrants, undocumented
writing. *See* border writing; literature
Wrobel, David, xii

Yarbro-Bejarano, Yvonne, xiii
Ybarra-Frausto, Tomás, 113, 116
Yúdice, George, 129

Zamora, Bernice: *Restless Serpents*, 63–66; "So Not to Be Mottled," 64–66
Zapata, Emiliano, 193
zoot suit riots, 59

Index:	Carol Roberts
Composition:	Integrated Composition Systems
Text:	10/13 Sabon
Display:	Sabon
Printing and binding:	BookCrafters